ECONOMIC SOCIETY

THIRD EDITION

K B MARDER & L P ALDERSON

Oxford University Press

Preface

The book provides a complete course in economics for students in the 14-16 age group. It assumes no previous knowledge of the subject and specialist terms are not introduced without explanation. The content is mainly descriptive and much of the abstract theory found in other textbooks is omitted.

The timing of a third edition made it possible to review the content of the book in the light of new syllabuses issued by the examining groups constituted for the General Certificate of Secondary Education. The text has thus been revised not only to bring it up to date but also to conform as closely as possible to syllabus requirements. In its treatment of the descriptive areas of economic study the book could also be used as an introduction to students taking their first courses in economics at A level or its equivalent, though it does not attempt to cover the body of pure theory normally required at that level.

Exercises are integrated into the text to test comprehension and as an aid to revision, while each chapter is followed by multiple choice questions, a data response exercise, and some questions of an essay type to give practice in dealing with such questions in examinations. Some guidance on the coursework component of the GCSE examination is provided in an appendix. Answers to the multiple choice questions and purely numerical questions are to be found at the end of the book.

Oxford University Press, Walton Street, Oxford OX2 6DP

Oxford New York Toronto
Delhi Bombay Calcutta Madras Karachi
Petaling Jaya Singapore Hong Kong Tokyo
Nairobi Dar es Salaam Cape Town
Melbourne Auckland

and associated companies in
Berlin Ibadan

Oxford is a trade mark of Oxford University Press

ISBN 0 19 913311 5

First published 1987
Reprinted 1989, 1990

Typeset by Christie Typeset (UK) Ltd, Bristol
Printed in Great Britain at The Bath Press, Avon

Contents

Chapter 1

Introducing economics

1.1 Economic resources

The problem of scarcity

Economics is clearly concerned with scarcity since without scarcity there would be no need to economize. Economics is studied because society does not have the resources to provide people with all the material things they need and want. This is obviously true of poor countries that do not have enough food for their people. But even rich Western nations have never produced enough to satisfy all the wants of their inhabitants. Indeed, history shows that as a society becomes more prosperous its wants increase more rapidly than the means of production. Compare, for example, the wants and expectations of people today with those of people living fifty or a hundred years ago.

The purpose of economics is to show how society can make the best use of scarce resources. Since there are not enough resources to satisfy all our wants, it is necessary to decide which should be satisfied at any time. These are basic economic decisions. For example, it is necessary to decide whether available labour and materials should be used for building more roads, shops, hotels, schools, hospitals, houses, or some other alternative. More of one thing means less of something else. These basic economic facts of scarcity and *choice* are expressed in the idea of opportunity cost.

Opportunity cost

The real cost of satisfying any want consists of the other wants that might have been satisfied instead. This is what we mean by opportunity cost. The opportunity cost to the country of a new airport is perhaps the power station that could have been built with the same quantity of resources.

Individuals are continually faced with similar

economic decisions. Each has a limited income and relatively unlimited wants. A decision to buy, say, a colour television set may mean doing without the suite of furniture or perhaps the holiday abroad that would have been chosen as an alternative. *The opportunity cost is the forfeited alternative.*

In the modern world, most economic decisions involve money, and cost is normally measured in money. The part played by money in the economy will be considered later. At this stage, our emphasis is on an essential economic fact: it is from real resources and not money that our needs are met.

Money is merely the means with which we buy resources for our use. If we spend more money on clothes, more resources will be attracted into the clothing industry. If the government spends more on the health service and less on defence, there will be a corresponding shift in the use of the country's resources. In each case, the real cost is not the money spent but the alternatives that could have been produced with the same resources.

Factors of production

The resources on which the economy depends are called factors of production. These are usually divided into three groups under the headings of land, labour, and capital. A fourth factor, *enterprise*, is sometimes added to represent the contribution of those who own businesses and bear the risks of production. We consider the role of enterprise in Chapter 4.

1 *Land*

Land has a much wider meaning in economics than in everyday language. It means not only the soil but also all other natural resources. It thus includes climatic conditions of rainfall and temperature which may be as important to agriculture as the fertility of the soil itself. It obviously includes mineral deposits such as coal, oil, and metal ores. The term is also extended to seas and rivers which are a natural source of fisheries, water transport, hydroelectric power, and so on. All such resources are provided by nature and used by people to meet their own needs.

2 *Labour*

Natural resources cannot be used for production without some human effort. The farmer must plough, sow, and reap, or employ workers for the purpose. He must also use his own knowledge and intelligence to plan the work.

All human contributions to production, whether manual or mental, skilled or unskilled, are classified as labour. In the world of business, it is common to distinguish between management and labour. But people working in any kind of job form part of the manpower resources available to the community. Managers, salesmen, teachers, entertainers, and every other occupational group are included in the labour force.

3 *Capital*

People rarely work with their bare hands. Even in primitive farming societies, ploughs and other simple tools were used. The capital of modern industry includes factories, machines, and complicated equipment of many kinds.

Capital differs from other factors of production in that it is itself created by production. It consists of goods that are not directly consumed but are available for further production or use in the future.

i) Capital goods such as factory buildings and machines are called *fixed capital*.

ii) Firms also hold stocks of goods or materials to

Identify three factors of production shown in this photograph.

be used when required in the future. Such stocks are called working or *circulating capital*.
iii) The capital stocks of the community also include such things as houses, schools, hospitals, and roads. This group is called *social capital*.

Whereas the amount of land and labour available at any time is more or less fixed, the quantity of capital can be increased simply by producing more goods of that type. The production of capital goods is called *investment*. Investment is clearly an important means of increasing productive capacity and so improving the standard of living. The richest countries are generally those that have used most resources for investment and consequently possess most capital.

It should be noticed that everyday terms are sometimes given a special meaning in economics. For example, people sometimes refer to their bank or building society deposits as capital, and investment often means purchases of shares on the Stock Exchange. But in economics, these terms are normally used to refer to real resources and not paper wealth such as money or shares.

Goods and services

Factors of production combine to produce goods and services to satisfy our wants. Goods are broadly classified into consumer and capital goods. We defined *capital goods* above. *Consumer goods* are those which directly satisfy the wants of people. They include foodstuffs and all the other goods bought in shops. Some of them, such as cars and television sets, are called consumer durables because they are used or consumed over a number of years.

Part of the nation's resources is used to supply *services* which people want to consume as well as goods. In an advanced society there is always a need for professional services such as those of lawyers, doctors, accountants, and architects. People with a high standard of living also make extensive use of services such as transport and entertainment. A large share of resources is employed by the government and local authorities to provide essential public services such as education, health, and law and order. The wholesale and retail trades are also sometimes included with the service industries.

Production

In everyday speech production usually refers to the process of making or manufacturing goods. In economics it has a wider meaning. Production includes all activities that help to make goods and services available for people to consume. It therefore covers every stage from the supply of raw materials to the delivery of finished products to the consumer (Fig. 1.1).

The productive process thus extends to the wholesale and retail stages and includes the transport

Fig. 1.1 The process of production

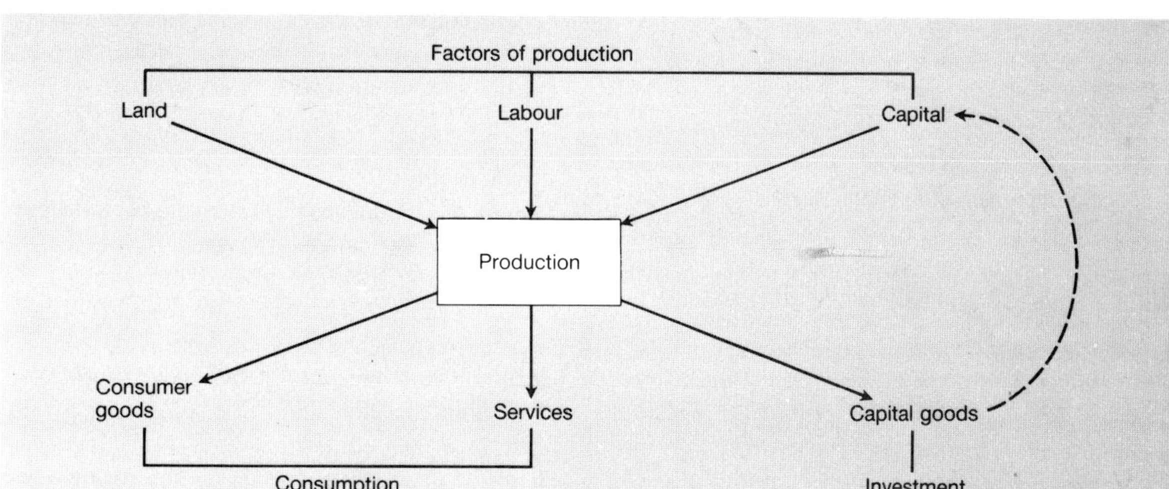

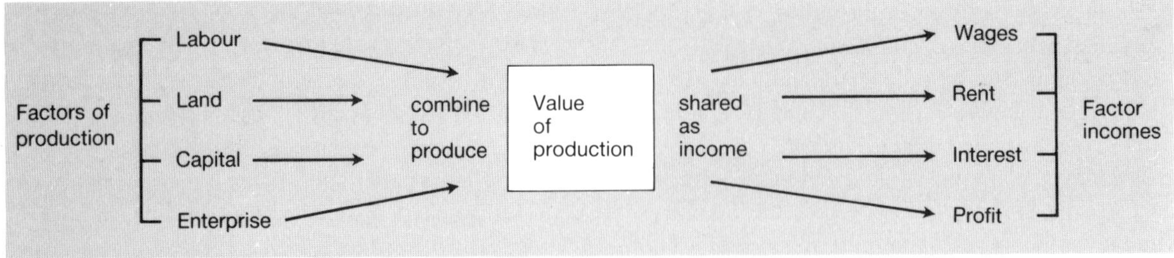

Fig. 1.2 Factor incomes

of products between each stage. It also includes the service industries such as banking and insurance which may assist other stages of production or provide services direct to the consumer. In this sense everyone who works for a living is engaged in production and all incomes are obtained in return for contributions to production.

The normal classification of income into *wages*, *rent*, *interest*, and *profit* corresponds to our classification of factors of production – into labour, land, capital, and enterprise – and represents the money payments to those factors for their respective contributions to production (Fig. 1.2). We return to this relationship shortly under the heading of *national income* (p.10).

Economic organization of society

There are broadly two ways of determining the allocation of economic resources. Control may either be left in private hands under a system of private enterprise or it may be exercised by the state on behalf of the community as a whole. In the former case the use made of resources depends on the mechanism of the market. In the latter case it is determined by central planning.

In practice most economies (including that of the United Kingdom) fall between these two extremes, involving elements from each. Consideration may thus be given to three possible forms of economic organization – the market economy, the planned economy, and the mixed economy (Fig. 1.3).

1 The market economy

The essential feature of a market economy is that the resources of the country are privately owned and production is undertaken by private firms working for profit. The prospects of profit are indicated by forces operating in the markets where goods (or services) are bought and sold and their prices are determined. Since people are generally prepared to pay for what they want, products in demand will sell well at good prices and so be profitable for firms to produce. Moreover, the producers will be able and willing to pay generously for labour and other factors of production. Wages and other factor prices should therefore be comparatively high, attracting resources into the industries concerned. By a similar but opposite process, resources will tend to be drawn out of industries in which demand is slack.

It would seem that, through the market mechanism, an economy based on private enterprise automatically ensures that resources are used to satisfy the wants of the population as consumers. This reasoning formed the basis of *laissez-faire* economic theory which prevailed in the nineteenth century and has been used to resist government interference with the working of the economy. However, the fact that such interference is commonplace even in countries strongly committed to private enterprise suggests that complete reliance should not be placed on market forces. The efficiency of a market economy is examined more closely in connection with the operation of the price system in Chapter 8.

2 The planned economy

The reverse of the free market economy is the kind of centralized planning in which resources are entirely under the control and direction of the government. Such a system is associated with communist countries and was also closely approached by Britain's economy during the Second World War.

Whether the allocation of resources in a fully planned economy meets the real needs of the people as consumers depends on the foresight and efficiency of the planners. Errors in planning could

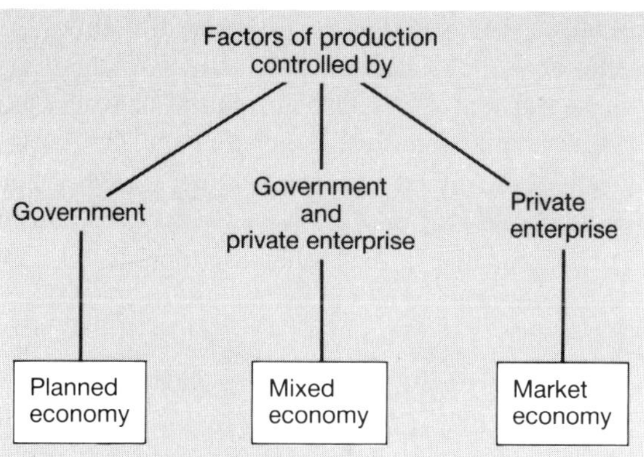

Fig. 1.3 Economic systems

lead to the production of large surpluses of unsaleable goods. Even communist countries have consequently made some concessions to market forces, and more decisions are allowed to be made by local factory managers. From the viewpoint of most Western nations there are also objections to the communist form of planning on grounds of freedom and democracy, and we often refer to such systems as *command* economies.

Nevertheless, central control over resources offers solutions for some of the problems of market economies. For example, unemployment can be avoided since factors of production may be kept at work even at a financial loss. Again, the problem of the trade balance disappears when the government itself controls both exports and imports. Similarly, central direction can ensure that a sufficient proportion of national resources is devoted to investment.

3 The mixed economy

Most modern economies are mixed in the sense that control over resources is divided between the government and private enterprise. The mixture varies from country to country but, in the Western world generally, the trend has been towards the enlargement of the economic role of governments. Thus, in Britain, the *public sector* of the economy – including central and local government together with the nationalized industries – accounts for more than 40 per cent of the total spending on goods and services of all kinds. At the same time, there remains a substantial *private sector* of business where market forces continue to operate though influenced by the government through taxation and other policies. Recent Conservative government policies have aimed at reversing the historic trend by shifting the balance back towards a larger private sector.

Social costs and benefits

Economic decisions based purely on market forces may fail to secure the best use of productive resources because they do not take into account all the possible effects on society. Businesses seek profit and are concerned essentially with *private* costs and benefits. These are costs and benefits that directly affect the individual or firm making the decision. Thus, in the case of a manufacturing firm, private costs consist of wages, costs of materials, and other factor costs, while private benefits are the revenues received from the sale of its products.

Firms do not normally consider the wider (external) effects of their actions on other members of society. These effects are called *externalities*. For example, location of a factory in an urban area may impose evironmental costs on the community such as pollution and traffic congestion. It may also confer external benefits in the form of reduced unemployment and greater local prosperity.

Social costs and benefits are defined as the sum of all the private costs and benefits plus externalities (costs and benefits) resulting from an economic decision. Before starting on large government projects such as the construction of motorways or airports, it is now normal procedure to undertake a study of the social costs and benefits. In effect, estimates are made of the values of all the gains and losses to society as a whole. This is called *cost benefit analysis*. If social benefits exceed social costs it may be assumed that the project is worth pursuing.

1 Explain the connection between economics and scarcity.

2 Explain the meaning of opportunity cost. Give examples that might occur (a) for you personally, (b) for the government or country as a whole.

3 Draw Fig. 1.1 and explain each of the terms, adding examples wherever possible.

4 How is the use of factors of production determined in (a) a planned economy, (b) a market economy?

5 Why is Britain described as a mixed economy? Give

at least three examples each of major British industries that are (a) privately owned, (b) nationalized.

6 What is meant by cost benefit analysis? Suggest factors that might be considered in such an analysis of a plan to construct a large new airport on the outskirts of London.

1.2 Standard of living

A person's standard of living depends on the quantity of goods and services he can afford to consume. Similarly, a community's standard of living is indicated by its level of consumption.

To judge living standards in a modern society we would look at a number of things: the space and comfort enjoyed by people in their homes; the proportion of households with hot running water, baths, central heating, telephones, refrigerators, and other modern appliances; the extent to which people can afford to travel, take holidays, buy consumer goods, visit theatres, and so on. We would also take into account the standard of education, medical treatment, and other social services.

Since the quantity of goods and services that a community consumes largely depends on how much it produces, an obvious guide to a nation's standard of living is the total value of its production or output. This total is known as the national income.

National income

The national income is the total value of goods and services produced by a community's resources over a given period of time, usually one year.

Why do we refer to the value of production or output as income? The answer is that they amount to the same thing. In fact we can arrive at the same total in three different ways. The value of goods and services produced by a country can be measured by adding up either the total incomes received from producing them or all the money spent on purchasing them or the value of the outputs of all the industries concerned in producing them.

This is illustrated in Fig. 1.4 which shows the flow of money in a simple community. There is no trade with the outside world, and the inhabitants spend all their income on the output of their own firms or farms. Measured over any period of time, the value of output must equal the money expenditure on it, and that value also forms the community's income shared out as wages, profits, etc. Of course, the modern economy is much more complex, but the principle still applies:

income = expenditure = output

Measurements of all three kinds are made annually by the British government and published in a Blue Book entitled *National Income and Expenditure*. The basis of the measurements can be briefly outlined.

1 Income

The income of the community incudes the wages and salaries of all employees, profits of firms (including nationalized industries), and rents received by owners of property. But students' grants, pensions, sickness benefits, unemployment pay, and other social security payments do not count as incomes because they are not obtained in return for goods and services produced and sold. They are called *transfer payments*.

2 Expenditure

The total includes all consumer spending in shops, etc., the spending of firms on capital goods such as machines, and spending by the government. These three are called *consumption, investment*, and *public spending* respectively. We must also add foreign spending on our *exports* since they are part of our output and provide us with income. But we deduct our own expenditure on imports because that portion goes to provide income in other countries.

Finally, a deduction is made on account of taxes such as value-added tax (VAT) which artificially raise the prices of goods and services. This leaves a total figure of expenditure at *factor cost* which is equal to the incomes received by people as producers.

3 Output

An estimate is made of the value of the production of every industry. But care is necessary to avoid counting the same output more than once. For example, if we count the output of the steel industry and also the final output of the motor car industry, which uses a lot of steel, we would be counting the same steel twice. The figure for each industry is therefore its *value-added* output—that is, its final

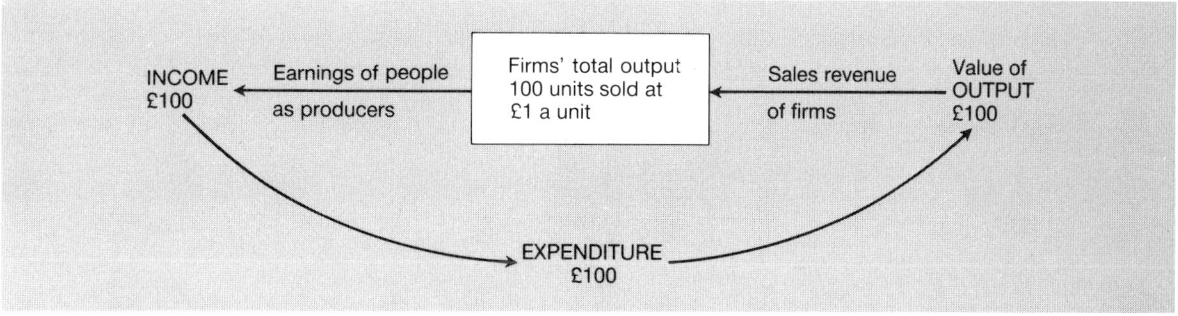

Fig. 1.4 Income flow

output minus purchases from other industries. Free government services such as education and health are valued at their cost to the government.

National income totals

It is useful to be aware of the meaning of certain terms used in national income calculations. The following definitions should be noted.

Gross domestic product (GDP) is the total value of all goods and services produced within the nation's borders.

Gross national product (GNP) is the total value produced by all British-owned factors of production at home and abroad. It is calculated by adding to GDP the income from British investments overseas and deducting similar payments to foreigners from their investments here. Such investments result from setting up factories, buying company shares, or making loans in foreign countries.

The *national income* is GNP minus an allowance for capital depreciation. This allowance corresponds to that part of our output that simply replaces worn-out buildings, machines, etc. and so does not make us any better off.

Personal disposable income is a related figure that shows the total spending power of households in the economy. It is derived from the GNP total by deducting direct taxes on income and adding government transfer payments, such as pensions which are omitted from other national income measurements.

Level of national income

In the long run, national income normally expands as a result of technical progress and the growth of productive capacity. This is the process of *economic growth* to which we return later (p. 14). However, any graph of movements of national income over a number of years shows that its growth is not steady but at a fluctuating rate, and in a period of economic depression or slump national income may fall.

What then determines its level at any time, and what causes its fluctuations? The answer is that national income depends on the total level of spending or *aggregate demand* in the economy. If expenditure rises, firms receive correspondingly more money to distribute in the form of incomes – wages, rents, interest, and profits. A fall in spending means correspondingly less income.

Fig. 1.5 illustrates the relationship between income and expenditure, in its simplest form, as a circular flow of money between firms (as producers) and households (as consumers). If household spending on consumption (in the bottom loop) is, say, £100 billion a year, it will generate income (in the top loop) equal to £100 billion. As long as households continue to spend all their income, there is no reason

Fig. 1.5 Circular flow of money

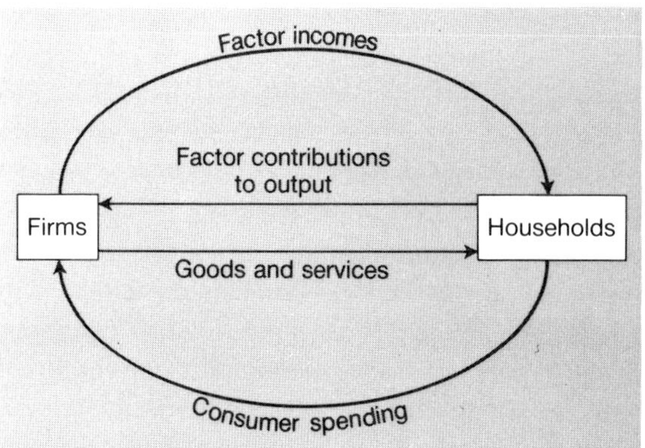

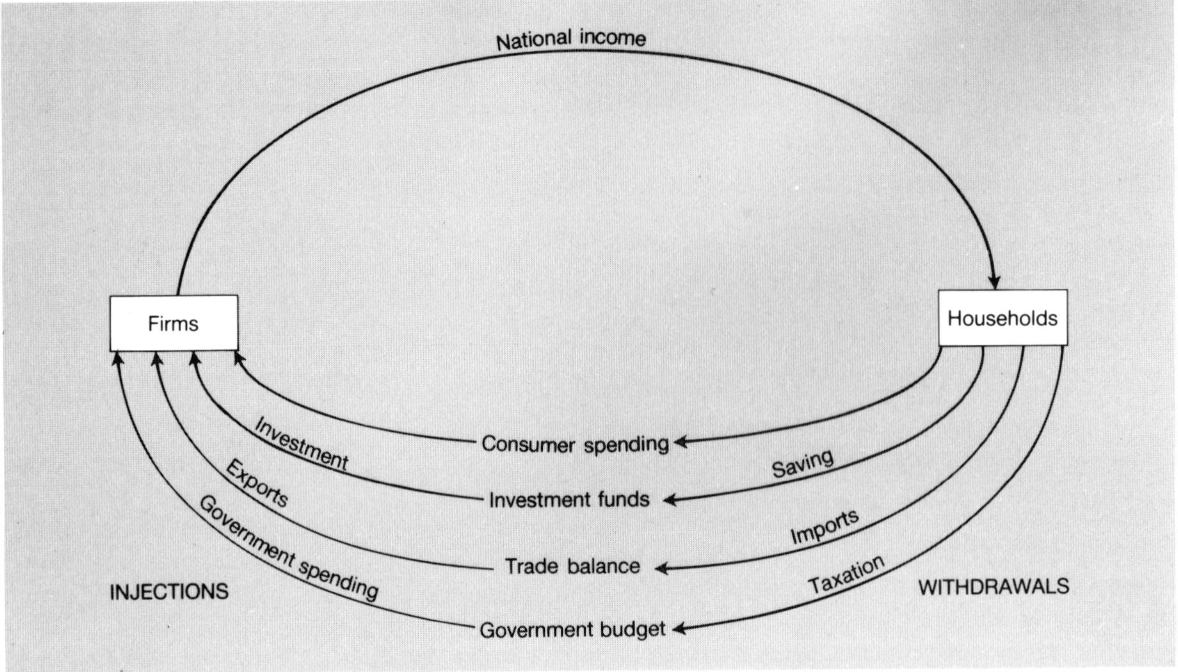

Fig. 1.6 Income flow with injections and withdrawals

why the flow of money should change and national income will remain at a constant level.

Now suppose that households decide to save some of their incomes (i.e. spend less). Clearly, national income will fall since firms consequently receive less money to pay out as incomes. Of course, in reality, many households regularly save without causing national income to fall. This is because consumer spending by households is not the only form of expenditure. Firms themselves spend by buying capital goods such as machines from other firms, and such capital expenditure (or investment) creates income in the same way as household spending on consumption.

Thus, while the income flow is being reduced by *withdrawals* or leakages through saving, it is also being increased by fresh *injections* of investment. The effect on national income depends on the balance between these two (Fig. 1.6).

Withdrawals and injections affecting the income flow also come about in two other ways – through international trade and the activities of government. In the process of trade, money spent on imported goods clearly escapes abroad while foreign expenditure on exports enters the income flow from outside. Thus imports cause a withdrawal and exports create an injection. Similarly, the government withdraws money by taxation but also injects through its own expenditure.

Fluctuations in national income may be caused by changes in either injections or withdrawals. The balance between them determines the level at any time. The government has a special role because by adjusting the balance of its own budget, it can offset other changes and exercise a degree of control over the total flow of national income. The use of the budget for this purpose is explained in Chapter 13.

Real income

An individual's standard of living depends on the quantity of goods and services he can afford to buy. It therefore depends on not only his money income but also the prices of the things on which it is spent. His standard of living only rises if his money income increases faster than the cost of living. In that case, we say that his *real* income has risen.

The same reasoning applies to the national standard of living. An increase in national income may be due simply to higher prices (inflation) without any increase in production. Larger pay packets are then offset by the increased cost of living and so people are no better off. Real national income depends on the volume of production and not just its value in money.

To calculate changes in real national income, it is necessary to allow for changes in the price level or cost of living. In Chapter 10 we shall see how changes in the general level of prices can be measured by means of *index numbers*. By allowing for price movements, it is possible to estimate the change that would have taken place in national income over a given period of time if prices had remained constant. This provides a measurement of real national income. During the 1970s for example, money national income more than trebled, but the increase was almost entirely due to higher prices. Consequently, real national income hardly increased.

Comparisons of living standards

Most governments publish figures of national income which are used to show what is happening to living standards in their own countries and to make comparisons with other countries. The relevant figures are clearly those of *real national income*, measuring quantity rather than value of output. A number of other allowances should also be made in interpreting the figures, particularly for international comparisons.

1 Population

A higher national income clearly does not mean a higher standard of living if the extra income is shared among more people. The standard of living depends on the average real income per head or *per capita*—that is, real national income divided by the population.

2 Composition of output

In ancient Egypt productive resources were squandered on building pyramids. Similarly, a modern society may use an excessive part of its resources for military purposes that contribute little to the welfare of the people. Moreover, societies differ in their needs. For example, a cold country has to use a portion of its productive capacity just to keep warm. At a particular time much of a country's output may be devoted to repairing damage due to floods or earthquakes. Less production is then available for satisfying other needs. During the Second World War the national income rose sharply but the standard of living fell.

3 Distribution of income

The wealth of a country may belong to only a small number of very rich people and so a high national income can conceal widespread poverty. Living standards within a society depend partly on how wealth and income are shared among its inhabitants.

4 Different national currencies

In order to compare the national incomes of different countries, it is necessary to convert the figures into the same currency. For instance, the United States's figures are in dollars whereas Britain's figures are in pounds sterling. To compare them, we must either change the former into pounds or the latter into dollars. This is done by using the exchange rate at which pounds can be changed into dollars.

For example, at a rate of £1 to $2, a UK national income of, say, £100 billion would be expressed as $200 billion. If the USA national income is then $400 billion, it would be taken as double that of the UK. But this assumes that £1 can actually buy the same amount of goods in Britain as it could if changed into $2 and spent in the United States. Anyone who travels abroad knows that currency exchange rates are rarely such an accurate reflection of prices. International comparisons of this kind can therefore be misleading.

5 Statistical limitations

Methods of calculation and reliability of national statistics inevitably vary, particularly between countries at different stages of economic development. Thus the welfare of people in a less developed farming community may be underrated by national income figures because production is based largely on family self-sufficiency and not measurable in money terms. Even in advanced economies the measurements can be misleading because they take no account of non-monetary pursuits such as the do-it-yourself activities of British households.

Wealth and income

Income should be clearly distinguished from wealth. Large amounts of wealth usually go with large incomes, but not necessarily so.

The real wealth of a nation consists of its capital – roads, railways, houses, factories, machines, and other stocks of capital goods available to use or consume in the future. The real income of a nation consists of the goods and services produced by its resources (including capital) over a given period of time. Wealth is essentially a *stock* of goods that has been accumulated, whereas income is a *flow* of both goods and services measured over time.

An individual would normally measure his wealth and income in money. But the distinction is the same. Wealth is a stock whereas income is a continuous flow. A person's income could thus include wages, interest, profit, and rent from ownership of property. Personal wealth might include savings deposits, stocks and shares, and the value of a house or other forms of property.

Differences of wealth and income not only enable some people to enjoy much higher living standards than others but also give them social advantages such as the ability to buy privileged educational opportunities for their children. On the other hand, inequalities are defended on the grounds that they are necessary to reward ability and encourage people to work, save, and take on responsibility.

Inequalities are reduced to some extent by a tax system that falls most heavily on the rich, and social services designed to give greatest help to the poorest in the community. Nevertheless, our society still contains wide differences between rich and poor. This is illustrated by figures published in reports of the Board of Inland Revenue. According to its calculations, the richest 10 per cent of Britain's population owned 47 per cent of the nation's wealth in 1982. House ownership is the most widespread form of wealth and nearly 40 per cent of the population, living in rented accommodation, possessed virtually no wealth at all. Income distribution is less unequal with the top 10 per cent receiving 28·3 per cent (falling to 26·8 after tax deductions) of national income in 1981/2.

1. What is meant by the national income? Note the three ways in which it can be measured and explain why they should each give the same total.
2. What are transfer payments? Give examples. Why are they not included in the national income?
3. Note the definitions of gross domestic product and gross national product. What is the difference between them? What further allowance is made to give the figure of national income?
4. What determines the level of national income? Draw Fig. 1.6 and explain how injections and withdrawals affect the level of national income.
5. What is meant by real income? How can money incomes change without a corresponding change in real incomes?
6. USA national income: 1200 billion dollars. UK national income (measured in dollars): 200 billion. List the points you would make to correct someone who assumed that the United States's standard of living was six times that of the United Kingdom.
7. Distinguish between wealth and income, giving examples of each.

1.3 Economic growth

An important aim of most societies is to increase the living standards or real incomes of their inhabitants as rapidly as possible. This is what we call economic growth. It is normally calculated as a percentage increase in national income, GNP, or GDP measured at constant prices.

Britain's rate of economic growth averaged about 2 per cent a year over the last two decades. This was considerably less than most other industrial countries and so Britain fell lower down the league table of real national incomes. A great deal of attention has consequently been given to methods of increasing the rate of growth.

Means of growth

It is possible to achieve a high rate of economic growth in any one year by taking up slack in the economy due to unemployment. But once the economy is working at full stretch, output can only be increased by increasing productive capacity or making it more efficient. This may be done in a number of ways.

1 More investment

Productive capacity can be increased by producing more capital goods such as factories and machines. While more resources are being used in this way, there may be some reduction in the output of consumer goods, but the extra capacity should make more available in the future.

2 Technical progress

Research and invention are means to greater efficiency. More efficient machines and equipment lead to more production. Computers and automation are obvious means of accelerating growth at the present time.

3 More labour

The supply of labour can be increased by attracting immigrant workers into the country, increasing the employment of women, or encouraging more overtime work. Another possibility is to make labour more efficient through improvements in education and training. The output of labour can also be increased by providing incentives for people to work harder.

Problems of growth

Economic growth enables a higher standard of living but also brings social problems. In recent years many people (including economists) have begun to question the assumption that more production should be the dominant aim of society. For example, people may be healthier and happier with lower material standards but more leisure and relaxation. Furthermore, the experience of some of the richest nations indicates that rapid growth can be accompanied by acute social and economic problems. Two such problems are concerned with energy and pollution.

1 Energy

A growing economy requires increasing quantities of energy for industry, transport, and domestic consumption. Rapid economic growth in many industrial countries has caused mounting concern over the rate at which the world's energy resources are being used up. This was shown in 1973 and 1979 when the main oil-producing countries cut their supplies and raised prices sharply.

Fig. 1.7 illustrates Britain's energy situation. Note the reliance on mineral sources – oil, coal, and natural gas – which cannot last indefinitely. Electricity is a secondary source which depends on the others for its generation. Note how much it depends on coal, though nuclear power may become more important in the future.

Like other industrial countries, Britain has relied heavily on imported oil to supply both fuel for motor transport and power for industry. The offshore discoveries thus brought considerable economic advantages. The first discovery of oil in the British sector of the North Sea was made in 1969 and the first oil was brought ashore in 1975. The flow has since increased rapidly and made Britain self-sufficient in oil since 1980. The saving in imports is already making a large contribution to the balance of trade, and there is also a substantial gain in government revenue from the taxation of oil companies' profits. It must be remembered, however, that reserves of oil (and natural gas) are limited and

Fig. 1.7 UK energy sources (1983)

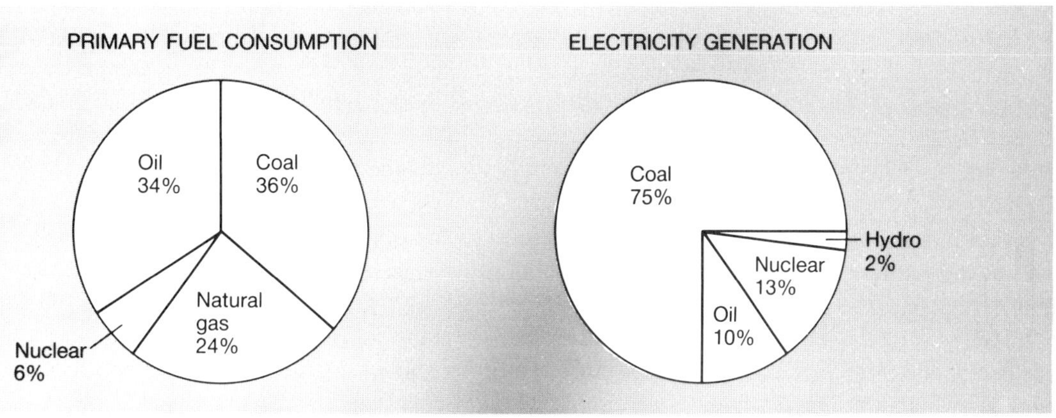

What alternative forms of energy could we use when this source runs dry?

the benefits are expected to fade by the end of the twentieth century.

Looking further ahead into the next century, we can predict that new forms of energy will eventually be required to replace mineral sources. Nuclear power faces obvious problems. Other possibilities being voiced include solar energy for heating and tidal energy for hydroelectricity.

2 Pollution

Problems of pollution are not new but they have been increasing and people have become more aware of them. There has consequently been pressure on governments to deal with pollution in its various forms.

Air pollution is largely due to fumes from factory chimneys, domestic coal fires, and the exhausts of motor vehicles. The effects can be serious in large industrial towns. In Britain, however, a great deal has been done through Clean Air Acts establishing zones in which households can use only smokeless fuel. Factory smoke is also more strictly controlled.

Waste disposal has caused serious pollution of water and land. Sewage and industrial waste poured into rivers and seas kill fish and, in some instances, have seriously affected human health. Areas of land have also been spoilt by the waste disposal of firms over years of industrial development. However, a close watch is now kept on industrial waste including dumping at sea. Illegal discharges of oil at sea are liable to heavy fines, and international co-operation is developing on sea pollution in general.

Noise has come to be associated with the problem of pollution. It may appear to be inconvenient rather than harmful, but medical evidence shows that excessive levels of noise can affect health. The most common offenders are motor vehicles and aircraft. However there are maximum permitted levels for cars and lorries, and aircraft noise is now an important factor in the design of aeroplanes and the siting of airports.

Developing economies

The highest rates of economic growth have been achieved in advanced industrial countries which also have high national incomes and living standards. An important international objective is to stimulate growth in those relatively poor countries – mainly in Africa, Asia, and South America – forming the so-called Third World and containing more than three-quarters of world population. The countries concerned are described as developing or less developed.

The reasons for low national income and lack of economic growth have already been indicated. A developing economy may have abundant labour, but its productivity is limited by backward technology and lack of capital. Efficiency may also be reduced by low standards of nutrition, health, and education. Programmes of international aid are intended to overcome these obstacles to economic growth.

Developing economies invariably rely on agriculture. They may be essentially *subsistence economies* in which people grow their own food and supply most of their own needs. Or the economy may depend on the export of a single crop. A harvest failure or decline of the market for its product can then cause widespread suffering and famine.

In such economies poverty is often made worse by rapidly expanding population. Unless economic growth runs ahead of population growth, living standards cannot rise. Clearly, the solution may lie partly in population control. We consider this aspect of the problem in the next chapter.

1 What is meant by economic growth and why is it considered desirable? What could the government do to increase Britain's rate of growth?

2 Explain why economic growth causes concern about (a) energy supplies, (b) the effect on environment and pollution.

3 Why are some countries much poorer than others?

Multiple choice

1 Which factors of production are used in the extraction of North Sea oil?
A labour only
B capital only
C labour and capital only
D land only
E land, labour, and capital

2 Which of the following would NOT be classified among factors of production?
A an oil tanker
B a company car
C a company share
D a coal seam
E a coal miner

3 John Doe obtained a new cricket bat with a £25 gift token which could also have been exchanged for a tennis racket that he liked or a radio that he did not want. The opportunity cost of the cricket bat was
A £25
B the gift token
C the radio
D the tennis racket
E zero

4 The opportunity cost of an unemployed building worker is
A his unemployment benefit
B his loss of wages
C the building work he would have done in employment
D not measurable
E zero

5 Which of the following would economists class as investment?
A buying shares on the Stock Exchange
B depositing money in a building society
C depositing money in a bank account
D buying a new coat
E building a new factory

6 The flow of national income will increase, other things remaining the same, if
A imports rise
B exports rise
C investment falls
D taxation rises
E government expenditure falls

7 A state retirement pension is
A a social cost
B a transfer payment
C an opportunity cost
D a factor cost
E a factor income

8 Which of the following is an economic decision?
1 determining the safety of a coal mine
2 deciding whether to sack and replace the mine manager
3 deciding whether to close the mine

A 1, 2 and 3 are correct
B 1 and 2 only are correct
C 2 and 3 only are correct
D 1 only is correct
E 3 only is correct

9 Which of the following statements do NOT apply to a mixed economy?
1 Profit is the motive for all business activity.
2 The use of resources is determined entirely by market forces.
3 The economy includes a public sector.

A 1, 2 and 3 are correct
B 1 and 2 only are correct
C 2 and 3 only are correct
D 1 only is correct
E 3 only is correct

10 A country's standard of living automatically rises when
A prices fall
B taxes fall
C wages rise
D consumption increases
E national income increases

Data response

The economy of Grottoland, using all its resources, can produce two products, blodgets and widgets, in the following combinations:

Blodgets	50	40	30	20	10	0
Widgets	0	5	10	15	20	25

These combinations can be plotted on a graph (with one product measured on each axis) which economists call a production possibility curve.

1 Draw the production possibility curve for Grottoland.

2 If it decided to produce 30 blodgets, how many widgets could it produce?

3 What would be the opportunity cost of producing one more widget, and what combination would the economy then have?

4 If blodgets are consumer goods and widgets are capital goods, what would be the probable effect on the country's standard of living, (a) immediately and (b) in the future, of using more of its resources for the production of widgets?

5 How would economic growth affect the position of the production possibility curve on your diagram?

6 Suppose that the country was producing 20 blodgets and 10 widgets. Show this combination by a point P on your diagram. What could you now say about the state of Grottoland's economy?

Essays

1 The basic economic problem is how to allocate scarce resources. Describe the resources concerned and explain the problem of allocation with reference to the concept of opportunity cost.

2 What are the distinguishing features of market and planned economies? Which kind of economy would you prefer to live in, and why?

3 'An increase in the national income of a country means an increase in the welfare of the citizens of that country'. Do you agree?

4 Explain how the level of national income is determined by injections and withdrawals. How would national income be affected if (a) people decide to save a larger proportion of their incomes, (b) the government cuts its spending on social services, (c) industry succeeds in expanding its exports?

Chapter 2
Population

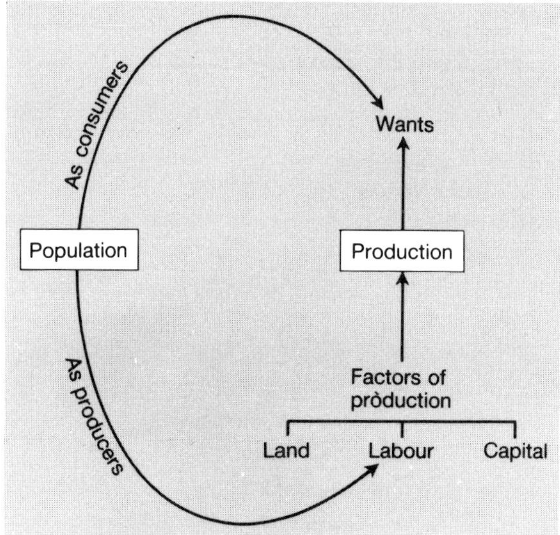

Fig. 2.1 People as consumers and producers

Since people are both consumers and producers, population has a double significance for economists (Fig. 2.1). It is the source of demand for goods and services and, at the same time, it provides the labour employed in producing those goods and services. The growth of population also causes social problems such as overcrowding and pollution.

Changes in the size and composition of the population therefore have important economic and social effects. A key set of figures providing information on many aspects of Britain's population is based on the census taken every ten years. The last census was in 1981.

2.1 Size of the population

Changes in size

A country's population is increased by births and decreased by deaths. Similarly, it is increased when

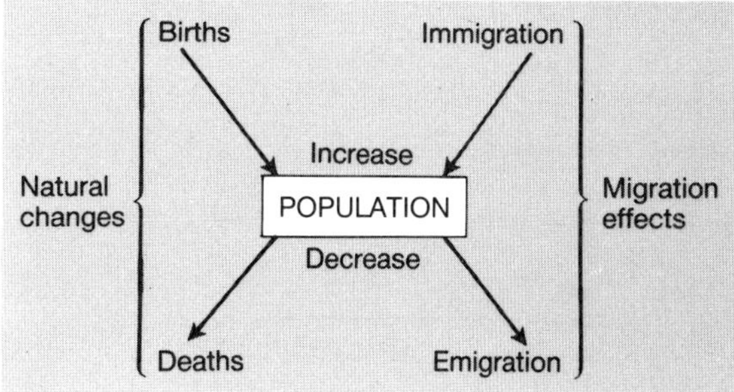

Fig. 2.2 Causes of population change

people from abroad come to live in the country (immigration) and decreased when people leave the country to live abroad (emigration).

A rise in population due to births exceeding deaths is known as a *natural increase*. If deaths exceeded births there would be a *natural decrease*. If a country were completely isolated from the rest of the world, the size of its population would depend simply on the balance between births and deaths. But with people able to move from one country to another, it is necessary to take account of *migration*—that is, the balance between emigration and immigration.

The population can change in size either because the number of births is greater or less than the number of deaths or because of migration (Fig. 2.2).

Birth-rate

A straightforward measurement of the birth-rate is *the number of live births per thousand of the population*. Thus, if a community has a population of 10 000 at the beginning of the year and 200 babies are born during the year, the birth-rate would be 20 per thousand. The answer is obtained by dividing the number of births (200) by the number of thousands (10) in the population.

The two main influences on the birth-rate are the number of marriages and the size of families.

1 Number of marriages

Most marriages occur between the ages of 16 and 50, and so the rates of both marriages and births are likely to be higher if a large proportion of the population is within this range.

Another factor that could affect the number of marriages is the ratio of men to women in the marrying age group. Obviously, fewer marriages would be possible if the numbers of the two sexes did not roughly balance. This situation has sometimes arisen, particularly after a war has caused a large number of male deaths. However, the sex ratio is less important in a society that recognizes polygamy – the practice of allowing each person more than one marriage partner.

2 Size of families

A reduction in family size was the principal cause of Britain's falling birth-rate during the last hundred years. Thus, the average number of children in a family has fallen from nearly six in the Victorian period to between two and three since the 1930s.

Two major influences on family size are the age at which people normally marry and the extent to which they use birth control to restrict the number of children.

The age of marriage affects the birth-rate through the number of marriages and also because younger marriages extend longer over the period when women can have children. A minimum age is fixed by law in most countries – in England, at 16 with the consent of parents or 18 without consent. But the average marrying age depends largely on social custom and may also be affected by economic circumstances. For example, the depression and unemployment of the 1930s caused some people to postpone marriage, and the birth-rate fell.

Improved methods and wider knowledge of birth control now make it possible for people to plan the size of their families to a great extent. However, such knowledge only affects the birth-rate if people are willing to make practical use of it. In other words, the birth-rate largely depends on the number of children that people, in general, decide to have.

Decisions about family size are influenced by various social, economic, and political factors. All the following are likely to affect the attitude of people towards having children: the women's liberation movement; more employment opportunities for women; religious objections to birth control; greater opportunities for travel and other forms of leisure; government aid to parents in the form of tax reliefs, child benefits, and free health services; economic depression and unemployment; the outbreak or threat of war.

The experience of Britain and other advanced industrial nations is that people tend to have smaller families as their living standards improve. A probable explanation is that a large family reduces the ability to buy consumer goods and enjoy the full fruits of prosperity. Modern methods of birth control are also more widely understood and available in richer countries.

Death-rate

Corresponding with the birth-rate, a country's death-rate is usually measured by *the number of deaths per thousand of the population*. Most countries have experienced falling death-rates over a considerable period of time. This explains why population has continued to increase in industrial countries, such as the United Kingdom, even when the birth-rate has been declining.

A falling death-rate is the normal consequence of improvements in health and general living standards. Obvious contributory factors include advances in medical science, better hospital and health services, higher standards of sanitation and hygiene, and improved nutrition. Greater international co-operation may also help to reduce deaths from famine in some parts of the world. Another possible factor would be the absence of major wars over a period of time.

In countries such as Britain, with death-rates already very low, any future decline in the rates is likely to be gradual. But in many developing countries death-rates could fall much faster if living standards improved and the medical skills of the advanced nations became available to them.

Migration

Migration affects the size of the population through the balance between immigration and emigration. In the United Kingdom there has usually been an excess of emigration (Fig. 2.3), but migration in general has only been a minor influence on the total

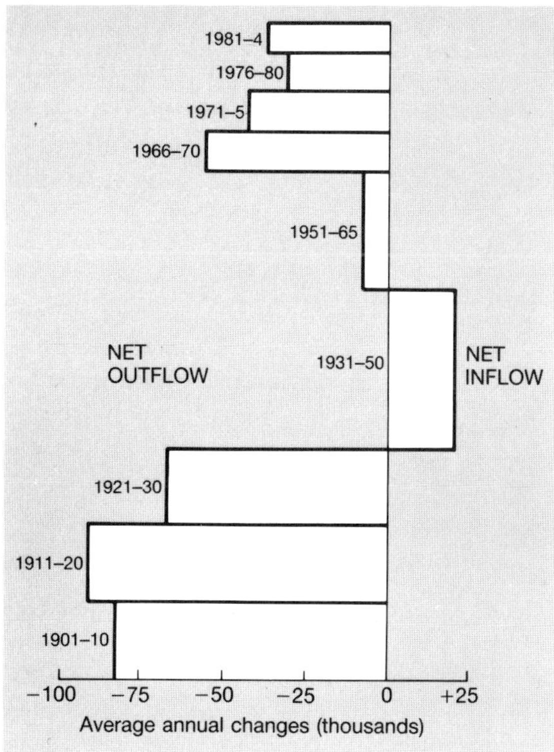

Fig. 2.3 UK migration: balance of gains and losses

numbers. The flow of Commonwealth immigrants into Britain, which began in the late 1950s, was soon checked by the adoption of strict immigration controls. However, immigration has played an important part in the development of some comparatively young nations such as the United States. Conversely, Ireland provides an exceptional example of a country whose population fell due to emigration over many years.

1 Causes of migration

Political and religious persecutions have been a cause of emigration for centuries. A recent illustration was the mass movement of Jews from Germany under Hitler. Emigration also results from harsh social and economic conditions in the home country. This explains, for example, the large-scale emigration from Ireland in the famines of the 1840s.

In addition to discontent with their countries of origin, emigrants must feel that the countries to which they are going offer them more freedom or greater opportunities.

In the 1960s immigration into Britain from the new countries of the Commonwealth was largely due to the attraction of a higher standard of living. During the same period the so-called 'brain drain' of British scientists and doctors to the United States was explained by the attraction of higher salaries, lower taxation, or superior facilities for work.

2 Effects of immigration

The economic effects depend partly on the size of the existing population. If a country is already overpopulated, it will obviously suffer from a large inflow of immigrants. On the other hand, an underpopulated economy should benefit from immigration. For example, immigration into the United States during the nineteenth century provided the labour needed to develop its economy and make full use of its vast natural resources.

Much also depends on the age composition of the immigrants and the contribution they can make as workers. A large inflow of old people or young children would clearly be a burden to the receiving country. But a country should benefit from immigration consisting mainly of people of working age, particularly if they were skilled in occupations it needed.

In practice those who seek new lives in other countries tend to be young workers, and recent immigration into Britain has supplied valuable labour for

How does immigration affect Britain's economy?

essential services such as transport and hospitals. The community as a whole gains from such immigration though wages may be held back in some occupations because immigrant workers are often willing to accept less pay.

In general, immigration should bring economic advantages to a country that is underpopulated and/or short of labour. But it can also create social problems and tensions.

The social consequences are likely to be most serious if the newcomers differ sharply from the existing population in race, colour, and culture. The difficulties of integration are also accentuated if the immigrants concentrate in certain localities. Housing shortages, overcrowded schools, and other signs of congestion then add to the problems of achieving harmony in a mixed community. Such problems became acute in some parts of Britain in the 1960s and Parliament passed Acts to check the inflow and also to deal with racial discrimination. Forecasts suggest continued net emigration from Britain until at least the end of the century.

Optimum population

In theory there must be for every country a population size that is just right in relation to area and resources. This is the ideal or *optimum* number of inhabitants. *Economists define the optimum as the number of people that enables a country to achieve the maximum average output per person and therefore the highest possible standard of living.*

If a country's population exceeds the optimum level it is said to be overpopulated, and if it is below that level it is underpopulated. On this basis, India is clearly overpopulated and its people would be better fed if there were fewer of them. On the other hand, Australia is underpopulated and wants more people to develop its resources.

However, the optimum population of a country is difficult to estimate and, in any case, does not remain fixed. For instance, India would probably be able to support more people if its natural resources were used more fully and efficiently.

Even if a country gains economically from a rise in its population, there may be social disadvantages due to overcrowding. But overcrowding can be caused by uneven distribution of inhabitants rather than excessive numbers. In the United Kingdom, for example, congestion occurs in London and a few industrial areas where a large proportion of the population is concentrated. Many other parts of the country, including large areas of Scotland and Wales, are sparsely populated.

Table 2.1 UK population trends

	Birth-rate (per 000)	*Death-rate (per 000)*	*Rate of increase (per 000)*	*Total population (millions)*
1871	35	23	12	27·4
1891	31	21	10	34·3
1911	25	15	10	42·0
1931	16	13	3	46·0
1951	16	13	3	50·2
1971	16	12	4	55·6
1981	13	12	1	55·8

Britain's population trends

The history of Britain's population can be divided roughly into three periods. First, there was a period of very slow growth lasting until the eighteenth century. The growth was slow because, though the birth-rate was high, life was short for most people and so the death-rate was also high. Secondly, a period of rapid growth occurred in the nineteenth century when the birth-rate remained high at about 35 per thousand while the death-rate was falling to about 20 per thousand. Finally, the rate of growth slowed down again in the twentieth century (Table 2.1).

Since the Second World War, the UK death-rate has remained fairly constant at about 12 per thousand and population growth has depended mainly on the birth-rate. This rose sharply during the war, reaching a peak (20·7) in 1947, but then resumed its general decline. In the 1970s, with the birth-rate hardly exceeding the death-rate, the population remained virtually stable at about 56 million. On present forecasts, it is expected to rise slowly to about 58 million by the end of the century. This is based on assumptions of steady net emigration and death-rates, and a small increase in the birth-rate.

1 What is meant by a natural increase or decrease in population? What is the other possible cause of a change in the size of the population?

2 How is a country's birth-rate measured? List the main influences affecting the birth-rate and indicate any you think particularly important at the present time.

3 How is the death-rate measured? Why would you normally expect the death-rate to fall? Suggest circumstances in which it might rise.

4 Why do people emigrate? How can a country benefit from immigration? What problems might it create?

5 What do economists mean by the optimum population of a country? Why is it difficult to estimate?

6 Draw graphs of the UK birth-rate and death-rate (Table 2.1). How do the graphs explain (a) the rapid growth of population towards the end of the nineteenth century, (b) the much slower rate of growth in this century?

2.2 Composition of the population

Age distribution

A useful classification of the population is into three broad age groups – those below school-leaving age, the working age group, and those above retirement age. The main dividing lines between these groups, in the United Kingdom, are the minimum school-leaving age of 16 and the retirement age of 65 for men.

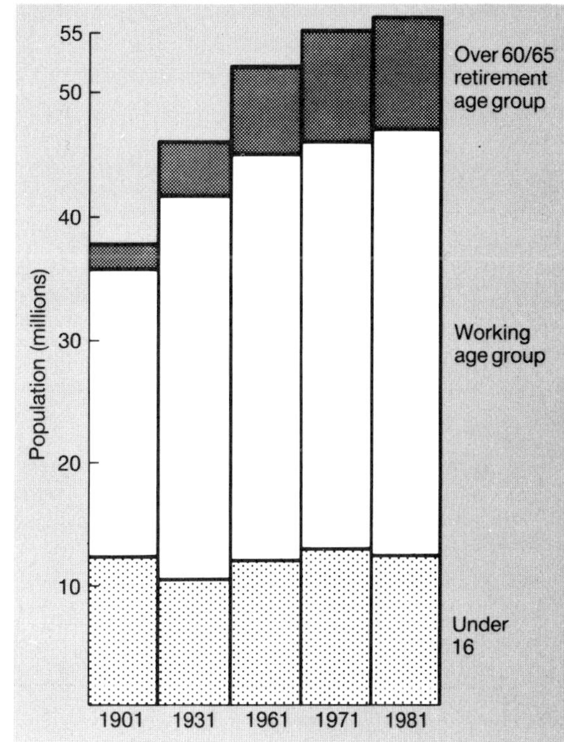

Fig. 2.4 Age distribution of UK population

1 Economic effects

i) The pattern of spending reflects the age distribution. An ageing population – one that contains a rising proportion of old people – requires an increasing quantity of products connected with old age and relatively fewer connected with the young. The industrial system has to adjust itself to the changing demand for goods and services. This adjustment could cause problems, particularly because the labour force is less adaptable in an ageing population.

ii) Young workers are generally more productive and adaptable. Although older people may have the advantage of experience, they are likely to be less energetic and enterprising. Moreover, in an ageing population, the young may have to wait longer to reach positions of responsibility and this could have a discouraging effect.

Of course the assertion that young people are more productive is open to contradiction (especially by their elders). However, few would question the view that they are more adaptable and easier to train for new jobs. A young population should also provide a larger flow of school-leavers able to start work in the industries where labour is most needed. The difficulty and expense involved in the movement of workers between industries are thus avoided.

The ability of workers to move easily from one job to another or one area to another is called *mobility of labour*. It is particularly important in economies such as that of Britain which must respond not only to changes of demand at home but also to foreign demand and competition.

iii) Production depends on the working age group. It is obviously possible to produce more goods and services and so achieve a higher standard of living if a larger proportion of the population is in the working age group – between school-leaving and retirement ages – which must provide the bulk of the country's labour force. Moreover, this group bears the burden of supporting the non-working members of the community. If a larger proportion of the population is either retired or at school, the extra cost of pensions or education falls on relatively smaller numbers who are working and earning.

2 Age distribution in the UK
The age distribution of the population, like its size, depends on what has been happening to the birth-rate and death-rate, and also migration, over a period of time. Since Britain's population growth is chiefly due to a falling death-rate, with people living longer, the largest increase has been in the group above retirement age. Its proportion of the total population has more than doubled since the beginning of this century (Fig. 2.4).

Both pensioners and children depend on the working population to supply the products they consume. Clearly, a larger dependent population means a greater burden of maintenance on the working population. The proportion of dependants in the population rose to a peak in the mid-1970s. It has since declined because the increasing number of retired people has been more than offset by a decreasing proportion of dependent children due to the falling birth-rate. This trend is expected to be reversed during the 1990s. A major factor is the rising percentage of very elderly (over 75) who make the greatest calls on health and social services.

Sex distribution

Women outnumber men in Britain's population because they live longer on average and also fewer were killed in the two World Wars. However, male births have exceeded female births over a number of years and males are consequently more numerous in all age groups up to about 50. If the present sex ratio of births continues, men will eventually outnumber women in the population as a whole. Nevertheless, women will remain in a majority among the very old as long as their average expectation of life exceeds that of men (Table 2.2).

In a society that condemns polygamy, it is obviously desirable to have roughly equal numbers of men and women of marriageable age. Inequality of numbers may reduce the chance of personal happiness for some who are deprived of marriage. As we have seen, the marriage-rate in turn affects the birth-rate – with all its consequences.

As well as influencing the birth-rate, sex distribution also affects the economy through the labour supply. Since women retire earlier than men and fewer are generally at work, a country with a relatively large number of women is likely to have a smaller working population. In Britain today, as the proportion of men rises, one can expect the benefits of a larger working population.

Table 2.2 UK expectation of life at birth

	Men	*Women*
1901	46	50
1931	58	63
1951	66	71
1981	70	76

Apart from numbers at work, there are also differences in the type of work done by men and women. Thus, a smaller proportion of women in the working age group could lead to shortages of certain kinds of labour for which women are most suited.

1 Refer to Fig. 2.4 and note the three main age groups into which the population is divided. Which age group has been growing most rapidly?
2 What are the likely economic effects of an ageing population?
3 Why do males outnumber females in the younger age range of Britain's population but not among retired people?

2.3 World population

The population explosion

At the end of the eighteenth century, the economist Malthus wrote a gloomy essay on the future of Britain's population in which he foresaw probable starvation as the rapidly expanding number of people outgrew the country's food supply. This prediction did not come true, mainly because newly developed areas of the world, such as America and Australia, were able to provide Britain with extra food in exchange for manufactured goods. At the same time, improvements in farming methods brought about a large increase in home food production.

Many people feel that the problems of overpopula-

Table 2.3 The growth of world population

Year	Population (millions)
1650	550
1750	750
1800	900
1850	1150
1900	1600
1950	2500
1980	4430
2000	6400 (estimated)

tion that Malthus expected to occur in Britain are now really facing the world as a whole. Of course, figures of world population can only be rough estimates, particularly for earlier periods of history, but the trend shown in Table 2.3 would not be disputed.

The increasing rate of population growth in the nineteenth century took place chiefly in Western Europe where the pattern was similar to that of Britain. The new explosion which started about 1945 is concentrated in the less developed areas of the world, particularly in Asia and Africa (Fig. 2.5). The explanation is that birth-rates have remained high in those areas while their death-rates have fallen with the spread of medical knowledge from the West. Thus, the countries concerned generally have birth-rates in the region of 40 per thousand and death-rates around 15 per thousand.

Population is now multiplying fastest in areas of the world that already have the greatest food shortage and are least able to support additional numbers. Unfortunately, population growth in these areas has not been accompanied by a corresponding increase in their food production. Nor has it been linked with industrialization and technical progress on the scale that enabled the Western nations to support extra people. Moreover, one cannot assume that, without a similar rise in living standards, birth-rates will automatically fall as they did in Western Europe.

Food shortage is due either to insufficient quantity (undernutrition) or a deficiency of essential ingredients (malnutrition). Some recent estimates suggest that up to half the human race may be suffering from undernutrition and as much as two-thirds from malnutrition.

Both kinds of shortage are concentrated in areas

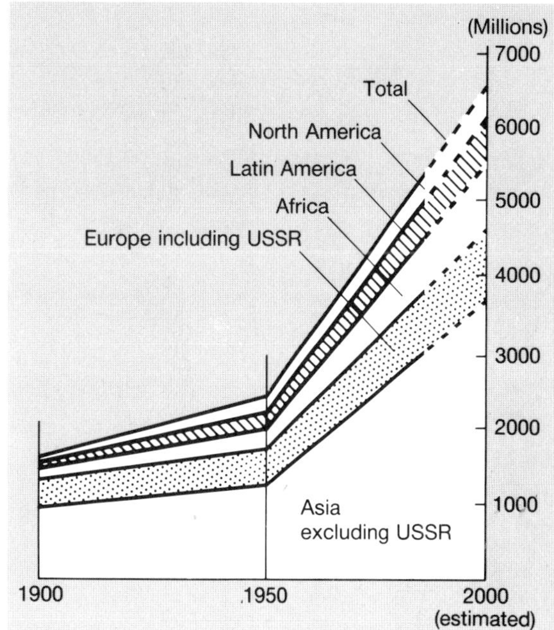

Fig. 2.5 World population growth

of Asia, Africa, the Middle East, and South America, containing nearly three-quarters of the world population and experiencing the fastest rates of population growth. The widespread hunger and poverty of these 'have-not' areas make a disturbing contrast with the expanding wealth of the 'haves' of Europe and North America.

Possible solutions

Population obviously cannot continue to grow at its recent rate for ever. The ultimate solution could be war or famine on a scale not yet experienced. The question is: what can people do to avoid the starvation that continues to threaten a large part of the world's population?

1 Reducing the birth-rate

International organizations and governments, such as those of India and China, have already done a lot to promote birth control. But modern methods are expensive for poor people, and knowledge is difficult to spread in places where the inhabitants are widely scattered and poorly educated.

It is possible that the birth-rate would be most strongly influenced by better education and a higher standard of living. Western experience indicates that

family size is reduced as people become better off and have more leisure opportunities. Progress in education would not only help the spread of birth control but also help to overcome poverty by increasing the efficiency of the people.

2 Increasing agricultural production

Farming methods remain primitive in many parts of the world, particularly in the areas of greatest food shortage. Considerable progress has been made in recent years, but there is still great scope for development of the world's agricultural resources.

3 Overseas aid

It should be apparent that many of the proposed solutions depend on assistance from rich to poor countries. Assistance is given through voluntary organizations such as Oxfam, through international agencies, or directly by governments. It can take many forms: providing advisers, technicians, or teachers; supplying machinery or equipment; making grants or loans of money.

What problems of a developing economy are illustrated by the poster and two farming photographs?

The main purpose of government aid to other countries is to help them to develop their own agricultural and industrial resources. Industrial development should enable those countries to sell products abroad and so buy food or other things needed by their people. Aid should therefore be accompanied by the development of trade between the countries of the world.

One problem is that developing economies often find it difficult to make headway in competition with the already developed industries of more advanced economies. There is a case for helping them to expand their exports by giving them favourable treatment such as lower tariff duties on their products.

1 What is meant by the population explosion and what has caused it? Use Table 2.3 to draw a graph showing the growth of the world's population. Describe the trend shown by your graph.

2 Why has there been a revival of the ideas put forward by Malthus two centuries ago? What can be done to ease the problems of the poorer developing countries in Asia, Africa, and South America?

Multiple choice

1 A natural increase in population occurs if
1 the birth-rate exceeds the death-rate
2 immigration exceeds emigration
3 the number of births exceeds the number of deaths

A 1, 2 and 3 are correct
B 1 and 2 only are correct
C 2 and 3 only are correct
D 1 and 3 only are correct
E 1 only is correct

2 A country's population would tend to decrease if
A the death-rate falls
B immigation increases
C the birth-rate falls
D there is a rise in the average family size
E there is a fall in the average age of marriage

3 Which of the following is true of the UK population?
A Immigration usually exceeds emigration.
B Men outnumber women in the population as a whole.
C The proportion of retired people has risen in this century.
D The working population has fallen in this century.
E The proportion of children has risen continuously.

4 The term 'optimum population' refers to the size of population that
A can be adequately fed
B maximizes total output
C creates fewest social problems
D maximizes output per head
E can achieve self-sufficiency

5 The effects of an ageing population include
1 an increase in labour mobility
2 a decrease in the dependent population
3 a change in the pattern of spending in the economy

A 1 only is correct
B 1 and 2 only are correct
C 1 and 3 only are correct
D 2 and 3 only are correct
E 3 only is correct

6 The size of the working population would NOT be affected by a change in
A its geographical distribution
B its sex distribution
C the retirement age
D the school-leaving age
E opportunities for higher education

7 A change in sex distribution is likely to affect all the following EXCEPT
A the supply of labour
B the birth-rate
C the composition of the labour force
D the level of immigration
E the size of the working population

8 A country's total population remains stable if
A birth-rate equals death-rate
B birth-rate is zero
C natural increase equals net immigration
D natural increase equals net emigration
E immigration is zero

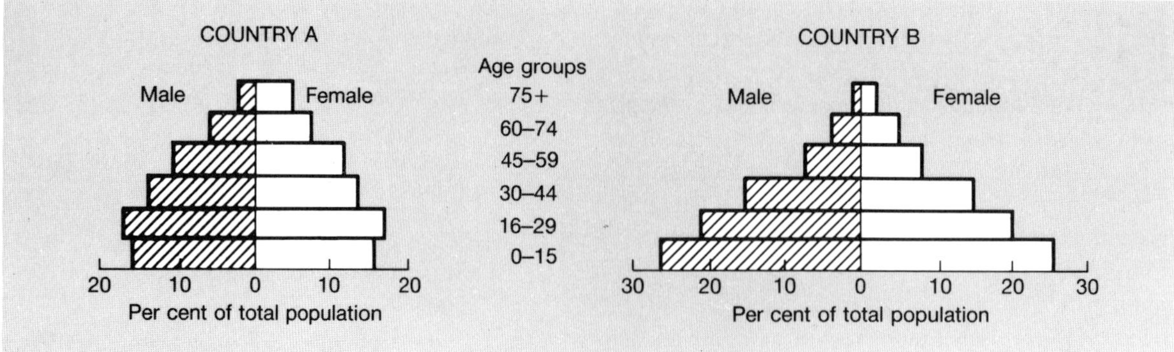

Fig. 2.6 Population pyramids

Data response

The pyramid diagrams in Fig. 2.6 show the age and sex composition of two countries. In both, the school-leaving age is 15 and retirement is at 60.

1 Which country has experienced (a) the highest death-rate, (b) the highest birth-rate, (c) a falling birth-rate?

2 What is meant by an ageing population? Which pyramid provides evidence of an ageing population and what is the evidence?

3 Suggest three likely effects of an ageing population.

4 Define the working age group in the two countries. How could this age group be increased quickly in an emergency such as war-time?

5 Suggest three reasons why the number of workers or working population of a country might differ from the number in the working age group.

6 Which of the two pyramids is most likely to represent a less developed country in Africa or Asia? Explain your choice.

7 What happens to the sex distribution of population in both countries above retirement age? How can it be explained?

Essays

1 World population has increased rapidly since 1945 while that of the UK has increased only slowly. Account for the difference.

2 Why has the average age of Britain's population shown a rising trend over a number of years? Describe the probable effects of such a trend.

3 Explain the concept of optimum population. In the light of this concept, discuss the likely economic effects of substantial immigration into the UK.

Chapter 3

Working population

3.1 Supply of labour

Number of workers

The working population of a country consists of all its inhabitants who either are at work or offer themselves as available for work. It thus includes all those who are out of work but registered as unemployed. The latter normally qualify for unemployment benefit (the dole) while waiting to be found jobs.

The basis of the working population is the working age group of the population comprising everyone between the official ages for school leaving and retirement. To these must be added people who continue to work beyond the retirement age. However, the number of workers is reduced by full-time students, housewives, and others of working age who do not make themselves available for work. Out of a total United Kingdom population of 56 million in 1981, there were 33 million in the working age group and a working population of 26 million.

1 Determining the numbers

The main factors determining the size of the working population are indicated in Fig. 3.1 and can be briefly stated.

Fig. 3.1 The working population

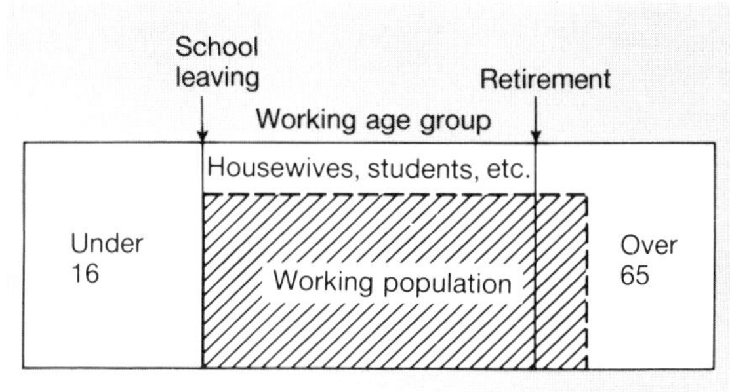

i) *Total population.* A larger population generally contains more workers, though this may be offset by other factors listed below.
ii) *Ages of school leaving and retirement.* These determine the lower and upper limits of the working age group of the population.
iii) *Proportion of non-workers within the working age group.* These are mainly full-time students above the age of 16 and housewives who do not go out to work.
iv) *Number at work beyond retirement age.* In Britain, old age pensions are paid to men at 65 and women at 60, but a number continue to work beyond these ages.
v) *Age distribution of the population.* The working population of a country should obviously be larger if more of its people are in the working age group.
vi) *Sex composition of the population.* The effect of sex distribution on the size of the working population depends on the laws and customs of the country. If the social customs discourage women from going out to work or cause them to retire earlier than men, then a larger proportion of women results in a smaller proportion of workers. In Britain, the excess of male births over female births should help to expand the working population, though this is offset by the fact that more women now go out to work.

2 Government influence

The size and composition of the working population can be influenced by government policies in a variety of ways. Laws relating to compulsory education and retirement clearly affect the size of the working age group. Changes in rates of pension, the scale of student grants, the number of university places, and provision of nursery education are all examples of measures that could affect the size of the labour force by influencing personal choices such as retirement and further education.

Productivity of labour

A country's manpower resources depend not only on the number of workers but also on the amount that each worker on average produces – that is, the productivity of labour. Productivity in turn depends on the hours of work including overtime, how hard people work during those hours, and their efficiency as workers.

Longer holidays and a shorter working week normally mean less production unless people work harder during the reduced hours of work. The efficiency of the working population is also affected by such things as standards of education and training, conditions of work, and the ability of managements to make good use of their workers.

In addition, productivity depends very much on the efficiency of other factors of production with which labour is combined. Thus, the output of farm workers depends to a great extent on the fertility of the land they cultivate. Similarly, the higher productivity of factory workers in advanced industrial countries is largely due to superior machinery and other capital equipment with which they work.

1 Note the definition of the working population. Draw Fig. 3.1 and note how the working population differs from the working age group of the population.

2 Make a list of changes that could bring about an increase in the country's working population.

3 What is meant by the productivity of labour? How could productivity be increased?

3.2 Industries and occupations

Industrial distribution

For the purpose of looking at its industrial distribution, the working population is conveniently classified into three main groups – primary, secondary, and tertiary industries (Table 3.1).

The primary or extractive industries are generally concerned with obtaining food or raw materials. They consist of agriculture, forestry, and fishing, together with mining and quarrying.

The secondary industries cover the whole range of manufacturing, and also building and construction.

Table 3.1 Distribution of employment

	Percentages		
	1961	*1971*	*1984*
Primary (extractive)	6	4	3
Secondary (manufacturing and construction)	46	42	31
Tertiary (services and public utilities)	48	54	66

The tertiary industries are those that provide services. They include public utilities (gas, electricity, and water), transport and commmunications, distributive trades, banking and financial services, professional and scientific activities, catering, and all the services of central and local government.

1 Primary industries

An outstanding feature of industrial distribution in the United Kingdom is the small percentage of workers in the primary industries. The proportion of the working population employed in these industries has fallen almost continuously since the nineteenth century (Fig. 3.2). The decline is explained by the contraction of employment in agriculture and coal mining, the two main industries in the group.

The diminishing role of *agriculture* in the British economy reflects the trend towards industrialization over a long period of history. The number of farm workers has also fallen in the twentieth century because of difficulties facing the industry through foreign competition.

Though British farmers have received substantial assistance from the government since the Second World War, the number employed in the industry

Fig. 3.2 Changing distribution of employment

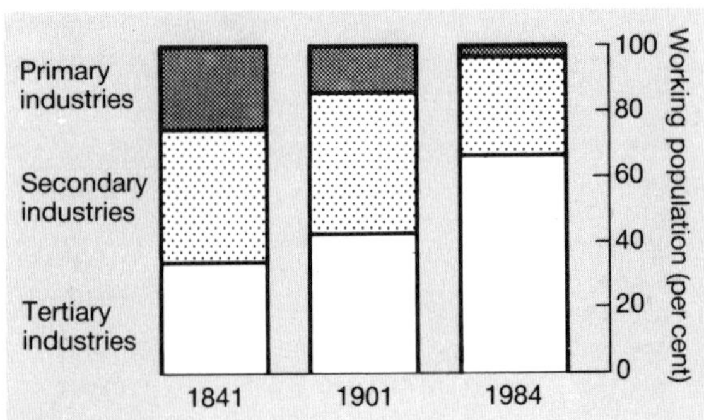

These photographs show primary, secondary, and tertiary stages of industry. Which stage does each represent? What is the basic material in all three?

has continued to fall, rural workers being attracted by the higher wages and better conditions to be found in towns. Agricultural production has in fact expanded in recent years, but this has been achieved by mechanization and higher productivity per worker.

Coal mining has declined because of competition from other sources of energy. Britain's coal production has been falling since the 1950s, and the industry has drastically reduced the size of its labour force.

2 Secondary industries

A notable feature of the British economy in recent years has been the decline of the once dominant manufacturing sector-a process know as *de-industrialization*. Output of manufactured goods fell sharply in the early 1980s, and secondary industries now employ less than one-third of workers in employment. Significant changes have also taken place in the pattern of manufacturing. In particular, the old basic industries such as textiles and shipbuilding have declined in importance as employers of labour compared with the modern technological or science-based industries such as motor vehicles, engineering and chemicals.

3 Tertiary industries

Perhaps the most striking fact revealed by the figures of industrial distribution is the importance of this group in the economy today (Table 3.1). Services have been the most rapidly expanding part of the economy and now employ more workers than there are in manufacturing. There has been a substantial growth of numbers in nearly every category in this group. A notable exception is in the number of domestic servants, a category that once provided the main opportunities of employment for working women.

In general, the growth of the service industries is a reflection of the development of society. The growth of the welfare state and the educational system has meant an expanding demand for doctors, nurses, social workers, and teachers. State intervention in the economic and social life of the country has likewise resulted in an expanding number of civil servants and local government employees.

The numbers engaged in banking, insurance, accountancy, law, and other professions have multiplied with the growth of business and trade. At the same time, rising standards of living have been accompanied by an expanding demand for services concerned with such things as entertainment, travel, and catering.

Effects of economic progress

A comparison with the industrial distribution of Britain's working population in the eighteenth century (before industrialization) or with a developing country today would bring out several points. In a developing economy a much larger proportion of the workers is employed in primary industries, particularly agriculture. The numbers engaged in manufacturing and services are correspondingly less. This is because low incomes are spent chiefly on essential foodstuffs. People need to be relatively well off before they can afford to buy manufactured products or services on a large scale.

As an economy develops and the living standards of the people rise, employment expands first in manufacturing industries and then in services. With continued progress, the latter group eventually surpasses manufacturing as a source of employment. This sequence of events explains the present distribution of workers in the United Kingdom.

Occupational distribution

An alternative way of looking at the working population is according to jobs rather than industries. This classification has the advantage of distinguishing groups such as clerks and unskilled workers who are scattered among many different industries. However, the occupational grouping generally corresponds with the features already observed in connection with industrial distribution.

The comparatively small share of the primary industries in Britain's economy is indicated by the small numbers of farm workers and miners in relation to other groups. The importance of manufacturing is shown by the fact that factory workers are the largest single occupational group. Moreover, many members of other occupations, such as clerks, are actually in manufacturing industries. The extent of the service industries can be realized when it is considered that they include nearly all professional workers (doctors, lawyers, teachers, etc.) as well as all those engaged in transport, selling and distribution, recreation and entertainment, and numerous office workers.

1 Explain, with examples, the classification of industries into primary, secondary, and tertiary. Note the percentages of the population employed in each of these three sectors, using the most recent figures available (Table 3.1).

2 Describe and account for the changing distribution of employment illustrated in Fig 3.2.

3.3 Mobility of labour

In an industrial society, the demand for products is always changing and new products are constantly coming into existence. Thus, at any moment of time, some industries and occupations will be growing in importance while others are declining. This requires a continuous movement of labour between jobs. It may also require geographical movements since the expanding industries that need labour are not necessarily in the same areas as the declining industries where jobs are disappearing.

An economy such as Britain's therefore requires labour to move easily between industries, occupations, and areas. These three kinds of mobility are illustrated in Fig. 3.3.

Fig. 3.3 Types of labour mobility

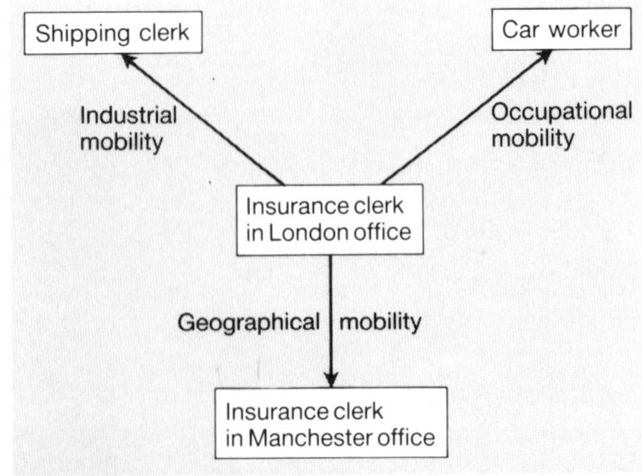

How do job centres contribute to mobility of labour?

Obstacles to mobility

Economic efficiency requires that labour should not remain idle and should move rapidly into jobs for which it is most suited. But there are many obstacles to mobility. What are the difficulties involved in each of the three types of movement illustrated?

Industrial mobility is obviously most straightforward when the worker is going into a similar job in the same area, though even this involves adjustment to the conditions of another industry. Occupational mobility is often obstructed by the delays, costs, and difficulties of retraining, and this can be particularly hard for older workers. Geographical mobility can entail all the personal problems of uprooting home and family. Frequently, all three kinds of mobility are combined in a single move.

Aids to mobility

1 Government policies

If workers are reluctant to move to the jobs, it may be easier for jobs to be moved to the workers. Thus, governments have tried to meet some of the problems of the geographical immobility of labour by encouraging firms to expand or build new factories in areas of exceptionally high unemployment. These *assisted areas* are given favoured treatment through government regional policies.

Various methods are used to encourage workers to move to jobs where they are needed. Job centres in every area have the task of fitting the unemployed workers on their registers into suitable vacancies notified by employers. School-leavers obtain advice and information from youth employment offices and are also helped by careers departments within the schools themselves. In certain cases financial help is given towards removal expenses and the cost of rehousing. Special importance is now also attached to training facilities to improve the mobility and efficiency of the working population.

2 Industrial training

Training increases the mobility of labour by fitting people for new jobs and helping to supply the new skills required by technical progress. Most industrial training is carried out by firms themselves, sometimes in co-operation with technical colleges. But many firms are too small to develop their own schemes. Substantial facilities are now provided by the government through the Department of Employment and Manpower Services Commission.

Full-time courses are arranged for unemployed workers or others who wish to train for new jobs. Courses lasting for up to a year are provided at government training centres, in the premises of firms, or at institutions such as further education colleges. The Youth Training Scheme, initiated by the government in 1983, guarantees all unemployed school-leavers two years of vocational education and work experience.

1 Distinguish the three types of mobility of labour illustrated in Fig. 3.3. Give an example of each type. Why is labour mobility important for an advanced industrial economy?
2 What obstacles may prevent people from changing their jobs? How does the government help to overcome obstacles?

3.4 Unemployment

The official figure of unemployment in Britain is obtained from a monthly count of the numbers registered as unemployed and claiming benefit at employment offices throughout the country. It is sometimes expressed as a percentage of the working population, called the rate of unemployment. However, the true level of unemployment is always higher than the published figures because there are a number of people, particularly women, who seek work but do not register as unemployed.

Types of unemployment

1 Voluntary

There are always some people who register as unemployed, in order to qualify for relief, but do not genuinely seek work. In some cases, their earning capacity may be so low that they are hardly worse off on unemployment pay. An obvious answer would be to ensure a minimum working wage well above the rate of unemployment benefit. However, there will always remain those who cannot find work owing to mental or physical incapacity.

2 Seasonal

In some industries the demand for labour varies during the year, causing unemployment at slack periods. Obvious examples are in tourist and holiday activities, agriculture, and industries with markets dependent on climate. In some cases the problem can be met by recruiting temporary labour at peak periods – for instance, the employment of student labour by the Post Office at Christmas.

3 Frictional

A proportion of the unemployed at any time consists of people who are merely in the process of changing their jobs. This is inevitable in a developed economy where industry is constantly adapting to new techniques and changing demand for products. Thus, while the demand for labour is declining in some industries, it is expanding in others. The resulting unemployment is usually temporary and may involve no severe hardship. Such frictional unemployment cannot be eliminated but may be reduced by measures to accelerate the mobility of labour.

4 Structural

Structural unemployment, like frictional, is largely caused by the changing demand for products. It can also arise from technological changes, including automation, leading to the substitution of machinery for labour in certain industries. A major cause in Britain has been the growth of foreign competition in some important industries.

The main difference between structural and frictional unemployment is that the structural type is generally associated with the decline of major industries, such as cotton and shipbuilding, which are concentrated in certain parts of the country. It therefore tends to be unemployment of a regional or local nature, bearing heavily on areas dependent on the industries concerned.

For this reason, the workers affected find it hard to obtain alternative jobs and, compared with frictional unemployment, structural unemployment generally lasts longer and creates more hardship. The areas concerned are chiefly the *development areas* which receive special treatment under the government's regional policies (see Chapter 6).

5 General

Seasonal, frictional, and structural unemployment are confined to particular industries or occupations. Unemployment of a more widespread nature occurs when the total spending of the community on goods and services of all kinds is not enough to keep the resources of the economy fully occupied. This means that industry in general is forced to work below its full capacity with some factory space and machinery lying idle and a proportion of workers laid off.

Of course, all industries are not affected to an equal extent. The worst hit have usually been large investment industries such as steel and coal which depend on the demand of other industries. Food-producing industries are least affected since people generally maintain their spending on food even in lean times. But the effects are much wider than with other types of unemployment.

Unemployment of this kind is called *cyclical unemployment* because it is associated with ups and downs of the economy which are known to economists as the trade cycle. The conditions in which such unemployment occurs are those of slump or deflation. The remedy is for the government to stimulate spending through its own budget or by making more money available through the banking system.

Level of unemployment

In a country such as Britain unemployment could never fall to zero. Even when the economy is working at full stretch there is always some frictional unemployment due to the normal movement of labour between jobs. In addition, some seasonal, voluntary, and structural unemployment have always existed. When we talk of *full employment* we mean a situation in which the economy is working at close to its full capacity and unemployment is close to the minimum level attainable. Opinions differ about the actual figure, but recognizable symptoms are widespread labour shortages and rapidly rising wages and prices. The problems of the economy are then concerned with inflation, not unemployment.

Another way of looking at the employment situation is to compare the figure of unemployment with the number of unfilled jobs or vacancies notified by employers (Fig. 3.4). From this point of view, a state of full employment can be said broadly to exist when the number of unemployed falls below the number of vacancies. This is a clear indication of labour shortages with consequent inflationary pressures on wages and prices – a situation which economists sometimes call 'overfull employment'. However, the economy has not been even close to such a position since 1974.

Hardship of unemployment

From a purely economic point of view, unemployment is a waste of the community's scarce resources. The existence of unemployed labour also usually means that factory space and machinery are not being

Fig. 3.4 UK unemployment and vacancies (annual averages)

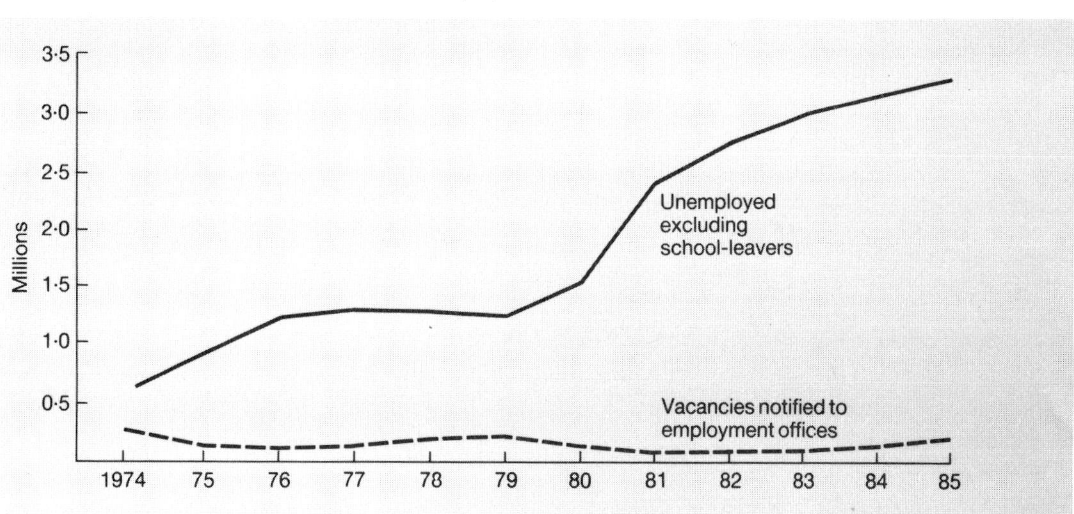

fully used. Production is consequently below maximum and society is not achieving the highest possible standard of living for its members. Moreover, production lost in this way is never regained.

To many, however, the worst consequences are social rather than economic. Long periods of enforced idleness can seriously affect personal attitudes and family relationships. Social problems are also created for the community as a whole.

The right to work is a recognized principle of modern society. Governments must give high priority to the maintenance of full employment and are expected to relieve the hardship of unemployment by adequate scales of benefit. In addition to the system of national insurance, employers in Britain are now required to make redundancy payments to workers who are laid off. The size of the payment is related to the length of service, age, and pay of the worker.

1 Note the main types of unemployment. Explain clearly the distinguishing features of frictional, structural, and general unemployment.

2 What is meant by full employment? How is it related to job vacancies?

3 By what methods does the government try (a) to reduce unemployment, (b) to relieve its hardship?

3.5 Division of labour

This term is used by eonomists to refer to a feature of modern life that we take for granted. This is the fact that nearly every worker earns his living from a particular trade or job at which he spends all his working hours. If there were no division of labour, each person would have to divide his time between different tasks, like Robinson Crusoe on his island, in order to produce for himself all the things he wanted. If a person does this he is said to be 'self-sufficient' because he does not then depend on others to supply his needs.

Division of labour is the reverse of self-sufficiency. It means that each worker concentrates on one job and relies on the work of others to supply most of his needs.

With division of labour, the work an individual does may make no contribution to his own personal needs. For example, the worker in a tobacco factory may not smoke himself. But in return for his specialized work he receives an income which can be used to buy from others all the goods and services he wants. Usually this income is in money, but money is not essential for division of labour. It would be possible for people to be paid for their work in actual goods which they then either use themselves or exchange for other things they want. This has happened in undeveloped economies.

Extent of division of labour

Even in simple farming communities where each family provided nearly all its own needs there was usually a certain amount of division of labour. This was likely to occur within the family, with the wife concentrating on tasks in the home while the husband worked on the land. Further division of labour has generally come about in stages as economies have developed (Fig. 3.5).

1 Division into occupations

The first significant steps towards the modern system took place when some members of early farming communities began to work full-time in certain occupations, such as those of millers and blacksmiths. These specialists would buy the various goods and services they needed with the income they received from their own work.

With the development of industry and trade, the number of specialist workers rapidly increased. The working population came to be divided into a growing number of industries such as textiles, coal mining, shipbuilding, and so on. It further divided into occupational groups such as clerical workers and engineers who could themselves be spread over many different industries. The distribution of the working population between both industries and occupations is described earlier in this chapter (p.30).

2 Division into processes

Another important development was the splitting up of the work in many industries and occupations into smaller processes with each worker specializing in a single task. In many cases this has been taken so far that an individual's special task may amount to only a small fraction of the final product. For example, it is common for factories to use a con-

What drawbacks of division of labour are illustrated by this production line?

veyor belt system where the product passes through successive stages with each worker making his own small contribution to the finished article. The worker on a car assembly line may thus spend all his time fixing just one small part into each car.

All jobs cannot be done on a conveyor belt, but an equivalent subdivision of work has taken place in most industries and occupations. One need only think of the number of specialized jobs in a hospital or a building site or even a school or college. There are few people today whose jobs do not depend on the co-operation of many other workers.

3 Geographical division

Division of labour occurs geographically when countries, or areas within countries, specialize in certain kinds of products. Britain as a whole traditionally specializes in the engineering products of which it is a large exporter. These international and regional aspects of division of labour are considered in later chapters on international trade and the location of industry.

Advantages

The great possibilities of division of labour were noted by the economist Adam Smith writing when Britain's industrial expansion had hardly started in the eighteenth century. Using pins as an example, he showed how production could be enormously increased. Instead of one man producing the whole pin, there would be several specialists – one preparing the wire, another cutting the lengths, another sharpening, and so on. The effect on skill and speed of work is obvious.

The specialization of the labour force generally enables a community to produce more and so attain a higher standard of living while also increasing its leisure time. These benefits come about through more efficient use of factors of production – capital as well as labour (Fig. 3.5).

1 Better use of labour

A society that provides opportunities for specialization allows individuals to choose the occupation for which they are best suited. More can be produced because workers do not have to divide their time between a variety of jobs many of which they may not do very well. Thus, a talented doctor can concentrate on his profession and leave a talented mechanic to look after his car. Furthermore, by working continuously at the same job a person improves his performance and learns how to overcome difficulties.

Output can also be increased because specialist workers do not waste time moving from one job to another, changing tools, and so on. In addition, by breaking up the work into simple tasks or processes,

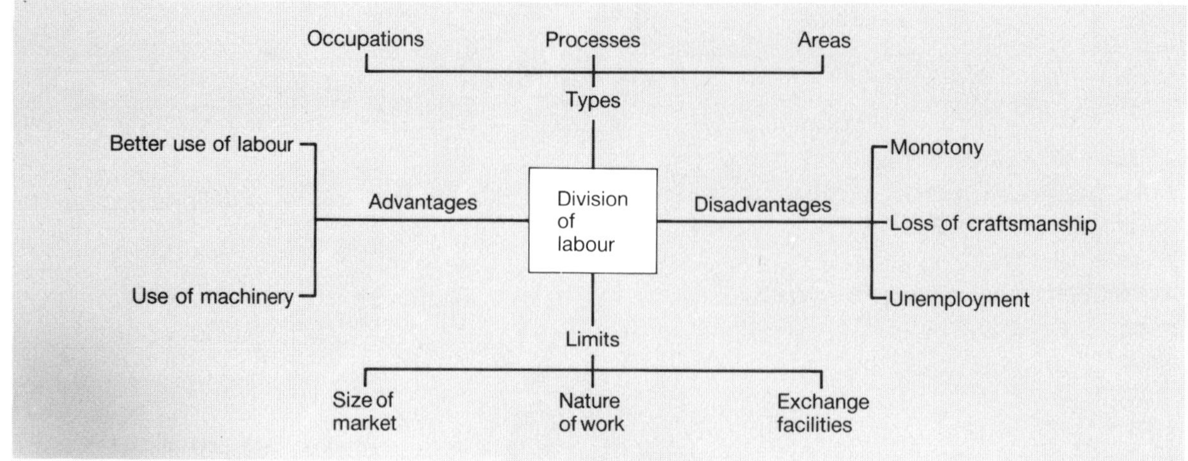

Fig. 3.5 Aspects of division of labour

some jobs are made easier to learn and time is saved in training. It should be remembered, however, that simple processes are sometimes taken over by machines and technical progress also requires more people with a high degree of skill and training.

2 More use of machinery

The simpler the process the easier it is to create a machine to perform it. It would thus be impossible for one machine to assemble a car completely, but separate machines can be designed to assist each process. Technical progress would have been much slower if not accompanied by division of labour.

Not only are machines easier to introduce but they can also be more fully used. If a worker does several different tasks, some tools and machines are likely to lie idle when he leaves them in order to carry out another task. Through division of labour, machinery can be kept running all the time with a continuous flow of production along the assembly line. Machinery increases production and may also relieve workers of heavy or tedious tasks.

Disadvantages

1 Monotony of work

We should ask ourselves whether society attaches too much importance to production and wealth. For instance, there is now serious concern about effects of the productive system such as pollution and noise. In connection with division of labour, the question is whether more production is worth achieving at the price of growing monotony in the working lives of many people.

The problem of monotony is most acute in the case of factory jobs that require continuous tedious repetition of a straightforward process in which there can be no personal satisfaction. Such work can have effects extending beyond the boredom of the job itself. For example, it may eventually narrow the worker's outlook and make communication with other people more difficult. The quality of personal and social life could thus be lowered. There could even be harmful effects on the health of workers.

Apart from its effects on the individual, the monotony of a narrow repetitive job may lead to increased absenteeism and reduced productivity, so defeating the object of division of labour. Some firms have consequently found it rewarding to reduce the degree of specialization in order to provide workers with more varied and interesting jobs. An individual worker or team of workers might be entrusted, for instance, with the assembly of a whole radio set instead of fitting just one component.

Nevertheless, there may be compensations to offset monotony. Many factory jobs are simple to learn and soon become automatic to the people doing them. If conditions allow, workers can easily learn to work and talk at the same time, so eliminating some of the boredom.

In addition, division of labour has helped to reduce the hours of work and provided workers with opportunities to pursue more varied interests through leisure. It should also be remembered that division into occupations has enabled a number of people to devote themselves to the jobs that they find most interesting and satisfying.

2 Loss of craftsmanship

Before industrialization, the typical occupations of town workers were in the skilled trades – printing, bootmaking, tailoring, baking, coachbuilding, watchmaking, and so on. The master craftsmen engaged in such trades provide an example of workers who could take a real pride in the quality of their products. The basis of this pride was that each worker did the whole job and could see the results of what he was doing. There are still occupations of this kind but they clearly do not include all the ordinary jobs in factories or offices in which the majority of people now work.

With the division of work into processes, particularly in manufacturing, most workers make only a small contribution to the final product and so have little incentive to take care or interest in their work.

The traditional type of craftsman would be willing to make goods to meet the requirements of individual customers. Workmanship of this kind is clearly impossible in a system based on division of labour and mass production. A feature of modern production is the standardization of products, with factories turning out large quantities of identical models. The variety of goods available is consequently restricted by division of labour.

However, the accompanying benefits should not be forgotten. In particular, expanding output and falling costs have brought manufactured consumer goods within the reach of masses of people who could never have afforded the products of individual craftsmen.

3 Insecurity of employment

Division of labour makes our jobs dependent on other people who buy our products or share in making them.

Jobs can be threatened by events in distant parts of the world. For example, Lancashire cotton workers became unemployed because overseas customers adopted new fashions in clothing or because foreign countries developed their own textile industries. The contraction of export markets has been a major cause of unemployment.

In many industries, workers have become dependent not only on unreliable markets but also on the actions of their fellow workers. If there are several processes in the production of an article, a strike among one group of workers can quickly affect those engaged in other processes. This kind of risk to employment is a familiar feature of the car industry where widespread stoppages have sometimes occurred as a result of the actions of a few workers perhaps producing one small car component.

The risks of unemployment may also be greater because many workers only get to know one job. Should there be a decline in the demand for their particular skills, they find it difficult to transfer to other occupations. For example, an unemployed miner in his forties or fifties does not find it easy to adapt himself to other work.

Scope and limits of specialization

1 Size of the market

The division of work into processes is a feature of large-scale production. Conditions are most favourable in industries where there is a large demand for a standardized or uniform product. The car industry is suitable because there is a mass market for popular models both at home and abroad. On the other hand, there is little scope for division of labour in the production of racing cars, which must be virtually handmade according to individual designs. The scope is similarly limited in firms making specialized instruments or machinery.

While recognizing the limits imposed by the size of the market, it should be noted that the demand for most products has increased over the years, so extending the opportunities for division of labour.

The growth of markets may be partly due to the fact that specialization has itself made people better off. Another factor is that the population of most countries has risen and is continuing to rise at a rapid rate. In addition, improvements in transport and communication have meant a substantial widening of both national and international markets. International markets have further expanded as a result of recent movements towards the reduction of trade restrictions and the formation of alliances such as the Common Market.

The growth of world trade has extended the scope for division of labour, but export markets are not always helpful in this respect. Though sales might be expanded in a number of countries, detailed variations in their national requirements sometimes act as an obstacle to mass production. Even a large market may provide only limited opportunities for division of labour if customers have different individual requirements.

It should be added that the obstacle of a limited market can sometimes be offset by reducing the number of firms or factories operating in an industry. In Britain and other industrial countries, the trend towards specialization has been assisted by the integration of firms through mergers and takeovers.

2 Nature of the work

Some occupations provide little opportunity for dividing the work into separate tasks or processes so that there is a limit to the development of division of labour. Obvious examples are doctors in general practice, teachers in primary schools, and skilled craftsmen such as carpenters or plumbers.

Even in occupations where there is a high degree of specialization, the number of processes cannot be indefinitely multiplied. The process of tightening a nut can hardly be further divided. Moreover, specialization can be limited by the number of workers available. Thus, labour shortages could compel a firm to reduce the number of processes and give each worker a wider span of duties.

3 System of exchange

The specialized worker lives by exchanging the products of his labour for all the other things he needs. In modern economies exchange is based on money. Each worker is paid a wage in money which he then uses to buy the things he wants. Without an efficient monetary system, division of labour on the modern scale would not have been possible. In a backward economy its development could still be obstructed through the lack of a satisfactory exchange system involving a stable unit of money, a reliable network of banks, and so on.

1 What do economists mean by division of labour? Indicate briefly the main stages of development to its modern form.

2 Note the ways in which division of labour is likely to lead to increased production.

3 Division of labour is often criticized from the viewpoint of employers as well as workers. Make a list of criticisms.

4 Explain, with examples, why division of labour is carried much further in some industries and occupations than in others.

Multiple choice

1 The working population includes all the following except

A policemen
B registered unemployed
C teachers
D full-time students
E insurance agents

2 The working population of a country is most likely to increase if

A retirement pensions are raised
B the age of retirement is reduced
C the school-leaving age is raised
D immigration is restricted
E more nursery schools are provided

3 The percentage of the total working population of Britain employed in primary industries is

A under 5
B 5-10
C 10-20
D 20-30
E more than 30

4 Which of the following is classed as a tertiary industry?

A coal mining
B agriculture
C engineering
D insurance
E cotton

5 The following figures show the distribution of the working population:

Agriculture	2 million
Mining	3 million
Manufacturing	12 million
Transport	1 million
Insurance and banking	2 million
Central and local government	2 million

The total number employed in tertiary production is

A 3 million
B 4 million
C 5 million
D 14 million
E 15 million

6 A person changes his job from a railway train driver in Liverpool to a railway signalman in London. This is an example of

1 geographical mobility
2 industrial mobility
3 occupational mobility

A 1, 2 and 3 are correct
B 1 and 2 only are correct
C 2 and 3 only are correct
D 1 and 3 only are correct
E 1 only is correct

7 A group of workers lose their jobs because an engineering factory closes down. After short periods of unemployment, all find new jobs in other factories close by. Economists call this type of unemployment

A voluntary
B seasonal
C frictional
D structural
E cyclical

8 The capital employed by a firm is fixed, but its labour force can be altered. Which of the following would signify increased productivity of labour?

1 Output decreases with an increase in the labour force.
2 Output remains constant with a smaller labour force.
3 Output increases with a smaller labour force.

A 1, 2 and 3 are correct
B 1 and 2 only are correct
C 2 and 3 only are correct
D 1 only is correct
E 3 only is correct

Data response

Employment by industry

Industry	*1971* (thousands)	*1981* (thousands)
Agriculture, forestry, and fishing	432	351
Mining and quarrying	396	338
Manufacturing	8 058	6 087
Construction	1 262	1 143
Gas, electricity, and water	377	347
Transport and communication	1 568	1 443
Distributive trades	2 610	2 767
Insurance, banking, and finance	976	1 316
Professional and scientific services	2 989	3 757
Miscellaneous services	1 946	2 579
Public administration	1 509	1 573
Total employment	22 122	21 701

1 Identify the primary industries in the table of employment. Calculate the approximate percentage of workers employed in those industries in 1981.

2 Why is employment in primary industries so low and evidently declining?

3 Identify the secondary industries and calculate their approximate percentage of total employment in 1981.

4 Referring to the figures, explain the term 'deindustrialization' as applied to the UK economy.

5 Why are services called tertiary industries? What is their approximate percentage of total employment in 1981?

6 Note and account for the trend of employment in service industries shown by the figures.

7 What group of people is included in the working population but not in the table? Explain the probable effect of a decline in the mobility of labour.

Essays

1 What is meant by the working population? By what means could the government try to increase its size, productivity, and mobility?

2 Unemployment is undesirable but unavoidable in a modern industrial society. Do you agree? Can governments do anything about it?

3 'Division of labour has brought economic benefits accompanied by social drawbacks'. Discuss.

Chapter 4

Organization of firms

We saw in Chapter 1 how goods and services are produced through the combined use of factors of production – land, labour, and capital. Economists sometimes add a fourth factor which they call *enterprise*. Enterprise is required to bring together the other factors and set them to work in a producing unit or firm. A person who does this is sometimes called an *entrepreneur*.

The traditional idea of an entrepreneur was an individual businessman who owned and controlled his own firm, gaining the profits if it succeeded but also risking the loss of his money if it failed. However, the growth of industry and increasing size of firms made it necessary to develop different kinds of business organization. These are classified in Fig. 4.1.

4.1 Private enterprise

Types of firms

Under private enterprise, firms are owned and controlled by individuals or groups of individuals seeking their own profit. Such firms vary in size and type from small family businesses to giant public companies. The company form of business organization is also described as *corporate* ownership or enterprise.

1 Sole proprietors

The simplest form of business organization is the small firm owned and managed by one person – *the sole proprietor.* He may work entirely on his own or employ other workers, but all decisions affecting the firm are made by him. He has probably put his own money into the business and takes on all the risks. Thus, if the firm does well he is rewarded with the profits, but if it fails he must bear the losses.

The main advantages are independence and adaptability. To many people, the attraction of the small firm is that the owner is the boss, makes his own decisions, and does not take orders from anyone else. Such a firm can usually adapt itself quickly to changing circumstances because decisions can be made by the owner on the spot and nobody else needs to be consulted. Another advantage is that the owner has a strong incentive to work hard for profits which he does not have to share with others.

Independence has drawbacks as well as advantages. An obvious drawback is that the sole proprietor often

Fig. 4.1 Types of business organization

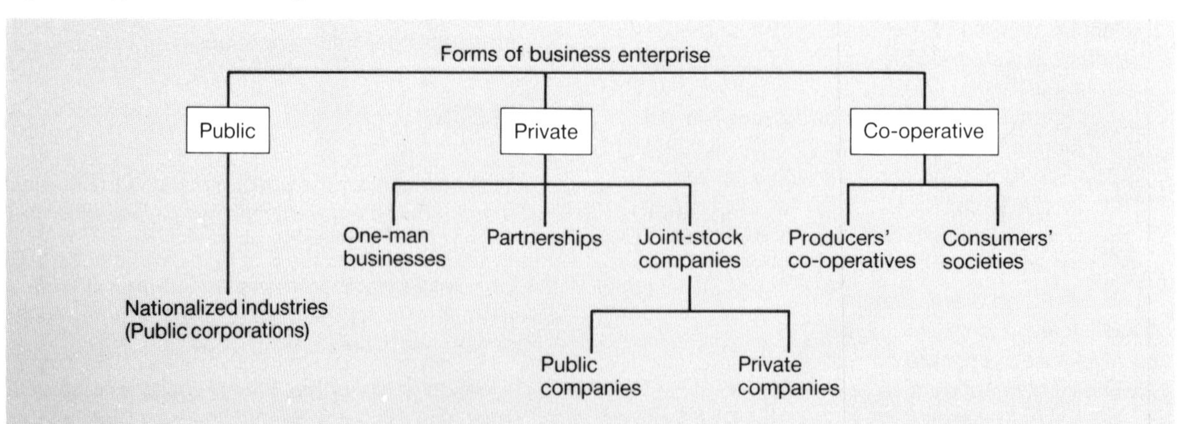

Why is this kind of business often run by a sole trader or partnership?

has nobody with the same interest in the business with whom he can discuss his problems. He may also have to rely on his own resources to improve or expand the business. This is because the small businessman frequently finds it difficult to raise money (capital) by borrowing. He can of course use his personal savings or put any profit he makes back into the business – a practice known as ploughing back the profits. But financial help from outside usually depends on his ability to inspire others with confidence.

A serious financial disadvantage of the sole proprietor is that he does not obtain the privilege of limited liability which the law gives to companies. This means that if the business fails the owner may be forced to pay his debts not only by selling the business property but also by giving up his own personal possessions. The risks of the sole proprietor are therefore greater than those undertaken by the owners of other kinds of business organizations.

Although the general tendency is for firms to become larger, being the sole proprietor continues to appeal to many people. A large number of such businesses starts up every year though experience shows that a fairly high proportion is also likely to fail.

The advantages and drawbacks of sole proprietors indicate the spheres of the economy in which they are most likely to flourish. Such firms are clearly suitable for businesses requiring close personal involvement and quick decisions but not too much capital. Two traditional fields are retailing and agriculture.

2 *Partnerships*

A partnership is a legally recognized association of between two and twenty people who have joined together to contribute the capital of a firm and share its profits.

The law lays down various rules about partnerships. In general, the number of partners is limited to twenty, though some exceptions are allowed. Decisions on basic matters such as the admission of new partners must be unanimous. Normal business decisions can usually be made by a majority vote and are then binding on all the partners. There are also rules applying to such circumstances as the death of a partner.

A partnership may originate in the desire of several people to share in a joint enterprise. Alternatively, it can come into existence because a sole proprietor needs more capital or wants to bring in new blood.

The obvious advantage is that it enables a firm to obtain more capital without becoming too large and impersonal. Partners can advise and consult each other, and it is also possible for each to specialize in certain aspects of the business.

Partnerships do not always run smoothly. Relations between partners can be difficult, particularly if business pressures mount up and there are wide differences of opinion. Partners must rely on each other and all will suffer if mistakes are made.

The dependence on each other is increased by the fact that, like sole proprietors, partners do not have the legal safeguard of limited liability and so their personal wealth is at risk if the firm fails. Limited liability is only allowed to a partner who has contributed capital but does not take any active part in running the business. Clearly, partnerships are unlikely to survive without a great deal of trust and confidence between the partners.

The disadvantages of partnerships explain why they have not proved a very suitable form of organization for firms engaged in industrial and commercial activities. Such businesses often involve a lot of risk and so there would have to be very close confidence between the partners to stand the strains.

Partnerships are most common in the professions where there are advantages to be gained from cooperation. Thus doctors, dentists, solicitors, accountants, architects, and other professional people are frequently grouped together. By forming partnerships, they can obtain more capital and also benefit by sharing their knowledge, advising each other, or specializing in particular matters.

3 Private companies

All companies are joint-stock organizations – that is, jointly owned by a number of shareholders or stockholders. *A private company is limited to a maximum of fifty members and its shares or stocks are not allowed to be sold to the general public.*

A great advantage of companies is that their members have limited liability – often indicated by 'Ltd' after the name of the company. We saw that this did not apply to either sole proprieters or partnerships. The term can now be more exactly defined. *Limited liability* means that if the company goes bankrupt, the holders of its stocks and shares can lose only the money they put in and cannot be required to give up personal property or savings to pay the debts of the company.

With more members and limited liability, a private company is in a position to raise more capital than either a sole proprietor or a partnership. It also has an advantage over larger public companies in that control over the company can be retained in the hands of a few people, as in the case of a family business.

These advantages explain why private companies are favoured for many commercial and industrial concerns of medium size. But their ability to raise large amounts of capital is restricted in two ways: first, because the number of shareholders is limited to fifty; secondly, because their shares cannot be sold publicly.

The restriction on selling shares publicly is a major disadvantage. It means that shares cannot be advertised for sale and cannot be sold through the Stock Exchange. A shareholder who wants to sell must find a private buyer. This may not be easy, particularly if the company is not well known. However, large financial institutions such as insurance companies are sometimes willing to invest in sound private companies.

4 Public companies

If the development of a private company is hindered by shortage of capital, its obvious answer is to become public. *A public company can raise capital by public issues of stocks and shares which may be quoted on the Stock Exchange, and there is no ceiling on the number of holders.* In fact, company law requires a minimum number of seven shareholders but no maximum.

Although private companies easily outnumber public ones in the United Kingdom, the latter are much more important in terms of total production and employment. If you look at the Stock Exchange prices listed in newspapers, you should be able to find the names of nearly all the giant industrial concerns whose products are familiar in almost every household. A public company can also be identified by the letters 'plc' after its name.

Company shares and debentures

The chief reason for forming companies is to raise more capital to pay for new factory buidings, machines, and so on. In the case of a public company, this is commonly done by issuing shares that any member of the public can buy.

When very large amounts of capital are required, the usual method is to advertise shares by means of a 'prospectus' outlining the state of the company and the terms of the issue. Such advertisements can be seen in newspapers from time to time. The shares are issued in units such as £1, and people are invited to apply for a quantity by a given date. Sometimes the existing shareholders of a company are favoured by being given the first chance to buy a new issue of shares in proportion to the amounts they already hold. This is called a 'rights' issue.

A share entitles its owner to a share of the profits of the company and perhaps also some say in the company's affairs. Part of the profits may be retained by the company to *plough back* into the business. The remainder is distributed to shareholders in the form of payments known as *dividends*. With limited liability, a shareholder can lose no more than the amount he paid for his shares. But if the company does badly there may be few or no dividends, and the value of its shares is also likely to fall.

Shares are classified according to the risk to the shareholder. The two main types are called ordinary and preference shares. We will also consider debentures – an alternative means by which companies can obtain capital from the public.

1 Ordinary shares

Ordinary shares involve the greatest risk to the shareholders but are also the most profitable if the company does well. The holders receive their dividends out of the profits left over after all other claims have been met. They may consequently get nothing, but also stand to gain most if the company earns a large surplus of profit. They are also the last to be compensated if the company goes bankrupt and has to be sold up to pay its debts.

Risk and profit go together with the ownership of business. Ordinary shareholders are consequently part-owners and share some of the responsibility of running the company. In practice, this means that they are entitled to vote at general meetings of the company and so have some power to influence major decisions such as the appointment of directors or perhaps a proposal to merge with another firm.

The voting power of a shareholder depends on the number of shares he holds. However, the practical influence of the mass of ordinary shareholders in public companies is generally very small. They are usually too numerous, scattered, and unorganized to exercise much pressure on the full-time directors.

In any case, a typical investor spreads his shares over several companies and has no time to take an active interest in any one. Most shareholders' meetings are thus thinly attended, and the directors, who may themselves be large shareholders can nearly always get their own way. Companies sometimes also issue non-voting ordinary shares which strengthen director control.

2 Preference shares

Preference shares earn a fixed dividend that must be paid before there can be any distribution of profit to ordinary shareholders. If a company does well it is the ordinary shareholders who are rewarded with the extra profit and not preference shareholders whose dividend remains unchanged. But the preference shareholders must be paid first and also have first claim on the company's property if it goes bankrupt. Since they take fewer risks, they do not have the same rights as ordinary shareholders to vote at company meetings.

Preference shares may be *cumulative*, that is, if no dividend is paid in an unprofitable year, the holder is entitled to have his payment made up in a future year. Another type of preference share is called *participating* and entitles the holder to an extra share of the profits on top of the fixed dividend, in a good year.

3 Debentures

Debentures are not shares but loans that earn a fixed rate of interest. They are not classed as shares because they do not depend on profits, and the interest must be paid before any profits are calculated. If a company fails to pay the interest on debentures, the holders can force it into bankruptcy and demand repayment of their loans from the sale of the company's property. In the event of failure, the company must repay its debts to debenture holders before anything is paid to shareholders. Debentures clearly do not involve the risk of shares and give no right to vote at meetings.

Sources of business finance

A firm may need finance either to start up or to expand. Expansion can be self-financed (from profits) or financed by borrowing of various kinds. The method of borrowing depends partly on the purpose for which it is required – for example, whether temporary or long term. It also depends on the type and size of the firm concerned. These factors affect the sources of finance outlined below.

1 Bank loans

Money required for temporary purposes can usually be borrowed from a bank in the form of an *overdraft* or short-period loan. Such a loan might be used to purchase raw materials or stocks of goods leading in due course to sales from which the loan can be repaid. More recently banks have been prepared to lend for longer periods (years rather than months) in the form of *term loans* used, for example, to buy machinery or equipment. Obviously a large established company is in a stronger position to borrow, and can usually secure a lower rate of interest, than a small comparatively unknown business.

2 Share issues

A public joint-stock company can raise additional capital through new issues of shares or debentures. This method is used to finance costly schemes of expansion or modernization. As we have seen, private companies can also raise share capital but are restricted to a maximum of fifty shareholders. Progression through the stages of sole proprietor, partnership, private company, and finally public company, provides a means of financing the growth of a business.

3 Retained profits

Profits are an important source of funds for firms of all types. The expansion of small businesses is frequently achieved through re-investment of profits. Companies do not have to distribute all their profits as dividends to shareholders and commonly retain part of their profits as reserves for future use. Such undistributed profit may be ploughed back into the business as long-term capital.

4 Financial institutions

The funds accumulated by financial institutions such as insurance companies provide an important source of long-term capital for industry, often through the purchase of shares in private or public companies.

Firms may also obtain long-term capital from *Finance for Industry*, a government-backed organization combining two distinct agencies: the Industrial and Commercial Finance Corporation which specializes in providing capital for comparatively small businesses; the Finance Corporation for Industry which generally caters for the needs of larger firms. Both corporations obtain funds mainly from banks to be used for loans or the purchase of shares. They run on business lines, and firms are carefully investigated before capital is provided.

5 Government funds

Industry has benefited from substantial government funds – including funds provided by the European Economic Community – in connection with *regional policy*, mainly designed to stimulate industrial development in areas of high unemployment. This subject is pursued in Chapter 6.

Governments have sometimes given special financial assistance to particular firms to avoid closure or increase efficiency. Emphasis has recently been placed on encouraging the development of modern technology. An example of this is the British Technology Group, set up in 1981, with funds available for lending to firms applying new technology or developing new products.

A strong influence on recent government policy is the belief that small firms can make a significant contribution to production and employment. Recognizing that finance is a major problem for small firms, the government provides assistance in several ways. The *business expansion scheme* offers generous tax reliefs to investors in new or expanding firms. The *loan guarantee scheme* provides undertakings to offset the risks of lending to small businesses. The Council for Small Industries in Rural Areas (COSIRA) was set up to promote prosperity in rural areas by encouraging the growth of small businesses.

6 Other sources of finance

Firms can obtain short-term finance in a variety of ways. Purchases of machinery, equipment, and vehicles, for example, may be arranged through *hire-purchase* agreements with finance companies. Alternatively, payment can be made on an instalment basis through *lease* or rental arrangements. *Trade credit* allows firms time in which to pay for deliveries of goods or materials by suppliers. Such credit is equivalent to a short-term loan and is particularly helpful to small firms operating with limited funds.

1 What is meant by private enterprise? Note the various forms it takes. Refer to Fig. 4.1.
2 Explain, with examples, the advantages and drawbacks of being a sole proprietor.
3 Note the definition of a partnership. Why do people form business partnerships? What are the possible drawbacks?
4 All companies are joint-stock organizations with limited liability. Explain the terms *joint-stock* and *limited liability*.
5 Note the differences between a private and a public company. Why do firms remain private when they could expand by turning public?
6 Distinguish clearly between ordinary shares, preference shares, and debentures. Why do ordinary shareholders generally exercise little influence over boards of directors?
7 Make a list of the various methods by which a company can raise capital to expand its business.

4.2 Co-operative enterprise

There are broadly two kinds of co-operative enterprise – producers and consumers. Producers' co-operatives consist of groups of workers who jointly run their own businesses through elected committees or managers. Some of these have been formed in Britain though the idea has not generally flourished. There are obvious problems of finance and management facing workers who try to run their own businesses on a co-operative basis. Yet producers' co-operatives have proved successful in other countries. A well-known example is the co-operative farm or kibbutz of Israel.

Britain's co-operative movement is an organization of consumers formed into co-operative societies. These have the legal status of public companies but differ radically from the forms of private enterprise that we have considered so far. The distinguishing feature of the co-operative societies is that they are owned by their own customers, and it is they who largely share the profits.

The origin of the consumer co-operative movement was in the Lancashire town of Rochdale in 1844. A group of weavers put their money together to open up their own retail store. The idea was simple

How does ownership of this store differ from that of other supermarket chains?

and ingenious. They would buy groceries from their own store and share the retail profits. Furthermore, as an incentive to use their own store, the profits would be shared according to the value of their purchases instead of the normal joint-stock principle of sharing according to the capital contributed.

This method of distributing profits has remained the basic principle of the consumers' co-operative movement. Meanwhile, the single shop of the Rochdale pioneers has grown into a nationwide movement that covers retailing, wholesaling, and manufacturing activities.

Retail societies

In 1983, 149 retail co-operative societies in the United Kingdom had a total membership of about 9 million and ran about 7000 shops. Between them, they accounted for about 6 per cent of all retail sales. However, their share of the market has been declining for some time as a result of growing competition in retailing (see Chapter 7). To meet the competition, societies have merged into larger units. The number of separate societies has consequently fallen from a peak of over 1000 in the 1950s.

The societies do not compete with each other. Each serves a particular area with its own network of shops. Though independent, they are linked loosely together by the central Co-operative Union and also their connection with the wholesale society.

1 Distribution of profit

According to the original co-operative principle of profit sharing, each society would periodically declare the amount of the dividend payable to members for every pound they spent in its shops. However, competition in retailing has forced societies to seek new methods of attracting customers who are not necessarily members. These have included the introduction of trading stamps and direct price discounts.

2 Ownership and control

A person can join a co-operative society by buying one share. Shares are normally £1 in value and entitle the holders to vote at society meetings. A member can hold up to £1000 worth of shares but, whatever the value of his shares, he is allowed only one vote. The effect is to make all members equal and avoid the domination by large shareholders that occurs in many public companies. At meetings, the shareholders appoint directors and exercise functions similar to those of other public companies.

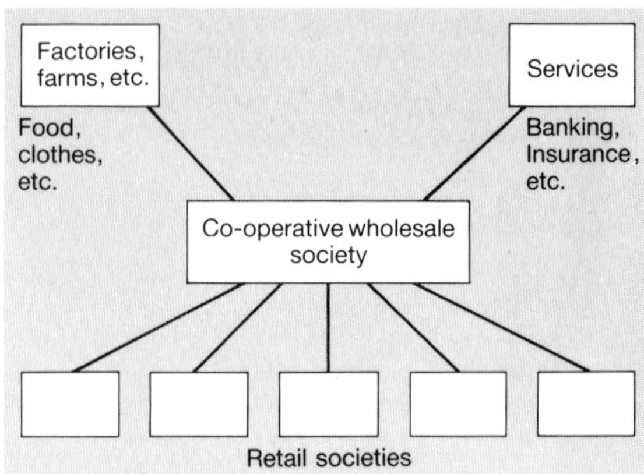

Fig. 4.2 The co-operative movement

The wholesale society

The Co-operative Wholesale Society (CWS) supplies a large proportion of all goods sold in co-operative shops. It is owned and controlled by the retail societies which share the profits in proportion to their purchases according to the co-operative principle. But contrary to the normal co-operative practice, the voting power of each retail society is also related to the value of its wholesale purchases. The larger retail societies consequently have more influence in the running of the wholesale business.

The activities of the CWS have steadily grown and now extend far beyond the wholesale function. For instance, it manufactures goods in its own factories, grows tea on its own plantations, and runs the Co-operative Bank (Fig. 4.2). The range and quantity of CWS-manufactured products is so great that they are sold not only through the retail societies but also other retail businesses.

1. What obstacles are likely to be met by workers forming a producer co-operative?
2. Why has there been a reduction in the number of retail co-operative societies in recent years?
3. How do shareholdings in a co-operative society differ from ordinary shareholdings in a company?
4. What is the CWS and how is it related to the retail societies?

4.3 Public enterprise

Public enterprise occurs when governments themselves enter into business activities, usually as a consequence of nationalization. It is called 'public' because governments act on behalf of the people or public. The industries or services concerned are thus publicly and not privately owned.

When an industry is nationalized, the ownership is transferred from private owners or shareholders to the government or state. The normal practice, in Britain, is to compensate the shareholders with government stocks that earn a fixed rate of interest in place of the varying profit or interest from shares. Whether the compensation is fair can only be judged separately in each case. However, if people prefer to hold shares, they can always sell government stocks on the Stock Exchange and buy shares in other companies.

Nationalization

Nationalization is an issue that has always deeply divided the main political parties. It is widely accepted that certain activities such as postal services should be carried out by the government. But the Labour party generally believes that public enterprise should be extended, whereas the Conservative party wants it to be as limited as possible.

Since industries vary greatly in their problems and circumstances, the arguments for and against nationalization should be related to each case separately. However, some general arguments are set out below as a basis for discussion. The arguments can also be related to Conservative government policies of denationalization or *privatization* which we consider at the end of the chapter.

1 Arguments for nationalization

i) Private profit is wrong. It encourages greed and widens the gap between rich and poor.

ii) Nationalization makes it possible to co-ordinate a whole industry, concentrate production in the most efficient units, and promote economies of scale.

iii) Some modern industries cannot attract enough private capital for research and development. A nationalized industry is in a better position to obtain government funds.

iv) Vital industries on which the life of the community depends should not be left to private enterprise. Nationalization protects the consumer from being exploited and ensures that the industry is run in the interests of the community. This argument is particularly applied to public utilities such as gas and water that are seen as *natural monopolies* in which profit should not be the main consideration.

What is the name of the public corporation associated with this photograph?

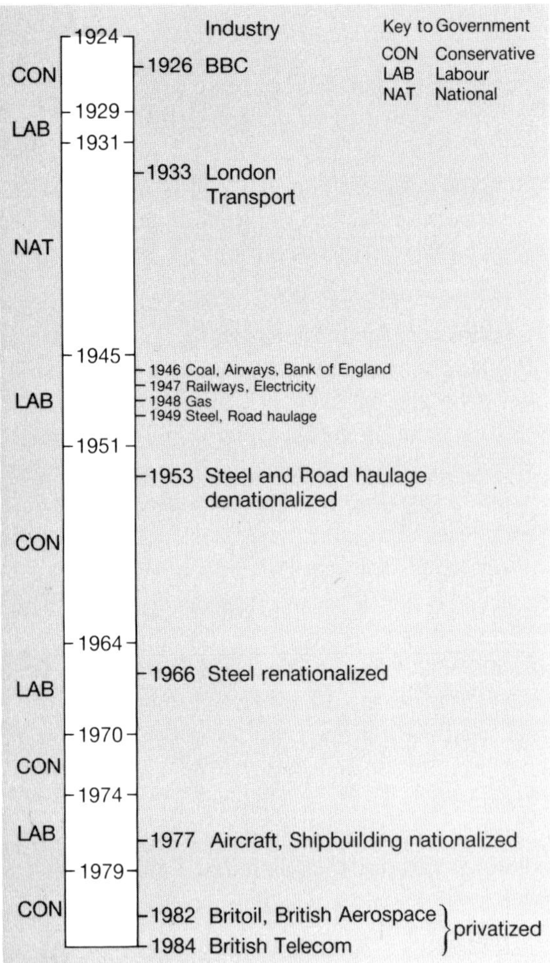

Fig. 4.3 Landmarks in public ownership

2 *Arguments against nationalization*

i) The management of nationalized industries becomes slack and inefficient because they lack the stimulus of working for private profit.
ii) Nationalization often leads to inefficiency because it destroys the initiative necessary for survival in an atmosphere of competition between firms.
iii) Many nationalized industries are too large and secure, and people are constantly irritated by mistakes and delays in the service they provide.
iv) Nationalized industries are supposed to belong to the public, but the public has little or no control over them.

Structure of public enterprise

Although most of the nationalized industries are of fairly recent origin, public enterprise is not new in Britain. Government industrial or commercial activities such as naval dockyards and postal services go back centuries. Several public enterprises were started by Conservative governments between the two World Wars, but most of Britain's large nationalized industries were created by Labour governments after 1945. The main landmarks are shown in Fig. 4.3.

1 *Public corporations*

We have seen that the main reason for nationalizing an industry is to enable the government to control it in the interests of the public. The main objection to nationalization is that it loses the urge for efficiency claimed on behalf of private enterprise.

The problem of nationalization is to secure government control with maximum efficiency. Whether this problem has been solved in Britain is open to argument, but the attempt to solve it has led to the development of a particular form of organization for nationalized industries. This is the public corporation.

A public corporation is the structure adopted for Britain's nationalized industries. Its essential feature is that the management of the industry is in the hands of a small board appointed by the government and under a limited degree of government control. Thus, the managing body of the nationalized coal mines consists of the Chairman and ten other members of British Coal.

The boards of public corporations resemble the boards of directors of privately owned companies and are expected to act in a similar manner. They are free to make all the ordinary decisions of management and are usually expected to aim at a certain level of profit. The theory is that by operating like businesses rather than government departments they will achieve the efficiency usually associated with private enterprise. A question to be considered is whether a nationalized industry such as the railways should be run as a business for profit or as a public service more on the lines of education and the health service.

In contrast with public companies, nationalized industries do not obtain finance by issuing shares and debentures for purchase by the general public. Their capital expenditure may be financed out of profits, and additional needs can be met by govern-

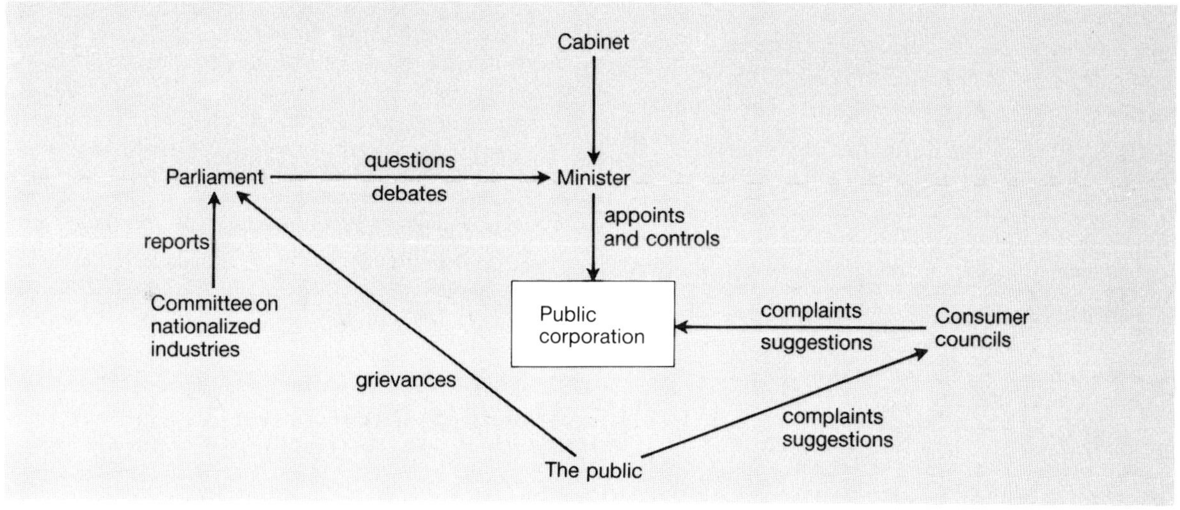

Fig. 4.4 Control of public corporations

ment loans on which interest is charged. Short-term capital is also obtained by borrowing from banks in the same way as other businesses.

2 Control over public corporations

Although public corporations are designed to work independently like privately owned companies, it would defeat the purpose of nationalization if there were not government control on behalf of the public. A certain degree of control over public corporations is exercised by government ministers, by Parliament, and by consumers themselves (Fig. 4.4).

There is a minister in the government responsible for each of the public corporations. He appoints the members of the board and lays down broad lines of policy for the industry. He is not expected to interfere in ordinary matters of management, but his approval is normally required for big decisions such as the building of a new power station or steelworks. The position of the minister is sometimes compared with that of voting shareholders in joint-stock companies, but his influence has generally been much greater in practice.

Members of Parliament can question the minister on the policies of a nationalized industry, though questions are not normally allowed on detailed matters of management. For example, the minister would be expected to answer questions on the broad issue of closing railway lines but not on the details of railway timetables. Apart from questions, the House of Commons occasionally has full debates on particular nationalized industries. The House also has a committee which examines and reports on particular public corporations from time to time.

Ministers and MPs are supposed to represent the interests of the public. Public corporations may also be influenced by the views of ordinary people expressed through newspapers, radio, and television. In addition, the public is directly represented on *consumers' councils* linked to those public corporations (notably in the field of transport and the power industries) that closely affect the lives of most people. The councils are set up by the minister in every area to represent the views of consumers and to act as a channel for complaints. Yet, in spite of these arrangements, there is a widespread impression that nationalized industries are too remote and not sufficiently sensitive to the needs of the public.

3 Government shareholdings

Full nationalization is not the only way of bringing industry under government control. An alternative would be for the government to buy enough shares in joint-stock companies to gain control and appoint the directors. In fact, state financial assistance to private industry became so great in the 1970s that the government acquired substantial shareholdings in such giants of private enterprise as Rolls-Royce and Austin Rover. This trend has since been reversed by the policy of privatization.

4 Municipalization

Public enterprise can be exercised through local authorities as well as the central government or its agencies. In the nineteenth century, for example, a number of local authorities were pioneers in the provision of gas and electricity. Many local councils provide facilities such as bus services, swimming baths, restaurants, seaside piers, and golf courses. These undertakings are generally operated on a commercial basis, though possibly subsidized from the rates, under managers appointed by council committees.

Privatization

The Conservative government, elected to power in 1979, adopted a policy aimed at reducing the size of the public sector and so reversing the general trend of the preceding fifty years. This involves selling back selected nationalized industries into private ownership (Fig. 4.3) and also, wherever practicable, transferring functions of central and local government to private enterprise. Hospital cleaning and local refuse collection are examples of services that have been taken over by private contractors in a number of areas. As part of the same policy, tenants of council houses have been given the right to buy their homes.

An industry is privatized by selling shares to the public at an estimated market price. Profitable industries, such as British Telecom, are obviously easiest to sell and are the main candidates for privatization. Each proposal revives the familiar arguments for and against nationalization already outlined.

The government lays stress on the greater efficiency claimed for private enterprise and competition. The large sums of money derived from the sales also give a temporary boost to government revenue. Opposition critics emphasize the loss of profitable assets to the nation as a whole and also argue that social needs will be subordinated to private profit, for example by closure of loss-making rural bus routes or telephone boxes.

1. What is meant by public enterprise? Examine the arguments for nationalization and state what you think were the main reasons for nationalizing (a) electricity, (b) the railways, (c) steel. Which arguments against nationalization do you consider most important?
2. Outline the main features of public corporations by showing how they both resemble and differ from company boards of directors.
3. What is privatization? Give examples. What reasons might be given to justify it?

Multiple choice

1. Which of the following is true?
   - **A** Shareholders in a private joint-stock company have limited liability.
   - **B** All members of a partnership have limited liability.
   - **C** There is no limit to the number of shareholders in a private joint-stock company.
   - **D** A sole proprietor can expand his business by selling more shares.
   - **E** A public joint-stock company is one owned by the state.
2. An ordinary share normally entitles its holder to each of the following EXCEPT
   - **A** limited liability
   - **B** voting at shareholders' meetings
   - **C** a share of the company's profits
   - **D** an annual payment of dividends
   - **E** a fixed annual rate of interest
3. A firm that is allowed to sell its shares to the public in general must be
   - **A** a public corporation
   - **B** a public joint-stock company
   - **C** a private joint-stock company
   - **D** a finance company
   - **E** a monopoly
4. Nationalized industries include
   - **A** agriculture
   - **B** banking
   - **C** chemicals
   - **D** railways
   - **E** motor vehicles

5 Which of the following sources of finance are available to a private joint-stock company?
 1 issue of shares to the general public
 2 retained profits
 3 bank overdrafts

 A 1, 2 and 3 are correct
 B 1 and 2 only are correct
 C 2 and 3 only are correct
 D 1 only is correct
 E 3 only is correct

6 A company's share capital consists of 500 000 8 per cent £1 preference shares and 1 million £1 ordinary shares. Its profit is £100 000. The sum available for distribution to its ordinary shareholders is
 A £40 000
 B £60 000
 C £80 000
 D £100 000
 E £500 000

7 Using the same information as in question 6 above, what rate of dividend (per cent) would be payable to ordinary shareholders?
 A 2 per cent
 B 4 per cent
 C 6 per cent
 D 8 per cent
 E 10 per cent

8 Which of the following does NOT apply to consumer co-operative societies in the United Kingdom?
 1 Profits are shared by members according to the number of shares held.
 2 The maximum number of shareholders is 50.
 3 Voting power depends on the number of shares held.

 A 1 only is correct
 B 1 and 2 only are correct
 C 1, 2 and 3 are correct
 D 2 and 3 only are correct
 E 3 only is correct

Data response

The pattern of ownership and organization in industry is varied. Personal, corporate, co-operative, and public enterprise all assume a number of different forms and all are important in the economy. Industrial enterprises vary from such large-scale organizations as the Ford Motor Company and public corporations such as British Coal to many thousands of small firms, some with fewer than 25 employees but accounting for something like one-fifth of the gross national product.

1 Distinguish between personal, corporate, co-operative, and public enterprise. What forms does each assume?

2 How does the passage show that Britain has a mixed economy?

3 What differences would you expect to find in the forms of ownership and organization between the Ford Motor Company and British Coal?

4 Why should coal be nationalized but not the car industry?

5 What is meant by privatization? What action would the government have to take if it decided to privatize coal mining? What obstacles, if any, might it encounter?

6 Which forms of business organization are most characteristic of the small firms mentioned in the passage? Give examples of industries in which such firms prevail. Why do they not exist in car manufacturing?

Essays

1 What changes in ownership, control, and finance occur when a public corporation is privatized?

2 The owner of a successful small firm wishes to expand. Advise him on the means by which he could raise more capital and the forms of business organization into which he could expand.

3 Distinguish between the types of stocks and shares that a company can issue. For what motives do people buy shares? What advice would you give a potential investor about the advantages and disadvantages of each type?

Chapter 5

Size of firms

5.1 Large-scale production

A hundred years ago, the typical manufacturing firm was a fairly small business owned and managed by one person. Today, most of the things we buy in shops are manufactured by huge companies each employing thousands of workers and owned by a large number of shareholders. Many of these giant firms started as small family businesses which either grew themselves or joined with other firms to form larger units.

An obvious explanation for the growth of firms is that as population increased and people became better off there was a rising demand for products of all kinds. However, this could have been met by having more firms rather than larger firms. The main reason for the growth in the size of firms is that, in many industries, larger firms are more efficient. They consequently produce more cheaply and can sell at a lower price.

In these circumstances, small firms find themselves unable to compete with the giants. The small ones are either eliminated or swallowed up or they join together to become large themselves. This has happened in modern industries such as motor vehicles and chemicals.

Economies of scale

Large firms dominate certain industries because their size gives them advantages over small firms. By producing large quantities they are able to reduce the cost of each unit produced. Reductions in costs due to the advantages of size are called economies of large-scale production or sometimes simply *economies of scale*. Let us consider how these economies arise.

1 Technical economies

Greater size gives more opportunities for division of labour, the use of machinery, and other ways of increasing efficiency. It also enables more to be spent on research and technical progress.

The scope for division of labour increases as a factory expands its output and employs more workers. We saw in Chapter 3 how the division of work into tasks or processes enables workers to become more efficient in their individual jobs and also makes it easier to introduce machinery.

Large firms can sometimes afford to buy machines and equipment that are too expensive for smaller firms. Furthermore, some machines are only worth operating at a minimum level of output which may be beyond the capacity of a small firm. Even if a machine is available in different sizes, a larger one is usually cheaper to operate in relation to output, in the same way as a loaded bus can carry each passenger more cheaply than a taxi can. Similar advantages are seen in the trend towards larger aeroplanes, oil tankers, container lorries, and so on.

Size can contribute to technical efficiency in a variety of ways. By carrying out all the processes of manufacture in one large factory it is often possible to save time and reduce costs. This is well illustrated in a modern integrated steelworks where the metal is moved through a series of processes from iron ore to the finished product without reheating at each stage. The technical advantages of large-scale production become strikingly apparent when one compares the assembly line of a modern car factory such as Ford with the way in which cars were handmade in workshops before the age of mass production.

2 Economies in management

Large firms employ the most professional managers. They are able to attract more qualified staff and may use specialists to manage particular departments. Able managers are likely to be attracted not only by higher salaries but also by the prestige and power of responsible positions in a large firm.

Which economies of scale are illustrated by this photograph?

The employment of specialist managers in charge of functions such as sales or accounts brings the advantages of division of labour. Small firms may not have enough work to justify separate departments for each of these functions so that managers and staff have to undertake a wider range of activities, losing the advantage of specialization. Indeed, the manager of a small firm might find himself doing work outside the field of management. For instance, he may have to spend valuable time dealing with complaints or inquiries that the manager of a larger concern would leave to other people.

3 Trading economies

Large firms are often able to buy materials at lower prices and also have advantages in selling their finished products.

Most shoppers have found that goods bought in large quantities or large sizes frequently turn out to be cheaper. Large firms are likely to pay less for their materials or components because suppliers naturally want to attract and keep important customers. Moreover, large orders are more convenient and cheaper to handle.

Similar advantages are obtained by the large firm when it comes to selling its finished products. In transport, for example, haulage contractors are willing to allow more favourable terms for bulk deliveries and full loads on their lorries. Alternatively, a big firm may find it worthwhile to provide its own transport. We have also seen how sales can be increased through the employment of specialist managers and staff to promote exports, advertising, and so on.

4 Financial economies

The advantages of being large include greater ability to raise money by borrowing and also to withstand the risks of business.

Firms commonly borrow money for short periods to meet expenses such as the purchase of raw materials. A loan of this kind can be paid off when the materials have been sold in the shape of finished products. Such temporary loans are usually obtainable from banks. From the banks' point of view, the large firm is better known and has more to fall back on. Its reputation enables it to borrow more easily and, being considered reliable, it may be charged a lower rate of interest.

Since big firms are generally public companies they can also borrow by selling shares to the public. Shares of a large concern such as ICI are more likely to attract public support than those of less well-known companies.

Firms, like people, can insure their property against ordinary risks such as fire and theft. But some of the financial risks of business are not normally insurable. These risks include changes in the demand for products, competition from other firms, and interruption of production due to strikes or shortages of essential materials.

A large firm usually has greater resources to meet business risks. It may also be in a position to reduce some of the uncertainties of business. For example, it might extend the range of its products and so not be dependent on the sale of a single product. It may further reduce its reliance on other firms by producing its own materials or components. The public alarm when a firm such as Rolls-Royce ran into severe difficulties, in 1971, shows how rare it is for a major firm to fail.

Table 5.1 Effect of internal and external economies

Firm	Stage 1 Output	Stage 1 Cost per unit	Stage 2 Output	Stage 2 Cost per unit	Stage 3 Output	Stage 3 Cost per unit
A	100	50p	1000	40p	1000	38p
B	100	50p	100	50p	100	48p
	Firms and industry small. No internal or external economies		Firm A expands and gains internal economies, reducing unit cost by 10p. No change in Firm B		Expansion of industry due to A leads to external economies, reducing unit costs of both firms by 2p	

External economies

The economies described above all occur inside a firm when it grows larger. Because they take place within the firm itself they are sometimes called internal economies. But firms can also obtain economies as a result of developments affecting the whole industry of which they form part. For instance, a new invention may be available to all the firms in an industry and not just one firm. Such economies are described as external (Table 5.1).

External economies of scale are achieved when the growth of an industry brings advantages to all the firms in it. This is likely to happen because expansion usually stimulates research, and new ideas tend to spread among the firms.

Advantages of this kind arise particularly when the growth is concentrated in one area. The area can then adapt itself to the special needs of that industry as in the case of the potteries of Staffordshire. External economies associated with local industries are called *economies of concentration* (see Chapter 6).

Integration

Firms become larger either by growing or by joining with other firms. Integration is the process of joining together. This can be done by an agreement between firms to combine or merge. Alternatively, it can result from a *takeover* bid when one firm gains control over another by buying its shares. Integration is normally classified into three kinds—horizontal, vertical, and lateral (Fig. 5.1).

Horizontal integration occurs when the firms joining together are in the same industry and at the same stage of production. This means that the same product is to be made by one large combined firm. It should thus be possible to obtain the advantages of large-scale production outlined above. Another motive could be to avoid competition.

Vertical integration is an amalgamation of firms in the same industry but at different stages of production. For example, hop farms, breweries, and public houses are all concerned with the supply of beer at different stages. If they join together, the integration is vertical. This type of integration can also be divided into *forward* and *backward*. Thus, a brewery that acquires its own public houses is said to be integrating forward because it is getting closer to its consumers. If it buys farms to grow its own hops the integration is backward—that is, back towards the raw material.

Firms may integrate vertically forward in order to expand their sales or backward to ensure the supply of their materials, instead of relying on other firms. They may also be able to obtain some of the economies of large-scale production.

When firms in different industries join together the integration is called lateral. This is most likely to happen when there is a connection between the industries—for instance, when the railways entered into the hotel and catering business. However, there has been a rising tendency towards integration between firms in unrelated industries. By joining together, the firms can make better use of their combined factory space or become less dependent on the sale of a particular product.

The following examples of integration are based on cases that have actually occurred: a merger between two oil companies (horizontal); a car manufacturer takes over a steel company (backward vertical); a paper manufacturer takes over a publishing business (forward vertical); a chocolate firm merges with a producer of soft drinks (lateral).

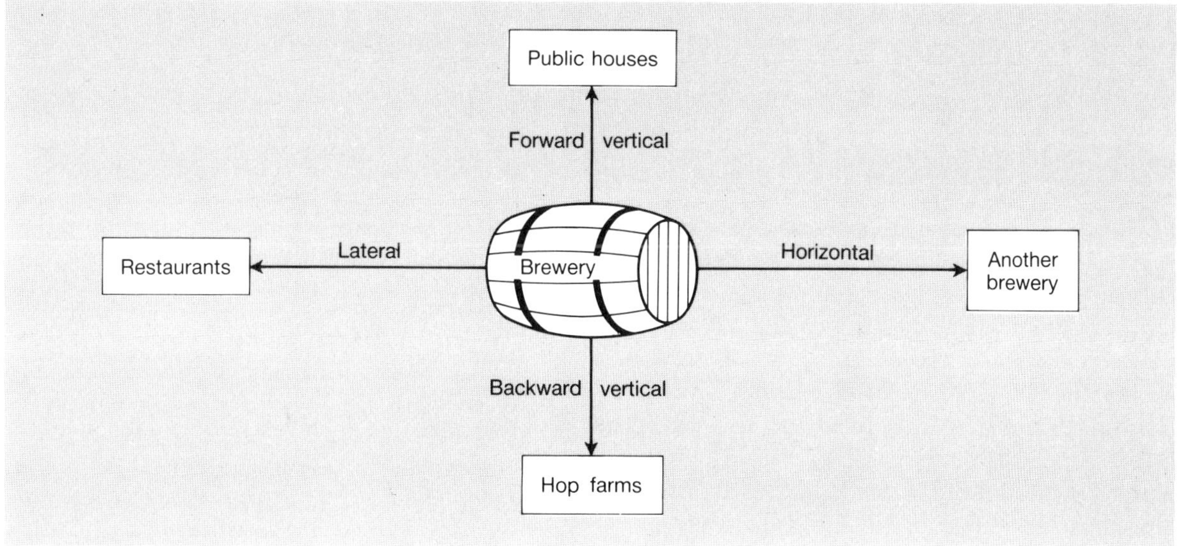

Fig. 5.1 Types of integration

Industrial giants

A striking feature of modern industry is the tendency for production to become increasingly concentrated in the hands of a relatively small number of very large firms. This is illustrated in Fig. 5.2 which shows the rising share of output produced by the hundred largest firms in the economy. If the recent trend continues, the degree of industrial concentration, measured in this way, will reach about 80 per cent by the end of the century.

The domination of a comparatively few large firms extends into the international field where there has been a rapid growth of great *multinational companies*—firms that operate in more than one country. The names of such firms in major industries such as motor vehicles, oil, and chemicals are known almost throughout the world. Their development has clearly been made possible by improvements in transport and communications and the accompanying expansion of world trade.

The rise of the industrial giants has certainly helped to gain substantial economies of scale, and they often have proud achievements in technical progress and the development of export markets. Their enormous power can, however, create problems for national governments, particularly in the case of multinational companies whose loyalties are divided between different countries.

Another feature of industrial development associated with increasing size is the growth of *conglomerates*—firms producing not one but a variety of distinct products. The variety of goods produced by these firms may be due to byproducts from the use of particular materials or result from integration between firms in different lines of production. An advantage of the conglomerate firm is that it no longer depends on the market for a single product and can thus become more flexible in its policies.

Fig. 5.2 The trend of industrial concentration

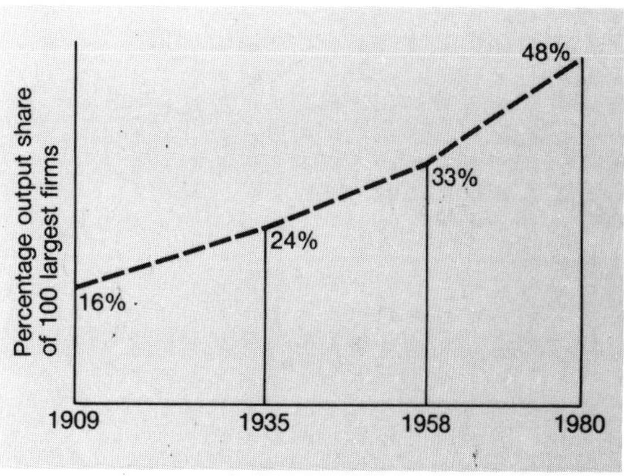

Diseconomies of scale

It is possible for firms to grow too large. Increasing size can bring drawbacks as well as advantages. Drawbacks that reduce efficiency and increase the cost per unit of output are called diseconomies of scale.

Diseconomies appear when a firm grows too big and unwieldy to organize. If one factory grows too big, it may be possible for the production to be divided between two or more separate factories of efficient size. But there is still the problem of controlling and co-ordinating the work of the several factories. This is largely a problem of management. The drawbacks or diseconomies of scale mainly arise through problems of management and human relationships in large complicated organizations.

The problems of a huge business organization are probably similar in nature to those of a large school or college. One can imagine the difficulties of arranging and supervising the work of very large numbers of people. Decisions are more difficult and take longer to reach when more people have to be consulted. In a large firm managers become more remote from the workers so that grievances and misunderstandings more often develop into disputes and perhaps lead to strikes.

Relations with customers may also compare unfavourably with customer relations in small firms where, for example, the owner or manager is personally available to attend to complaints.

1 What is meant by *economies of scale*? Classify the economies and note examples of each kind.

2 Distinguish between internal and external economies of scale. As an example of external economies suggest benefits gained by television manufacturers due to the growth of their industry.

3 Draw Fig. 5.1, preferably substituting a bakery or some other example. Write a sentence to explain the meaning of each type of integration.

4 Note the trend towards concentration of industry shown in Fig. 5.2, and suggest reasons for it.

5 What are (a) multinational companies, (b) conglomerate firms? Account for their development and give examples of each.

6 What are diseconomies of scale? Why are they mainly related to management?

5.2 Large and small firms

Optimum size

We have seen that as a firm grows in size and produces more it can benefit from economies of scale but, at some stage in its growth, diseconomies are also likely to develop. It is possible to imagine a point at which the advantages or economies resulting from further growth would be outweighed by the disadvantages or diseconomies. Beyond this point, further growth would make the firm less efficient. Instead of producing more cheaply, extra production would cause the average cost of each unit of output to rise (Fig. 5.3).

The optimum size of a firm is the size or output at which it can produce most efficiently and therefore at the lowest average cost.

Although the optimum is simple enough to define in theory, it may be very difficult to decide exactly where it lies in practice for any firm. In considering whether to expand and produce more, a business would have to weigh up all the likely economies and diseconomies and so estimate the effect on the firm's costs of production. Even if the optimum size is achieved it may soon be altered by the invention of new kinds of machinery or other changes in the techniques of production.

Fig. 5.3 Determining the optimum

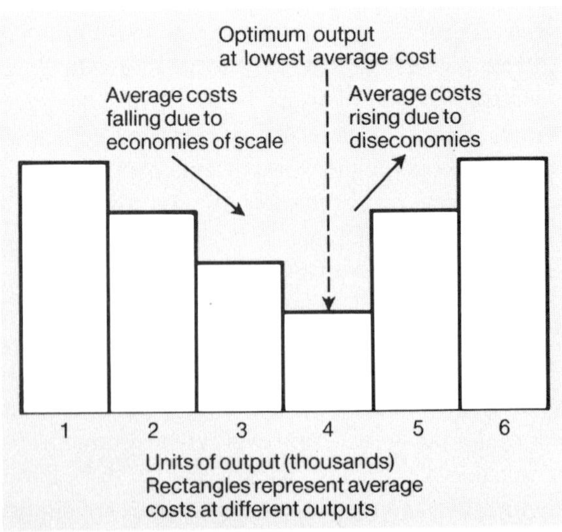

Table 5.2 Size distribution of manufacturing establishments in Britain (1980)

Size: number of employees	Number of establishments	Percentage of total establishments	Percentage of total employment
under 20	78 171	72	8·2
20–499	28 485	26	39·8
500–1499	1 651	1·5	20·6
over 1500	518	0·5	31·4

Differences in size

There are obviously wide differences between industries. The best size for an aircraft manufacturing firm is clearly very different from that of a bicycle-repair business. Small firms flourish in agriculture, retailing, the building industry, and professions such as law and architecture. On the other hand, most manufactured goods are produced by large firms because manufacturing allows the greatest scope for economies of scale.

If you think of familiar brands of manufactured goods such as cars, petrol, and television sets, the producing firms are probably all large and well-known. But if you look at the firms you pass daily on the road, the chances are that most of them will be small. Even in manufacturing, there are still many small factories or workshops to be seen.

A relatively few giant organizations produce the bulk of the nation's output and provide jobs for a majority of the population. Yet small firms greatly outnumber the large. This is illustrated in Table 5.2 which relates specifically to manufacturing establishments. (Establishments are not identical to firms, which may control several establishments).

A distinction can be made between industries in which the firms are (a) all large, (b) all small, and (c) a mixture of large and small. Aircraft, chemicals, and oil refining are examples of industries in which firms are invariably large. In hairdressing and market gardening the firms are all relatively small. In baking and building large and small firms exist together.

These works belong to ICI, a mass producer of chemicals. Why is it so large?

Reasons for smallness

In an age when the balance of advantage appears to be tilted strongly in favour of the giants, the survival of so many small firms may seem surprising. This particularly applies to industries where the dwarfs survive in competition with the giants. The explanation lies partly in the fact that some industries offer little scope for economies of scale and diseconomies become quickly apparent. In such industries size obviously brings few advantages and can sometimes be a real disadvantage. However, we must look more closely at the various factors that stop firms from growing larger.

1 The personal touch

Small firms generally flourish in industries where managerial decisions have to be quickly made and carried out, close individual attention to the customer is especially important, or personal trust and understanding is particularly essential between management and workers.

Such industries would include those that have to adapt themselves to frequent changes in tastes or fashions and also those requiring exceptionally high standards of skill or attention to detail on the part of the workers. Obvious examples are industries that provide personal or professional services such as dentistry and accountancy.

2 Business motives

Economists used to assume that all businessmen were ruthlessly concerned with obtaining as much profit as possible. If this were so there would be fewer small firms because fierce competition would result in the successful ones growing larger and the unsuccessful being eliminated. Many firms probably remain small because their owners have no further ambitions, preferring the security of a small business to the risk and anxiety of striving for expansion. Examples obviously occur in farming and retailing.

Another business motive is the desire for independence. A person who values independence may continue to run his own business as long as it provides a living even though the profit is so low that he would be better off financially working for someone else. For such reasons, small businessmen sometimes carry on through bad times and refuse good offers to sell out to larger firms.

3 Access to capital

Some firms are small merely because they are in the early stages of development and have not had time to grow large. Their growth may be delayed through lack of capital. As shown in the preceding chapter, small unknown firms can experience difficulty in borrowing from banks or other sources, and they lack the ability of large companies to raise money by selling shares to the public. They may therefore have to wait to build up enough reserves to finance their own expansion.

4 Market influences

In some industries the size of firms is limited by the extent of the market or the nature of the products they sell. The demand for a product is sometimes too small to justify large firms. The producers might also need to be small and adaptable in order to respond to a demand that is subject to rapid changes in tastes or fashions. Similarly, small firms are clearly at an advantage in industries, such as photography and dentures, where the products are not standardized and firms have to meet the different requirements of individual customers.

Even if a product has a large and stable demand it could be unsuitable for large firms. In the case of perishable foodstuffs, such as fresh vegetables, the market is limited by the fact that they cannot be transported long distances. Similarly, the cost of transporting very bulky or heavy goods, such as bricks, may limit the extent of the market. The market for such products is often divided up geographically with small firms supplying their own local areas.

Firms providing personal services – such as doctors' practices or firms of solicitors – are also small and local because they must be easily available to those who need them.

Importance of small firms

Small firms not only continue to make a useful contribution to production and employment but also help the economy in particular ways:

i) they provide a training ground for businessmen and managers who may later move on to larger concerns;

ii) they are sometimes most suitable for experimenting with new ideas and techniques;

iii) their competition can help to keep larger firms efficient and some small firms are themselves the large efficient firms of the future;
iv) as we have seen, in some industries smallness is itself an advantage from which the consumer benefits;
v) small firms increase the quantity and variety of products available to the consumer.

Government policy recognizes the importance of small firms and encourages them to start up and expand. Two particular requirements are financial resources and specialized knowledge. The sources of business finance outlined in the last chapter included facilities designed to meet the special needs of small firms. The system of taxation also gives certain advantages such as a reduced rate of tax on the profits of small companies. The need for information is met by the Department of Trade and Industry which has an advisory service catering particularly for small businesses. Most local authorities are also keen to assist business development in their areas.

1 What is meant by the optimum size of a firm? Why do average costs of production rise when a firm grows beyond its optimum size?

2 Note and briefly explain the reasons why small firms continue to exist. Give examples of industries in which all or most firms are still small.

3 Refer to Table 5.2 and comment on the place of small firms in the British economy.

4 The government has given tax reliefs and other forms of encouragement to small firms. Why should it do this?

Multiple choice

1 A car assembly firm takes over a firm that makes car bodies. This is an example of
- **A** horizontal integration
- **B** backward vertical integration
- **C** forward vertical integration
- **D** a conglomerate merger
- **E** lateral integration

2 The growth of the television industry stimulated research which in turn benefited all the firms in the industry. This is an example of
- **A** technical economies
- **B** managerial economies
- **C** trading economies
- **D** financial economies
- **E** external economies

3 Which of the following markets is most likely to be supplied by a few very large firms?
- **A** a rapidly fluctuating market for fashion clothes
- **B** an urban market for personal dental treatment
- **C** a standardized market for popular family cars
- **D** a widespread market in highly perishable goods
- **E** a luxury market for hand-made furniture

4 The optimum output of a firm is achieved when
- **A** it cannot sell any more
- **B** its output is at a maximum
- **C** its profit is at a maximum
- **D** its average costs are at a minimum
- **E** its total costs are at a minimum

5 Horizontal integration occurs when a firm
- **A** acquires a component supplier
- **B** expands its output
- **C** diversifies its output
- **D** acquires another firm in its industry at the same stage of production
- **E** merges with another firm in another industry

6 Which of the following would NOT restrict the growth of a firm?
- **A** lack of finance
- **B** a limited market
- **C** fierce competition in its market
- **D** possible economies of scale
- **E** possible diseconomies of scale

7 A firm could gain internal economies of scale if
1 specialist supply firms set up in its locality
2 the local transport system is improved
3 the firm invests in additional plant or machinery

A 1 only is correct
B 1 and 2 only are correct
C 1, 2 and 3 are correct
D 2 and 3 only are correct
E 3 only is correct

8 Advantages particularly associated with small firms include
1 opportunities for division of labour
2 personal service to customers
3 adaptability to changing circumstances

A 1, 2 and 3 are correct
B 1 and 2 only are correct
C 2 and 3 only are correct
D 1 only is correct
E 3 only is correct

Essays

1 Why do firms want to expand? Discuss the means by which expansion can be achieved in relation to the possible motives for expansion.

2 If large firms obtain economies of scale, why do small firms still exist and why does the government encourage their existence?

3 What is meant by the optimum size of a firm? How is it related to economies and diseconomies of scale? Indicate the problems that are likely to occur if a firm expands beyond its optimum size.

Data response

Refer to Table 5.2 (page 59).

1 In the light of the figures, assess the relative importance of very small firms (under 20 employees) and very large firms (over 1500 employees) in the UK economy.

2 Give examples of industries in which you would expect typical firms to be in the small, medium, and large categories respectively. Give reasons in each case.

3 What types of business organization (sole proprietor, etc.) would you expect to find in each size category shown?

4 How can small firms grow into large firms? What are the main obstacles to their growth?

5 If small firms employ so few people, why does the government encourage them to be set up?

6 Is the number of employees an appropriate measure of the size of a firm? What other standards might be used to judge the size of (a) manufacturing establishments, (b) retail businesses?

Chapter 6

Location of industry

6.1 Forces of location

Influences on location

Among the first decisions that a businessman has to make is where to set up his firm. Obviously, personal feelings could affect the decision. He may dislike certain parts of the country or, like the young Morris when locating his car factory, simply choose an area which he knows well. But business influences are likely to be the strongest. A firm usually aims to make as large a profit as possible and therefore seeks the location where it can produce most efficiently and cheaply.

If you were deciding where to build a house, you would probably weigh up a number of factors. These might include distance from work, access to shops, availability of schools, opportunities for leisure and entertainment, transport facilities, the attractiveness of the environment, and so on. Different locations would have different advantages. The influences affecting the location of a firm are different, but the nature of the choice is the same. The firm will be drawn to the area which offers the most favourable combination of advantages (Fig. 6.1). What advantages will it seek?

1 Access to materials and components

The need to be close to raw materials was an important factor in the original location of great industries such as woollen production in Yorkshire and cotton in Lancashire. Local sheep farming was clearly vital to the early growth of the woollen industry. In the case of the cotton industry, the location was greatly influenced by the fact that its basic material was imported from America. Firms therefore found it an advantage to be close to the port of Liverpool to which raw cotton could be most easily shipped.

With improvements in transport during this century, the pull towards raw materials has diminished. Transport costs of materials are now generally a much smaller part of the total costs of production than they would have been a century ago so that other factors have been more important in locating many of our newer industries. Synthetic materials, such as plastics, are now also widely used.

However, if an essential material is bulky and costly to transport, firms may still be attracted to its location. The ports are still an important attraction to industries dependent on imported materials. The location of raw materials also remains important in developing countries with inadequate transport systems.

As manufacturing processes have become more complex, the firms in some industries have become increasingly dependent on other firms to supply component parts for their production. For example, car manufacturers cannot do without a large and steady supply of components such as different kinds of electrical equipment. The need to be close to suppliers of components is a relevant factor in the location of some newer industries.

2 Access to power

Many of Britain's older industries grew up around the coalfields. The influence of coal on the location of British industry dates from the eighteenth-century invention of the steam engine. In the following century many industries consequently became reliant on coal fuel and steam power. Since coal was bulky and costly to transport, it was natural for firms to go where it could be easily obtained. Such traditional British industries as iron and steel, textiles, and shipbuilding thus continue to be found mainly within reach of the mining areas.

However, the attraction of the coalfields has greatly diminished since the beginning of this century. Electricity, gas, and oil are now obtainable in almost any part of the country at prices that hardly vary from area to area. With alternative sources of power widely available, access to power has become a less important influence on the location of newer industries. But it can still be a major factor in developing countries.

3 *Transport facilities*

A good transport system always makes an area more attractive to industry since it assists the delivery of both raw materials and finished products. Moreover, cheap and rapid transport can be particularly important to modern technological industries such as car manufacturing, which rely on a continuous supply of components from other specialist firms. Road improvements are among the means by which the government hopes to attract industry into areas of high unemployment.

4 *Climate and landscape*

The climate, soil and physical geography of an area are obviously vital to agriculture. They also help to explain the location of some manufacturing industries. A well-known example is the cotton industry. One of the original reasons for its location was that the damp climate on the west side of Britain reduced the chance of the thread breaking and so allowed more continuous production.

There are many examples of the relationship between industrial location and physical geography. For instance, coal mining can only be located on the coal seams. Timber must be associated with forestry. The location of water is often important: some industries such as shipbuilding need water to transport their products; others use water for production or to get rid of their waste products.

5 *Supply of labour*

Firms must take account of the fact that labour is an essential and sometimes scarce factor of production. Moreover, people cannot always be persuaded to move from one part of the country to another. Firms are therefore attracted to areas that can supply the kind of labour they require. For instance, the availability of suitable female labour helps to explain the growth of the Lancashire cotton industry. The establishment of so many car firms in the Midlands was also partly due to the local population possessing engineering skills acquired from the existence of cycle and motor cycle production in the area.

A recent influence on industrial location in Britain has been the concern of businessmen over loss of production due to strikes and absenteeism among their workers. There have been cases of firms avoiding areas noted for their bad labour relations.

6 *Access to markets*

Most of the influences on location so far mentioned have been concerned with the supply of factors of production. An influence that has particularly affected the location of newer industries is the desire of firms to be close to their customers and so reduce the cost of transporting their finished products. Thus, one of the effects of our rising standard of living is the growth of industries producing consumer goods and services in the densely populated areas where they sell most of their products. Similarly, industries producing mainly for export tend to be near the ports.

The pull of the market is obviously strong in the case of industries whose finished products are bulky and costly to transport. Furniture production and brick manufacture are therefore usually found close to towns. The same applies to perishable goods needing rapid transport to customers. People want food such as bread and vegetables as fresh as possible; so bakeries are invariably in towns and market gardeners flourish on the edge of towns.

Towns also attract firms that provide direct personal services to consumers. These include the retail trade and all kinds of professional services. People do not want to travel long distances to shop, get a haircut, visit the doctor, or draw money out of a bank.

Fig. 6.1 Forces of location

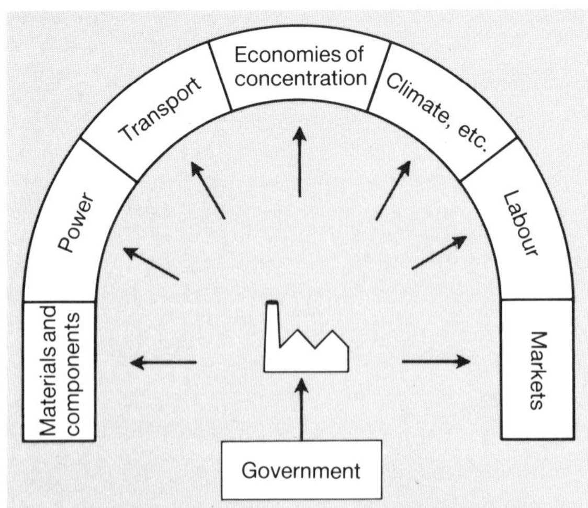

7 Economies of concentration

If an area is particularly suited to a certain industry, it is likely to attract a growing number of firms in the industry which then comes to be concentrated in that area. Having attracted the industry, there is then a tendency for the area to adapt itself to the special needs of that industry. Concentration thus brings its own advantages to the industry concerned.

The labour force in such an area becomes accustomed to the industry and responds to its requirements. School-leavers view it as a possible career and may learn about it even before starting work. In time, people become skilled at the particular jobs required by the industry. This is often assisted by schools and colleges which are encouraged to develop courses related to the local industry.

A concentrated industry may also benefit by attracting specialist firms providing materials, components, or services for the main industry by marketing its products, using its waste products, supplying or maintaining its machinery, and so on. At the same time, local firms such as banks and insurance companies are likely to become more familiar with the industry and so be able to offer services specially suited to its needs.

The fact that firms in the same industry exist side by side makes it easier for them to co-operate in ways that benefit them all. Information can be easily exchanged. A collective influence can be brought to bear on plans for the area such as the development of roads and transport. Firms may even benefit from a reputation for quality built up in the area as in the case of Sheffield steel.

8 Government influence

Since the heavy unemployment of the 1930s, successive governments have felt it necessary to interfere with the location of firms. Firms will choose the locations which suit their own interests but these may conflict with the interests of the community in general (Fig. 6.1).

For social and economic reasons, governments have restricted industrial development in some areas while encouraging it in others. No account of the influences on location would now be adequate without some explanation of government policies. We shall return to this later in the chapter.

Concentrated and dispersed industries

If we look at British industries as a whole, it can be seen that some are concentrated in a few areas while others are widely dispersed with firms in many parts of the country. Coal, steel, and shipbuilding are good examples of concentration or localization of industry. Obvious examples of dispersal are the retail trade, catering, and hotels.

Concentration occurs when an area has special attractions for an industry, which make it clearly superior to other parts of the country. Of course an area could have special advantages for more than one industry. In that case it will tend to concentrate on the industry in which its superiority is greatest compared with other areas. For example, Clydeside probably had great natural advantages for cotton production as well as shipbuilding: it concentrated on shipbuilding because of its greater 'comparative advantage'.

We have seen that concentration can give an industry advantages that add to the original attractions of the area. In time, the 'acquired advantages' or economies of concentration may become even more important than the natural advantages that originally attracted the industry. In some cases the original advantages have disappeared, but the industry continues to flourish in the area simply because of the advantages obtained from concentration itself. Sheffield steel and Staffordshire potteries are examples of industries remaining in established areas when their natural advantages have largely disappeared.

An industry is likely to be dispersed if there are no strong influences attracting it to certain areas or if the strongest influence on location is the attraction of a market composed of customers who are themselves widely scattered. Thus, we have seen that industries supplying consumer goods and services are often dispersed simply because the consuming population is spread throughout the country.

However, a widespread demand does not necessarily mean a widely distributed industry because other influences leading to concentration could be stronger than the pull of the market. For example, the demand for steel is nationwide but the industry is concentrated in only a few areas.

Take the case of an industry that sells its products

throughout the country but obtains its materials from certain limited areas. The influence of the market would then be towards dispersal while the raw material sources tend towards concentration. Whether the industry becomes dispersed or concentrated depends on the relative transport costs of finished products and raw materials.

In this connection, a distinction is sometimes made between *weight-gaining* and *weight-losing* industries. For example, brewing is weight-gaining because the finished product (beer) is heavier to transport than the basic materials (hops and malt). It is consequently a dispersed industry, with breweries generally located in densely populated areas. If beer could be transported more cheaply than hops, the breweries would be in the farming areas rather than the towns. Contrasting examples of weight-losing industries are provided by steelworks (originally close to coal and iron ore) and oil refineries (requiring dock facilities for tankers).

1 Note, with examples, each of the influences on location of industry.
2 Why are sources of raw materials and power supply now less important as locating influences than in the nineteenth century?
3 Which influences would you consider most important if you were setting up a factory to make (a) ice cream, (b) agricultural machinery? Give reasons.
4 What are the main forces causing (a) dispersal, (b) concentration or localization of any industry? Give examples.
5 Explain, with examples, why some industries are located near their markets while others are attracted to the sources of their raw materials.

6.2 The government and industrial location

Reasons for intervention

1 Local unemployment

The main reason for government interference has been the need to provide jobs in areas of exceptionally high unemployment. Thus, the government first began to be concerned during the great depression of the 1930s when unemployment rose to intolerable levels in some parts of the country. These were particularly the old industrial areas surrounding the coalfields. Unemployment has remained exceptionally high in some of these areas even when the national level has been very low. However, in recent years, most other regions have also had problems connected with unemployment (Fig. 6.2).

The problem of local or regional unemployment has its origins in the decline of traditional British industries such as coal mining, cotton, and shipbuilding. Their decline would not have been such a problem if new expanding industries had developed in the same areas, generally around the coalfields. Unfortunately, changing influences on location have tended to attract new industries to other parts of the country, particularly the South East. Governments have tried to halt this tendency.

Unemployment is not only a social problem for the community but also a waste of its economic resources. Idle manpower obviously means loss of output. Moreover, if labour is unemployed it is also likely that factories and machines are not fully used.

2 Urban congestion

The drift of industry and population can create problems in the areas where expansion is taking place as well as in those which are declining. Thus, serious problems of overcrowding have arisen in the South East and Midland regions where population has been growing rapidly.

Urban congestion leads to a shortage of housing accommodation and lack of space for recreation. It can also cause environmental problems connected with air pollution, waste disposal, and so on. Social services such as health and education are likely to come under increasing strain with overcrowding in hospitals and schools, etc. Local transport may have difficulty in coping with increased numbers, causing delays and frustrations, particularly at rush-hour periods. At the same time, social services, transport, and other local facilities are likely to become underused and wasted in the areas of falling population.

The social problems of overcrowding can also lead to economic problems. For example, the effect of overcrowding on health, and the strain of travelling to work, could reduce the efficiency of the working population. Where there is a heavy concentration of industry, costs of production may be higher. For

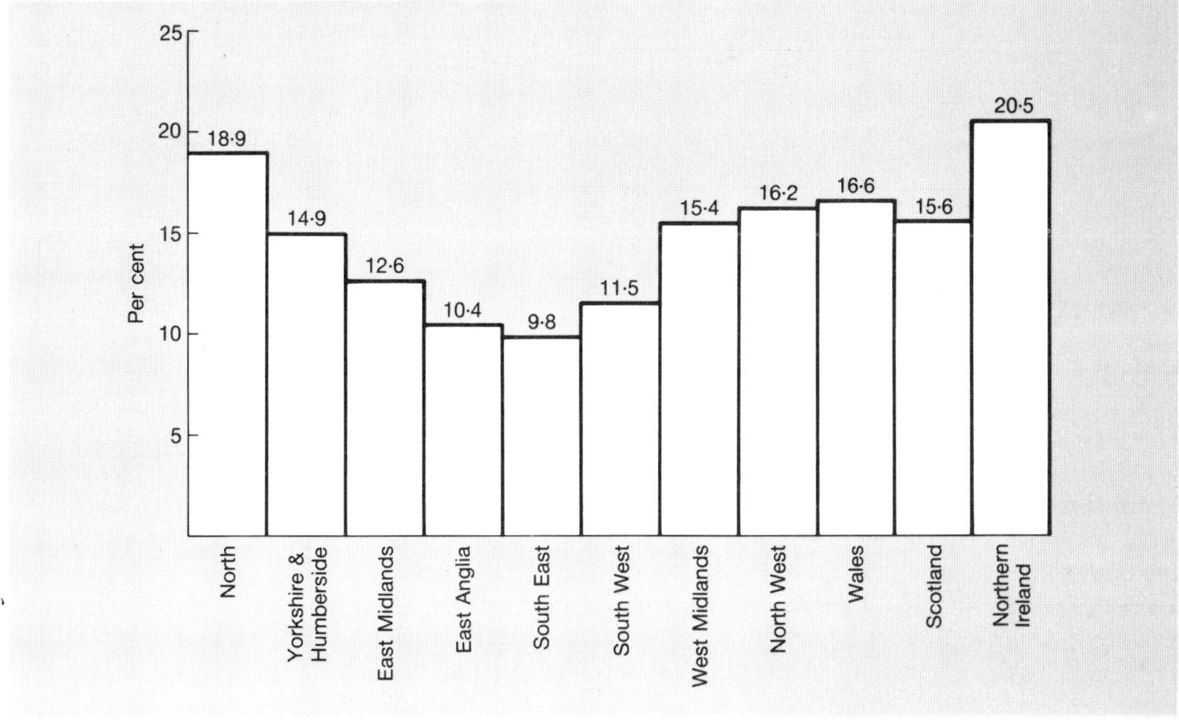

Fig. 6.2 Regional unemployment rates (July 1985)

instance, the great demand for skilled labour is likely to push up wage rates. Similarly, the shortage of factory sites will probably mean high land prices. Congestion and delays in transport could also be costly for industry.

3 *Drawbacks of specialization*

Special problems occur where the advantages of an area lead to the establishment of only one major industry. The local population becomes heavily reliant for jobs on the single industry. Should this industry decline, depression and unemployment are bound to spread into service industries such as retailing which supply the wants of people in the area. This problem was highlighted in the 1930s in towns such as Jarrow where the majority of the workers were made redundant due to the decline of the shipbuilding industry. Many coal-mining areas have had similar problems since the Second World War.

A further drawback of local specialization is that it limits employment opportunities in the area. People not wishing to work in the industry may be forced to leave the locality, and the industry may not provide enough jobs for groups such as women.

Methods of intervention

Every government has its own approach to the problems of industrial location so that the emphasis is constantly changing. The methods described below are simply intended to provide a broad outline of the policies used at various times (Fig. 6.3). Current policies are summarized in Chapter 16.

1 *Encouraging workers to move*

An obvious solution for local unemployment would be to persuade unemployed workers to move to areas where jobs are available. Movement could be encouraged by advertising the opportunities for work in other areas, by helping to pay the expenses of moving, and by providing cheap housing in the new areas.

However, governments in Britain have not put much reliance on this policy partly because of the natural reluctance of many workers to move and also because it might add to the problems of areas that are already overcrowded. The policy of the government has generally been to move industries rather than people. But people are helped to move into new occupations through government facilities for retraining.

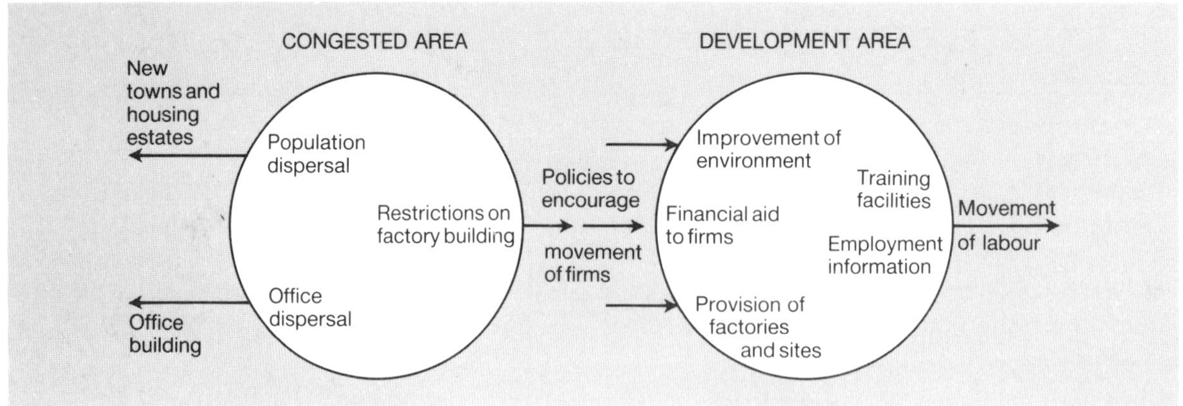

Fig. 6.3 Policies to control industrial location

2 *Encouraging industry to move*

Certain parts of the country that have suffered from high unemployment over a number of years are known as *development areas*. Various methods have been used to attract firms into them.

Governments have provided money to make development areas more attractive by generally improving their environment. For example, government expenditure has been used to improve social amenities such as parks, to clear away slum housing, and to develop transport facilities. This kind of spending not only helps to attract industry, but also directly creates work for people in the area.

Firms that establish themselves in development areas have been given certain financial advantages. In many cases, factories have been built with government money for firms to occupy at low rents. In addition, favourable treatment in the form of grants, loans, or tax allowances has been given to firms expanding or setting up in these areas. Firms in development areas have sometimes also received special payments related to the number of workers they employ.

Financial methods of encouraging movement have been backed up by actual restrictions on the location of firms. Governments have thus refused permission for new factories to be built in congested areas such as London in order to force them into other areas of higher unemployment. Since the government itself employs a large number of civil

Factory units are made available in a new town. How do they contribute to regional policy?

servants, it has been able to set an example by moving some of its own departments or offices away from London.

3 *Relieving urban congestion*

Industry and commerce are naturally attracted to the centres of large towns where most business activity is going on. This unfortunately creates severe problems of overcrowding and traffic congestion. Government influence has therefore been used to move firms away from congested city centres to outlying areas. The methods used include publicity, financial inducements, and occasionally direct restrictions on development in central areas.

These policies do not aim to bring about changes in the location of firms throughout the country but within specific areas. For example, in the case of the South East region, the policies mean an acceptance of the general drift in that direction while obtaining a better distribution of industry and population within the region.

In connection with the policy of relieving urban congestion, a number of *new towns* have been established since the Second World War (Fig. 6.4). New towns are planned to contain both housing and work for people moving out of overcrowded areas of old towns. They therefore combine both residential and industrial developments. In order to attract industry, factory space is provided on favourable terms.

Opposition to intervention

Criticism of government interference with industrial location comes largely from those who are opposed to government intervention in general. The basic argument is that firms know best where to locate themselves and should be left to make their own decisions. If the government tries to make firms build in areas which do not suit them, they may not build at all. Alternatively, if they do build in the wrong places, they will become less efficient so that their costs and prices will rise. A further argument is that the taxpayer pays for government intervention, and money intended to create jobs is sometimes wasted on firms that employ hardly any labour.

Another kind of criticism is that intervention is unnecessary because firms would themselves prefer areas of unemployment to overcrowded districts where labour and land are expensive and transport difficult. However, this argument is contradicted by the continuous drift of industry to already congested parts of the South East. The question is whether governments are justified in interfering with private business decisions on the grounds that such decisions are against the interests of society as a whole.

1 Why does the government try to influence the decisons of firms on where to locate their factories.

2 Refer to Fig. 6.3 and note the various methods by which the government (a) assists development areas where there is high unemployment, (b) relieves the pressure of industry and population in congested areas.

Fig. 6.4 Britain's conurbations and new towns

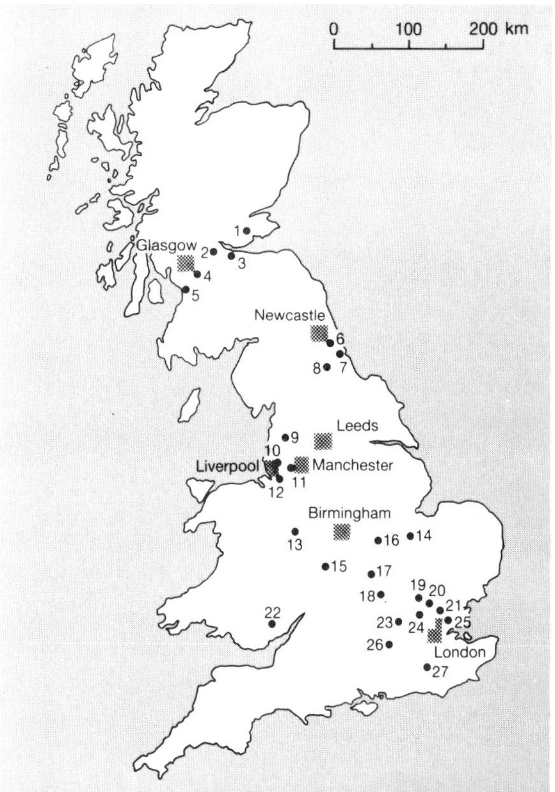

Conurbation

1 Glenrothes
2 Cumbernauld
3 Livingston
4 East Kilbride
5 Irvine
6 Washington
7 Peterlee
8 Aycliffe
9 Central Lancashire
10 Skelmersdale
11 Warrington
12 Runcorn
13 Telford
14 Peterborough
15 Redditch
16 Corby
17 Northampton
18 Milton Keynes
19 Stevenage
20 Welwyn Gdn. City
21 Harlow
22 Cwmbran
23 Hemel Hempstead
24 Hatfield
25 Basildon
26 Bracknell
27 Crawley

6.3 Distribution of population

People tend to move to parts of the country where they can find jobs. The geographical distribution of population thus corresponds fairly closely to the location of industry. If industry is spread fairly evenly throughout the country, population is also likely to be evenly distributed. This is generally the case where farming is the main occupation of the country and fertile land is widespread. But if, as in Britain, the main industries are concentrated in a limited number of areas, the population will also be unevenly distributed with heavy densities in those areas.

Britain's population distribution

Britain's population is largely concentrated in urban industrial areas traditionally centred around coalfields and ports. Outside these areas, there are still considerable stretches of sparsely populated countryside.

1 Concentrated areas

The concentration of population around the *coalfields* is explained by Britain's economic history since the beginning of the industrial revolution. During the nineteenth century coal became vital as a source of fuel to industries such as iron and steel and as a source of steam power to other industries. Manufacturing industries thus moved towards the coalfields and service industries followed them. Population was consequently attracted by the expanding employment opportunities in those areas.

The attraction of the coalfields faded during the period between the two World Wars when some of the older industries began to decline. Population growth then became strongest in the south of Britain where new industries were springing up.

Ports such as Liverpool and Glasgow are located in coalfield areas and their growth was closely linked to the rise of local industries. Other ports such as Belfast and Southampton, with large concentrations

How does a town such as Birmingham become a conurbation?

of population, owe their attraction entirely to their own advantages as ports providing easy access for imported raw materials and exported manufactured goods. London has had the huge additional advantage of being the political, social, and financial hub of the nation.

The vast majority of Britain's population lives in towns, and more than half the total lives in *conurbations* – areas where towns have spread and run into each other so that there is no longer any countryside separating them (Fig. 6.4). Greater London, with about 12 per cent of the country's population, is the outstanding example. Six other English conurbations are centred around Newcastle, Leeds, Sheffield, Liverpool, Manchester, and Birmingham.

2 Sparsely populated areas

In a manufacturing country agricultural areas are comparatively sparse in population. The most thinly populated parts of Britain are highland areas such as the Pennines and highlands of Scotland. These are relatively hard to farm and also least suitable for industry because of transport difficulties and lack of raw materials. However, higher wages and the social attractions of town life have drawn people away from agricultural areas in general. Less than 3 per cent of Britain's population is actually engaged in farming.

Recent population movements

Population is continuously on the move. During the Second World War there were substantial movements due to evacuation and the dispersal of industry as a precaution against bombing. Not all these movements were reversed when the war ended. However, considerable changes have taken place since then.

In general, the drift towards urban areas has continued, though the increase in car ownership has enabled more people to live on the fringe of towns in which they work. Population has in fact tended to move out of city centres to suburbs and surrounding areas. This trend has been assisted by policies to develop new towns and housing estates.

The most rapid population growth was in south-east England until the movement was checked in the 1970s partly by government regional policies. Britain's entry into the Common Market was expected to attract more industry and population to the South East, but this has not occurred on any significant scale.

1 Explain the main features of Britain's population distribution.

2 What movements of population have taken place in Britain in recent years? Are these movements likely to continue in the future?

Multiple choice

1 In selecting the location of a new factory, a firm is likely to be attracted by
  1 local availability of raw materials
  2 good transport facilities in the area
  3 an electricity power station in the area

  A 1 only is correct
  B 1 and 2 only are correct
  C 1, 2 and 3 are correct
  D 2 and 3 only are correct
  E 3 only is correct

2 For which of the following establishments is nearness to the market a more important locating influence than nearness to raw materials?
  1 a steel mill
  2 a bakery
  3 a shoe factory

  A 1 only is correct
  B 1 and 2 only are correct
  C 1, 2 and 3 are correct
  D 2 and 3 only are correct
  E 3 only is correct

3 Since the Second World War unemployment has been higher than the national average in all the following regions EXCEPT
  A North-east England
  B Wales
  C South-east England
  D Scotland
  E North-west England

4 Which of the following is a weight-gaining industry?
  A brewing
  B oil refining
  C steel
  D cotton
  E potteries

5 Features of the geographical distribution of population in the UK include
1 even dispersal throughout the country
2 concentration in urban areas
3 high density conurbations

A 1 only is correct
B 1 and 2 only are correct
C 2 only is correct
D 2 and 3 only are correct
E 3 only is correct

6 Which of the following is an example of an economy of concentration?
A bulk buying by a firm
B traffic congestion caused by the concentration of an industry in one area
C a skilled labour force suited to the needs of a main local industry
D atmospheric pollution caused by a local industry
E a highly automated local industry

7 Which of the following industries is LEAST geographically concentrated?
A cotton
B iron and steel
C shipbuilding
D furniture-making
E coal mining

8 Governments in Britain have tried to influence the location of industry by all the following methods EXCEPT
A nationalizing major industries
B improving derelict areas
C giving selective financial assistance to firms
D providing factory sites at low rents
E controlling new factory building

Essays

1 Why should location be important to a firm in setting up a new factory? What influences might affect the choice of location of a new car assembly plant?

2 Are owners and managers best qualified to decide the location of their firms or should industrial location be controlled by government?

3 Concentration of a large industry in a limited number of areas can have both advantages and disadvantages. Explain this statement. How can governments help to overcome the disadvantages?

Data response

UK regional unemployment

Region	*1979*	*1984*
	per cent	
South East	3·4	9·5
East Anglia	4·2	9·7
South West	5·4	10·9
North	8·3	17·9
Wales	7·3	15·6
Scotland	7·4	14·9
Northern Ireland	10·7	21·0
West Midlands	5·2	15·0
East Midlands	4·4	11·9
Yorkshire & Humberside	5·4	14·0
North West	6·5	15·7
United Kingdom	5·3	12·9

1 Which regions had rates of unemployment above the UK national level in both years?

2 In which regions did the percentage figure of unemployment increase by more than the national level?

3 How would you account for (a) the change in the national level of unemployment between the two years, (b) the wide regional variations?

4 Select one region of exceptionally high unemployment and suggest reasons for its particular problems.

5 Which two regions had the lowest percentage unemployment in both years? Suggest specific reasons in each case.

6 Does the comparison between the two years provide evidence of either success or failure for government regional policy?

Chapter 7

Distribution and markets

In Chapter 1 we defined production as including every stage in the process of making goods and services available to consumers. The final delivery of finished products to consumers normally involves two stages, wholesale and retail. Though workers at these stages are not actually making goods, they are productive workers in the economic sense of the term. Their part in production may be as important as the earlier processes. For example, the fish landed by trawlermen would be of little use without a wholesale and retail network to put the product within reach of consumers. Moreover, in the course of their activities other useful services are performed by both wholesalers and retailers.

7.1 Retail trade

Role of the retailer

The retailer is the final link in the chain of production. He is usually in personal contact with consumers and makes goods directly available to them. Let us see what this involves.

In the first place, *the retailer is there to save consumers time and trouble*. Without him, the consumer may have to travel long distances to factories or warehouses to find what he wants. It is important for retailers to be accessible to their customers and, in some cases, to provide a local delivery service.

The retailer should enable customers to choose what they want. He must therefore have facilities to display his goods. He should stock a selection of the types of goods he sells, offering a range of designs, qualities, etc. If necessary, he should have facilities for trying the goods – for example, by providing a fitting room in a clothing shop.

The quantity and range of goods kept by a retailer will depend on the demand of customers, storage space, and possibly financial considerations. But if he does not stock a particular item, he should know where it can be obtained and be prepared to order it for the customer. In the case of seasonal goods, such as fireworks or Easter eggs, it is the job of the retailer to anticipate the demand of consumers. He is in a unique position to know the requirements of the public and to inform manufacturers or suppliers. Thus, through sales representatives or wholesalers, he can keep manufacturers aware of consumer attitudes to products and suggest how products might be altered to suit demand.

Retailing is an aspect of division of labour. *Retailers are usually specialists* not only in their own stage of production but also in a particular type or range of products. As specialists, they are expected to advise customers and, where appropriate, provide or make arrangements for after-sales service such as maintenance or repairs. If required, they should be able to arrange hire-purchase or credit facilities.

Developments in retailing

1 Changes in demand

Considerable changes have taken place in the structure of retailing since the early 1950s. These have occurred in response to rapidly growing consumer demand and changes in the pattern of demand (Table 7.1). The changes in demand are themselves linked to other developments in society.

i) *Rising prosperity* has enabled the growth of consumer spending and also affected the type of goods demanded. In general, the demand for comparative luxuries has increased most rapidly. Rising expenditure on housing, durable consumer goods, and services (including travel and leisure activities) is clearly a reflection of higher real income and living standards. Since extra income is spent on other things, expenditure on necessities such as food and clothing falls as a proportion of total spending.

Table 7.1 The changing pattern of consumer spending

	Percentages of total household expenditure 1960	1983
Housing	9·3	16·8
Fuel, light, and power	5·9	6·5
Food	30·5	20·7
Alcoholic drink	3·2	4·9
Tobacco	5·9	3·0
Clothing and footwear	10·3	7·0
Durable household goods	6·4	7·2
Other goods	7·5	8·0
Transport and vehicles	12·2	14·7
Services	8·9	11·3

ii) *Advertising*, both in newspapers and on television, has stimulated consumer spending, particularly since the introduction of commercial television in the 1950s. Advertising can be *informative*, making consumers aware of available products and their characteristics. However, most modern advertising is *persuasive*, encouraging consumers to buy one brand of a product rather than another. Such advertising is frequently accompanied by special offers and other selling devices. Consumers may benefit from greater variety and choice, but advertising costs are likely to add to prices and could be regarded as a waste of resources.

iii) *New products* have significantly affected the pattern of family expenditure. Technical progress has created mass markets for a wide range of consumer durables, particularly household electrical products. Moreover, the purchase of one product often creates a demand for others – cars for petrol, recorders for tapes, freezers for frozen foods, computers for software.

iv) *Credit facilities* provided by banks and hire-purchase companies have helped to make expensive consumer durables available to a wide public. The government is able to influence this type of spending by control over bank lending and the level of interest rates charged to borrowers.

v) *The changing position of women and teenagers* in society has been an important influence on demand. The greater freedom and increased spending power of these two groups is reflected in the appeals of modern advertising and the development of new products and fashions.

2 *Structure of retailing*

In response to demand changes, retailing has become increasingly competitive. Competition has been further intensified since 1964 by the abolition of *resale price maintenance* – the system by which manufacturers could fix and legally enforce a uniform selling price for their products by all retailers. Many goods today carry the manufacturer's recommended price, but retailers are free to compete and sell below this price if they wish.

Increased competition among retailers has contributed to other developments. Since the 1950s retailing has become more professional and streamlined with emphasis on cut-price selling based on supermarkets, self-service, and generally larger organizations. Other effects of competition are longer and more flexible opening hours and a greater variety of products.

Supermarkets and self-service have also accelerated the trend towards pre-packing and branding of products. A lot of food now comes out of packets bearing the manufacturers' brand names.

The developments in retailing have reduced the importance of small neighbourhood shops. People are willing to go further afield for lower prices and a wider choice of goods. At the same time, the monopoly of the local shop has been broken by the greater mobility brought by the extension of car ownership. To many families, shopping now means the weekly excursion to the High Street instead of frequent visits to local shops. The effects go beyond retailing to town planning in the shape of pedestrian precincts, multi-storey car parks, out-of-town shopping facilities, and so on.

The trend is for supermarkets to grow not only in number but also in size and range of products. The large multiple retailers have competed in setting up superstores and *hypermarkets*. These cater for shoppers with cars and are sometimes situated on the outskirts of towns where ample parking space can be provided.

Retail organization

Retailers may be classified according to products sold or types of ownership and organization. The main forms of retail organization are outlined below and the changing pattern is shown in Table 7.2.

Why are shoppers attracted to a hypermarket like this one on the outskirts of a town?

1 *Independent owners*

Retailing is one of the traditional strongholds of the small business – shop, stall, or even barrow. The small corner shop always had the advantage of being conveniently situated and providing friendly personal service. But we have seen the effects of increasing competition in retail trade.

With limited sales and resources, the small shopkeeper often finds it hard to compete with larger organizations. He cannot obtain the same economies of scale and cannot buy in bulk or maintain such a wide range of products. With relatively small sales or turnover, he may not be able to afford to cut profit margins and prices to the same extent as larger rivals.

Despite the drawbacks, small shops visibly survive. Clearly, accessibility and personal service are still important to some people and in some lines of business. There has also been a movement towards co-operation to obtain some of the economies of scale – for instance, through bulk purchase of stocks.

Table 7.2 The structure of retail trade

	Percentages of total sales		
	1957	*1971*	*1982*
Department stores	5	4·9	5·2
Multiple shops	24	36·7	54·3
Co-operatives	12	7·1	4·8
Mail order	2	3·9	3·8
Independents	57	47·4	31·9

2 *Department stores*

These are large shops containing a number of specialist departments – in fact, shops within shops. Their attraction is that the shopper can buy a wide range of goods under one roof. They are usually situated near town centres and draw customers from a wide area. They have generally withstood the effects of competition and maintained their share of total retail trade.

3 *Chain stores*

A chain store or *multiple* organization consists of a number of distinct shops or branches under the same ownership. The owner may be an individual or partnership, but many of the large chains are limited companies. Some of the largest have branches in every part of the country. Some specialize in certain products, such as groceries, while others sell a wide variety of goods.

Chain stores have generally flourished in the competitive atmosphere of retail trade. They have been able to obtain the advantages of scale, bulk buying from manufacturers, and centralized organization. This has enabled them to cut prices and expand sales.

What advantages does a large chain store have over an independent shop?

4 Co-perative societies

The co-operative movement is dealt with in Chapter 4. It can be noted here that competition in retailing hit the co-operative shops. In recent years the movement has made great efforts to modernize its organization and image to compete more effectively with the chain stores, but its share of retail sales has continued to fall.

5 Mail-order firms

Customers choose their products from catalogues, sometimes through local agents (usually housewives) who visit their homes. The customer chooses his products at home and obtains the goods without having to leave home. The system is thus convenient for consumers and, at the same time, avoids the overhead costs of shops. Mail-order buying also has the advantage of allowing time for payment – perhaps twenty weeks or longer for expensive items. The practice has expanded rapidly, together with other forms of direct selling, but it remains a small proportion of total retail trade.

1 Explain the functions performed by retailers.

2 Identify and account for changes in consumer spending indicated in Table 7.1.

3 The last twenty-five years have brought a revolution in methods of shopping. Why has this occurred and in what ways has it affected the retail trade?

4 Note the types of organization now found in retailing and indicate the changes that have taken place in their relative importance (see Table 7.2).

7.2 Wholesale trade

Functions of the wholesaler

1 Distribution of goods

The wholesaler is the link between manufacturers and retailers. He receives goods from manufacturers in large quantities which are then broken down into smaller amounts for delivery to retailers.

The typical wholesaler buys from a number of manufacturers and distributes to many retailers. The

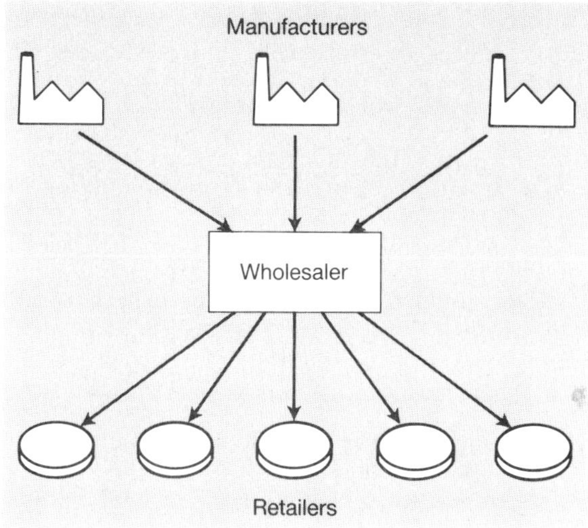

Fig. 7.1 Wholesale distribution

alternative would be for each manufacturer to deliver direct to every retailer. The saving that can be achieved by the wholesaler in transport and administration can be simply illustrated. Fig. 7.1 shows the journeys required to distribute products from three manufacturers to five retailers through an intermediate wholesaler. Note the multiplication of journeys if each manufacturer delivered direct to every retailer.

2 Storage of goods

Wholesalers normally hold stocks of a variety of goods in their warehouses. Both manufacturers and retailers are thus spared the need for storage space and are relieved of the expenses and problems of bulk storage. Retailers also have the advantage of being able to draw on the wholesaler's stocks quickly when required.

Through their holding of stocks, wholesalers are sometimes able to smooth out disturbing price fluctuations – for instance, in products affected by seasonal changes of demand or supply. Thus, stocks can be released to offset rising prices in periods of shortage or held back to check falling prices when supplies are plentiful.

3 Specialist services

As a specialist in his field, the wholesaler may perform a number of additional functions: he can advise both manufacturers and retailers, and act as communicating link between them; he may arrange imports and so make foreign products available to consumers; in some cases, he takes on the maintenance or servicing of products for the manufacturer.

In the past wholesalers often carried out tasks such as the grading and packing of goods for delivery to retailers, but this practice has become less common with more products being pre-packed and branded by manufacturers.

Elimination of the wholesaler

The existence of wholesalers and retailers, all with their profit margins, is sometimes seen as adding unnecessarily to the price of goods. But we have noted their functions, and the fact of their survival in competitive conditions suggests that the functions are still needed. Nevertheless, in certain areas of distribution – for example, where a manufacturer exists in close proximity to the retailers – separate wholesalers are less necessary. In such cases their functions may be taken over by either manufacturers or retailers.

Some of the changes we have observed in retail and wholesale trade have also led to the elimination of wholesalers. Larger retail organizations are capable of direct bulk buying from manufacturers and can provide their own storage facilities. For example, more than two-thirds of groceries are now delivered direct from manufacturers to the large food retailers, by-passing the traditional wholesaler.

On the manufacturing side, the practice of pre-packing and branding has deprived wholesalers of some of their former functions. Furthermore, the desire to ensure efficient and reliable distribution of their products has led some manufacturers to deal directly with a limited number of retailers or even to establish their own retail outlets. Oil companies have thus taken over garages, and breweries have acquired public houses.

Another development is the merging of wholesale and retail functions through mail-order business or direct discount selling from warehouses.

1 Explain the functions performed by wholesalers.

2 Why is there now less need for specialized wholesalers in the distribution of certain products?

7.3 Markets

Definition of a market

Between each stage of production, products are bought and sold. This is the business of markets in which wholesalers and retailers are often the professional dealers.

In everyday language a market usually means a place where a large variety of goods is retailed. Thus, the traditional market place of towns consists of a number of shops or stalls selling goods of many kinds. But in economics we generally mean a market in one particular product or group of products. For example, we speak of the markets for meat, wheat, fish, vegetables, houses, cars, gold, diamonds, and so on.

A market may be situated in a particular locality or building such as the London Stock Exchange – a market in stocks and shares. Some famous wholesale markets are associated with particular locations in London, and specialized markets are also located in other large towns.

If a product is perishable or bulky, and therefore costly to transport, the market is likely to be a local one comprising buyers and sellers from a fairly restricted area. However, improvements in transport and communication have enabled some markets to cover very wide areas, sometimes even worldwide. This generally applies to commodities such as wheat, cotton, and many raw materials that are wanted in almost every country and can be fairly easily transported. Buyers and sellers of these products are linked together by telephone and deals are frequently made across national boundaries.

A market may be either a place or an area where buyers and sellers of a product are in contact and its price is determined.

Degrees of competition

Markets can be classified according to product, stage of production, extent of area, or degree of competition. From the viewpoint of price, the degree of competition is of fundamental importance.

If a market consists of a number of buyers competing for the product but only one seller, the latter is obviously in a strong position to fix his own price. He cannot raise it indefinitely because buyers are likely to drop out if the product becomes too expensive. But he does not have to worry about being undercut by other sellers. This situation is called *monopoly* and is examined more closely in Chapter 8.

The reverse of monopoly is a situation in which there are not only many buyers but also a large number of firms competing fiercely with each other to sell the product. Between these two extremes there are varying degrees of competition – for example, markets where a very small number of firms compete, or one giant dominates the other firms, or where competition is restricted by agreements or understandings between firms.

Such forms of *imperfect competition* are in fact the most common market situations in the modern economy. However, to simplify at this stage, we concentrate on a situation in which there is the maximum degree of competition in the market. This we call *perfect competition*.

Perfect competition

To establish perfect competition, certain conditions must exist in the market.

i) *A large number of firms*. As we have seen, a market dominated by one firm or group of firms would be monopolistic, not competitive.

ii) *No government interference*. During and after the Second World War, the government rationed many foods and controlled their prices by law. Most of these products were scarce at the time, and competition among buyers would have forced prices up sharply. A more recent example is provided by incomes policy involving government intervention in the labour market (affecting wages).

iii) *Freedom of entry*. It would be a restriction of competition if new firms (or buyers) were obstructed in any way from entering the market to compete with those already in it.

iv) *Identical products*. Firms compete with each other to the greatest extent when they sell the same product in the same market. Any difference between the products makes competition imperfect because they are not perfect substitutes. The branding of products (called product differentiation) limits competition because buyers may prefer one brand name to another and so may continue to buy it even if the price is higher.

v) *Market perfection*. Competition is most intense when all buyers and sellers are fully informed about the prices being charged throughout the market and ruthless in their desire to get the best price. This is called a perfect market. A feature of such a market is that there can only be one price since no seller can risk raising his price above that of his competitors for fear of losing all his customers.

Retail markets are usually imperfect because housewives do not always have time to shop around for the lowest price and are sometimes willing to pay a higher price to save trouble. The most perfect markets are those in which the buyers as well as sellers are professional dealers who make a point of knowing about prices and getting the best bargain. Examples are commonly found among wholesale markets, commodity markets (dealing in raw materials), and other organized professional markets such as the Stock Exchange.

Two consequences of perfect competition can be noted: firstly, there will be a single uniform price, at any time, throughout the market since no firm can afford to charge more than its competitors; secondly, it will be fair to buyers because competition will prevent firms from making excessive profits by raising the price. In the next chapter we consider how the market price is determined under conditions of perfect competition.

Consumer protection

With living standards rising and more money to spend, people come under intense pressure to buy goods and services of all kinds. It consequently becomes important to protect consumers from inaccurate or misleading information, unfair methods of persuasion, and other unscrupulous selling practices.

To some extent consumers have organized to protect themselves by forming local consumer groups and through the national Consumers' Association. In every area there are Citizens' Advice Bureaux to help with particular individual problems or grievances. In the case of nationalized industries, consumers' councils have been set up to represent the views and interests of the public as consumers of the services concerned. In addition, since the end of the nineteenth century Parliament has passed a succession of laws to safeguard consumer interests in different ways.

Acts relating to *weights and measures* lay down uniform standards to ensure that the buyer obtains the quantity for which he pays. Quantities must also be correctly stated on packages. There are strict laws regulating the sale of *food and drugs* to ensure standards of cleanliness and quality, and similar controls also apply to *medicines*. Regulations are made to protect consumers from dangers caused by bad design or construction of goods. *Hire-purchase* and consumer credit is another area in which the law provides consumer protection.

The rapid growth of the *advertising* industry involves obvious risks to consumers. In an advanced economy advertising is a necessary means of informing consumers about products and their qualities or uses. But the real aim of most advertising is to persuade people to buy, and the effect can be to deceive rather than inform. However, under the Trade Descriptions Act 1968, it is an offence against the law to make false or misleading statements about goods or services or to misrepresent their prices in certain ways. In advertising or labelling products, firms may also be required to provide particular information for the benefit of consumers.

In 1972 a minister in the government was made specifically responsible for consumer affairs. In the following year the *Fair Trading Act* brought about the appointment of a Director-General of Fair Trading, with an office staff, to keep a general watch over all trading practices and activities in the interests of consumers. The Director-General can propose new laws to protect consumers against unreasonable pressure or other unfair trading practices.

1 Note the definition of a market in economics. Why are some markets purely local whereas others are worldwide?

2 How are markets classified according to degrees of competition? State the distinguishing features of monopoly and imperfect competition.

3 Note the conditions necessary to establish a perfectly competitive market. Why is competition generally less perfect in retail markets than in wholesale markets? What advantages are there to a consumer buying in a market where sellers are in perfect competition?

4 Make a list of the ways in which the law protects consumers against bad or unfair selling practices.

Multiple choice

1 The following statements relate to changes in the structure of retailing during the last twenty years. They are all true EXCEPT
- **A** Independent retailers' share of total retail sales has fallen.
- **B** The number of supermarkets has increased.
- **C** Mutiple chain stores have increased their share of total retail trade.
- **D** There has been a growth in the number of branded products.
- **E** Co-operative societies have increased their share of total retail sales.

2 Which of the following provides the best example of an imperfect market?
- **A** retail groceries
- **B** the Stock Exchange
- **C** the market in foreign currencies
- **D** wholesale markets
- **E** the international wheat market

3 Which of the following is NOT a condition of perfect competition?
- **A** a large number of firms in the market
- **B** branded products
- **C** freedom of entry for new firms
- **D** no government interference
- **E** no collaboration between firms

4 If one firm is the sole supplier of the product in a market, this situation can be described as
- **A** a black market
- **B** a supermarket
- **C** a sole proprietor
- **D** a monopoly
- **E** private enterprise

5 A large shop with many specialist departments under one roof is called
- **A** a warehouse
- **B** a department store
- **C** a mail-order firm
- **D** a chain store
- **E** a sole trader

6 Traditional functions of a wholesaler include
1 distributing goods
2 storing a variety of goods
3 advising retailers

- **A** 1 only is correct
- **B** 1 and 2 only are correct
- **C** 1, 2 and 3 are correct
- **D** 2 and 3 only are correct
- **E** 3 only is correct

Data response

Retail businesses (1980)

	Number	*Outlets*	*Total turnover (£ million)*
Single outlet retailers	197 884	197 884	18 118
Small multiples	28 932	76 920	8 451
Large multiples	1 261	73 797	31 915
Co-operative societies	191	8 556	3 869
Total retail trade	228 077	348 601	58 484

1 What is meant by a large multiple retailer? Give examples.

2 In what respects do co-operative societies differ from large multiple retailers?

3 What is meant by a single outlet retailer? Calculate their approximate percentage of (a) total retail outlets, (b) total retail turnover. What does this tell you about their average size?

4 Account for the survival of single outlet retailers in competition with the multiples.

5 What changes in the structure of retailing do you expect to see over the next decade, and why?

Essays

1 'Production does not end when goods leave the factory'. Explain this statement and show how wholesalers and retailers are an integral part of the productive process.

2 Distinguish the main types of retail organization now in existence and show how changes on both the demand and supply side of markets have affected the structure of retailing in recent years.

3 What do economists mean by a market? Note the main features of a perfect market and, with the aid of examples, show why such markets are exceptional in practice.

Chapter 8

The price system

The prices of most products are determined in the markets, where buyers and sellers come together. To understand how a price is determined, we must examine each of the two sides of a market – the demand side (composed of buyers) and the supply side (composed of sellers). Our explanation of the relationship between these two sides will generally assume conditions of perfect competition as described in the preceding chapter.

8.1 Demand

In the explanation of prices, demand must be given a precise meaning. *The demand for a product is the amount that people are prepared to buy in the market over a given period of time at any prevailing price.* This definition contains three distinct points:

i) It refers to the quantity that would actually be bought and not the amount that people need or desire (if only they could afford it). Demand in this sense is sometimes called 'effective demand'.

ii) Demand can only be calculated over a fixed period of time – say a week or a year – since the amount bought would vary when different lengths of time are considered.

Table 8.1 A demand schedule

Price per kg (pence)	*Quantity demanded per week (thousand kg)*
1	15
2	14
3	13
4	12
5	10
6	7
7	5
8	4
9	3
10	2

iii) Demand must be related to price since people are unlikely to buy the same amount of a product when its price changes.

Relationship between price and quantity demanded

In a market where the price is changing, it is possible to calculate the quantity demanded at different prices. Even if the price is stable, it is possible to estimate how much would be demanded at different prices. Such measurements or estimates can be set out in the form of a table called a *demand schedule*. Table 8.1 shows an imaginary demand schedule for apples in a local vegetable market.

Our demand schedule illustrates an important general rule about demand. *The quantity demanded of a product is usually greater at lower prices.* The reasons for this are obvious when it is remembered that the demand in a market is the total of the demands of individual purchasers. Think of how your own purchases of a product are likely to be affected by a change in its price. Firstly, if something you buy becomes cheaper, you can afford to buy

Fig. 8.1 A demand curve

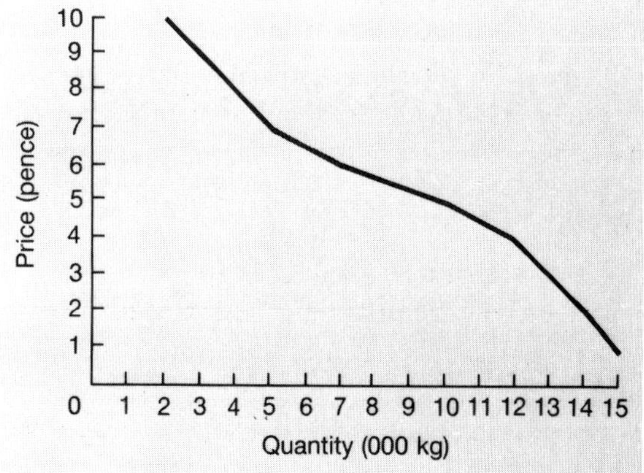

more. Secondly, you will tend to substitute the cheaper product for other things that are now comparatively more expensive. For example, if apples become cheaper, there would be a tendency for people to eat more apples and perhaps fewer pears.

1 The demand curve

Economists are fond of using graphs, and the information given in a demand schedule is often shown in the form of a graph called a demand curve. Fig. 8.1 shows the demand curve based on our demand schedule above.

The main feature of demand curves, in general, is that they slope down from left to right on the kind of diagrams we use. This simply reflects the fact that the quantity demanded is normally greater at lower prices.

2 Elasticity of demand

Although the quantity demanded is generally greater at lower prices, the effect of a change in price varies with different products. The quantity of milk or potatoes demanded probably does not change much when their prices change. On the other hand, that for lemonade or chocolates could change a great deal.

The extent to which a change in price leads to a change in the quantity demanded is called the elasticity of demand. If the quantity demanded is very sensitive to price changes it is said to be elastic. If price changes have little effect on the quantity demanded, it is relatively inelastic. If price changes have no effect at all on the quantity demanded, it is completely inelastic.

Economists measure elasticity of demand by comparing percentage changes in the quantity demanded with price, but there is no need for us to be so exact at this stage. If you examine the demand curve you will see that its slope indicates the degree of elasticity. The steeper the curve, the less its elasticity. A vertical demand curve is completely inelastic because it shows that exactly the same amount is bought at every price.

The elasticity of demand for any product depends mainly on how important the product is to the consumers and whether it has close substitutes. The demand for necessities is inelastic because people cannot do without them and cannot substitute other things if their prices rise. If products are close substitutes for each other, people will obviously switch their demand between them when there are changes in their relative prices, and so the demand for each will be elastic. However, at very low prices the demand for most products becomes inelastic because the expenditure on them is small and price changes may go unnoticed or seem insignificant to consumers.

Bearing in mind the above factors, it should be possible to estimate the elasticity of demand for different products. Two main questions should be asked in each case: how essential is it considered by consumers? to what extent are substitutes available? The demand for bread is inelastic because it is a comparative necessity with no close substitute.

Elasticity of demand is important in many practical ways. It obviously affects firms when they are deciding whether to raise or lower their prices. For instance, firms would be less willing to raise the prices of their products if the demand is elastic because price rises would then mean large reductions in their sales. In later chapters we shall also see how elasticity of demand is relevant to government policies such as tax changes and devaluation.

Influences other than price

The demand for any product also depends on influences that are independent of its price. Thus, an individual's purchases are obviously affected by his personal tastes, the size of his income, and the prices of other products. The total demand in a market is also affected by population influences and possibly by the policies of the government.

Though independent of the price charged for a product, these influences are important in determining the price and changes in them are a major cause of changes in price. We shall examine each in turn and, at a later stage, consider their part in the determination of the market price.

1 Personal tastes

The choices made by different people in spending their incomes depend essentially on their individual tastes and preferences. This is the basis of all demand. However, our tastes are not permanently fixed. They change by themselves and can also be affected by influences such as fashion, advertising, and the development of new products.

2 Incomes

Our demand clearly depends on how much we earn. This affects not only how much we buy but also what we buy. In a poor country the demand for luxury goods must be low. As incomes and living standards rise, the demand for most products increases – but not all to the same extent, and some may even decline in demand. In general, the demand for luxuries is obviously more responsive to changes in income than the demand for necessities.

The pattern of demand also depends on the way in which the wealth or income of a country is shared out among its inhabitants. The importance of this will be clear if you consider how the demand for different products would be affected by heavy tax increases on the rich in order to give more to old age pensioners.

3 Other prices

The demand for any product also depends on the prices of other goods, particularly if they are close substitutes or closely linked in demand. A fall in the price of a substitute would cause some consumers to switch over to it, and a rise in its price would have a reverse effect. For example, consider the effect of a substantial rise or fall in rail fares on the demand for bus or coach journeys.

There are many cases in which the demand for two products is closely linked – cars and petrol, pipes and tobacco, and so on. A rise in the price of one, causing the quantity demanded to contract, then leads to a fall in the demand for the other. Conversely, a fall in the price of one would cause purchases of both to increase. For example, consider the effect of a substantial rise or fall in the price of petrol on the demand for cars. This kind of connection between products is called 'joint demand'.

4 Population

A larger population means a greater demand for most products, but all products are not affected to the same degree. For example, the effect on demand of population growth due to immigration would be very different from that caused by a rising birth-rate. As we saw in Chapter 2, the pattern of demand depends on the composition of the population, including its age and sex distribution, as well as its total numbers.

5 Government policies

In countries such as Britain the government is a huge buyer of goods and services, and its policies are therefore an important factor in the demand for many products. This should become clearer if you think of all the things that have to be bought to equip, for example, a new hospital or school. The government also influences demand when it gives pensions, unemployment benefits, and other similar payments, thus adding to the income and spending of many people. Changes in taxation similarly affect the income and demand of taxpayers.

1 Note the definition of demand and explain the reference to *effective demand*.

2 Use Table 8.1 to draw the demand curve for yourself. (Remember that, for graphs of this kind, price is always measured on the vertical axis and quantity on the horizontal axis.)

3 Your demand curve should slope down from left to right. What does this show and why is it the normal case?

4 Define elasticity of demand. How is it indicated by the slope of a demand curve?

5 What determines the elasticity of demand for a product? Note examples of products for which the demand is (a) elastic and (b) inelastic, giving reasons in each case.

6 List and briefly explain the main influences on demand other than price.

8.2 Supply

In dealing with demand we were concerned with the buying side of markets. Supply is derived from the sellers. Its definition is similar to that of demand, but on the selling side. *The supply of a product is the quantity that sellers would make available for purchase in the market over a given period of time at any prevailing price.*

Extra stocks of the product may be lying in warehouses, but our definition refers to the amount that would actually be offered for sale in the market. It should also be noted that, corresponding with demand, the supply of a product is only conceivable if related to price and measured over a given period of time.

Table 8.2 A supply schedule

Price per kg (pence)	*Quantity supplied per week (thousand kg)*
1	0
2	1
3	2
4	3
5	5
6	7
7	10
8	12
9	14
10	15

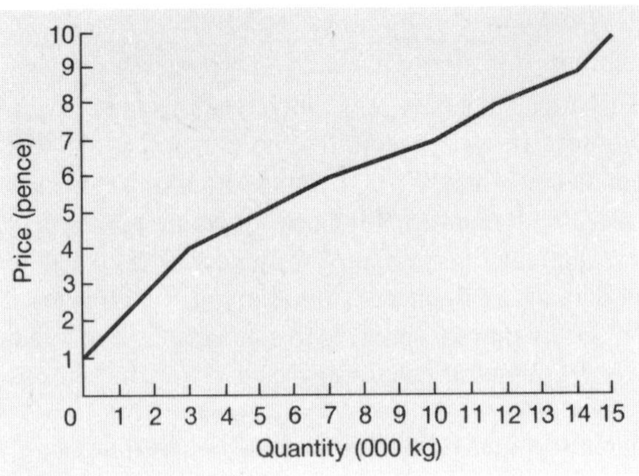

Fig. 8.2 A supply curve

As with demand, the quantity supplied of any product depends on its price and also on other influences independent of its price. These two kinds of influences need to be examined.

Relationship between price and quantity supplied

To understand this relationship we must consider how firms are likely to react to changes in the prices of their products. Let us suppose that the market price of a product rises because it is in great demand and people are clamouring to buy it. At the higher price the product has obviously become more profitable to produce and sell. The quantity is then likely to expand in two ways. In the first place, firms in the industry will want to take advantage of the opportunity to make more profit by increasing their outputs. This could involve expensive overtime payments or even raising wages to attract more labour, but these costs could be met from expanding profits. Secondly, new firms will be attracted into the market by the high profit.

Reversing the process, a fall in the market price would make the product less profitable. Firms might then cut production, switch to other products or even be forced out of business.

The effect of a price change on production indicates an important general rule about supply. *The quantity supplied of a product is usually greater at higher prices*. This can be illustrated by a supply schedule (Table 8.2) on similar lines to our earlier demand schedule (for apples). In the case of apples, it can be assumed that the quantity supplied to the market will expand if the price rises because farmers will find it worthwhile to gather more and (in the long run) will convert more land to growing apples.

1 The supply curve

The information in the supply schedule can be used to draw a supply curve on a diagram corresponding to the one used for the demand curve previously constructed. We show this is in Fig. 8.2. The supply curve slopes upwards from left to right – that is, in the opposite direction to the demand curve. This follows the normal rule that the quantity supplied is greater at higher prices.

2 Elasticity of supply

The extent to which a change in price affects the quantity supplied varies from product to product. For example, it might be very difficult and costly for miners to dig more coal out of the ground even if it were in great demand and the price were to rise. On the other hand, shirt manufacturers could easily and cheaply expand the quantity of striped shirts supplied if these became fashionable and their prices consequently rose. The supply of coal is inelastic; the supply of striped shirts is elastic. *Elasticity of supply is the extent to which a change in price leads to a change in the quantity supplied.*

As with demand, elasticity is indicated by the slope of the supply curve. The steeper the curve, the less its elasticity. A vertical supply curve is completely inelastic because it shows exactly the same amount supplied at every level of price.

Time can have an important influence on elasticity of supply. For example, the supply of fresh fish in a local market is likely to be absolutely inelastic on a particular day but may be very elastic if time is allowed to catch and deliver more (or less). Given time, it is possible to expand the quantity supplied of most products by building new factories, or, in the case of agriculture, by using more land. The period of time required to enable an industry to adjust itself fully to a change in price is called the long period or the long run. In farming the long run is usually a year. Supply is generally more elastic in the long run than in the short run.

Influences other than price

As with demand, the quantity supplied does not depend only on price. The output of firms is affected by anything that helps or hinders production or alters the costs of production. The following influences obviously affect supply and can cause supply to change without any change in price:

i) The cost of labour (wages), materials, and equipment used in the industry.

ii) Weather conditions (particularly affecting agriculture) and events such as fire or floods.

iii) Taxes on production or government subsidies to encourage production.

iv) The standard of technical efficiency including the effects of inventions or new methods of production.

v) The efficiency of managements and their relations with workers.

In general, any change in the costs or efficiency of factors of production is likely to affect supply.

1. Note the definition of supply. Why is the quantity supplied of a product usually greater at a higher price?
2. Use Table 8.2 to draw a supply curve on the same diagram as the demand curve you have already drawn for Exercise 2, p.83.
3. What is meant by elasticity of supply and how is it indicated by the slope of a supply curve?
4. List the main factors other than price that influence the supply of a product.

8.3 Market price

Having looked at demand and supply separately, we now have to bring them together in order to understand how the price of a product is established in the market. We can start by stating a basic principle applying to the price in any competitive market. *The price will settle at a level that makes the quantities demanded and supplied equal.* This level is illustrated in Fig. 8.3 by using demand and supply curves similar to those already drawn. (For the purpose of illustration it is customary to draw demand and supply curves smoothly.)

Market equilibrium

If you examine Fig. 8.3, you will see that at the price OP – determined by the point at which the two curves cut each other – demand and supply are both equal to the quantity OQ. This is known as the point of equilibrium and the price is the equilibrium price.

Economists use the term equilibrium to indicate a state of balance in which there are no forces causing change in either direction. If the price differed from the equilibrium level, market forces would push it back towards that level. This is usually illustrated by looking at the consequences of departures from the equilibrium. Fig. 8.4 shows how the forces of demand and supply would restore the market price to equilibrium if, for any reason, it fell below or

Fig. 8.3 Market equilibrium

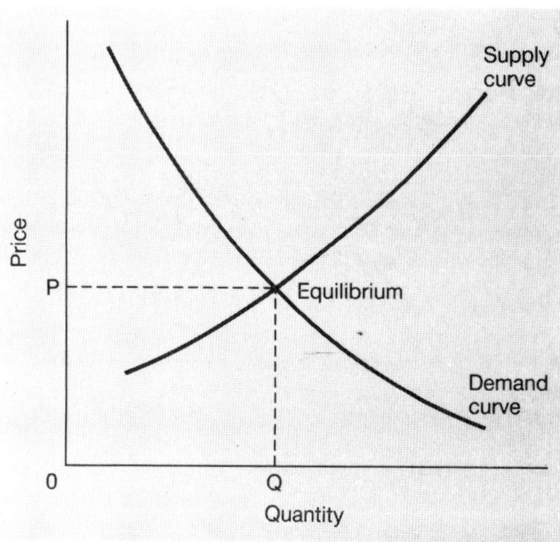

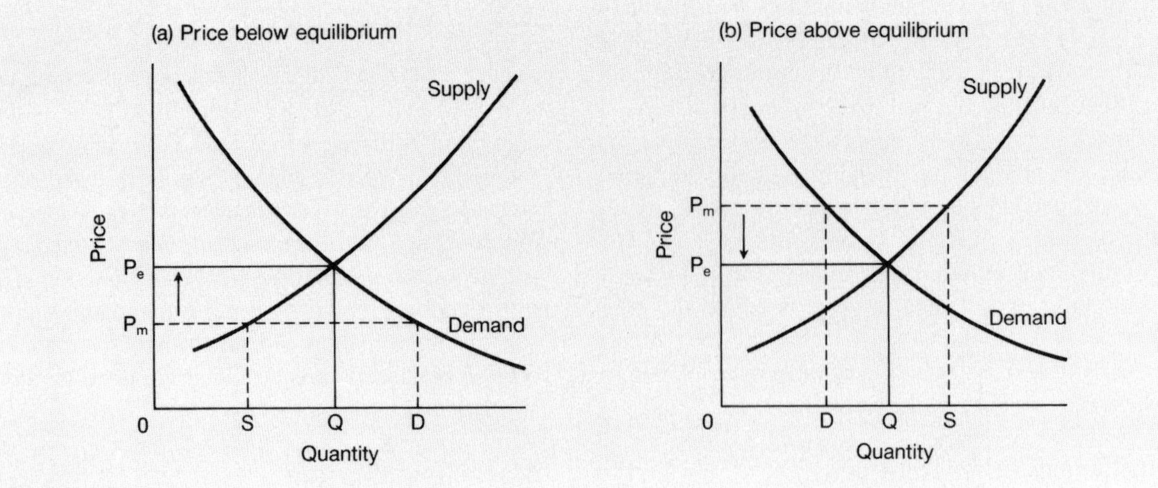

Fig. 8.4 Movements to equilibrium

rose above that level. In each case P_e is the equilibrium price and P_m is the temporary market price.

In Fig. 8.4a, with the market price below equilibrium at P_m:
i) the quantity demanded (OD) exceeds the quantity supplied (OS);
ii) the resulting market shortage causes the price to rise;
iii) the rising price causes supply to expand and demand to contract until equilibrium is restored at price P_e and quantity OQ.

In Fig. 8.4b, with the market price above equilibrium at P_m, the resulting surplus of supply over demand causes equilibrium to be restored by exactly the reverse process.

Changes in equilibrium

The equilibrium is determined by the state of demand and supply in the market at that time. If conditions change on either the demand or supply side, the market must adjust itself to a new equilibrium and a new price. The causes of any such change are to be found among the influences on demand and supply outlined in the early part of the chapter. Fig. 8.5 is a reminder of those influences and shows how they are related to price.

Since changes in equilibrium are brought about by changes in demand or supply, the process of adjustment can be shown through shifts of the curves on the diagrams we have already used. For this purpose, we look separately at the effects of changes in demand and changes in supply which are the cause of such shifts. It should be noted that price changes themselves are an effect and not a cause.

Fig. 8.5 Influences on price

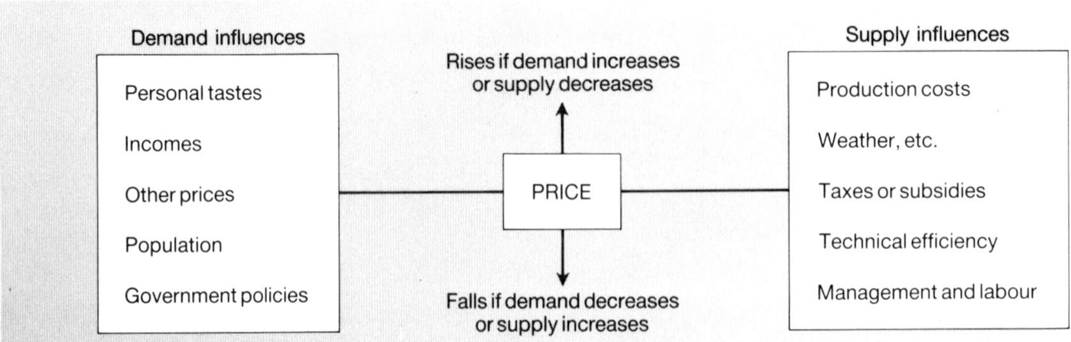

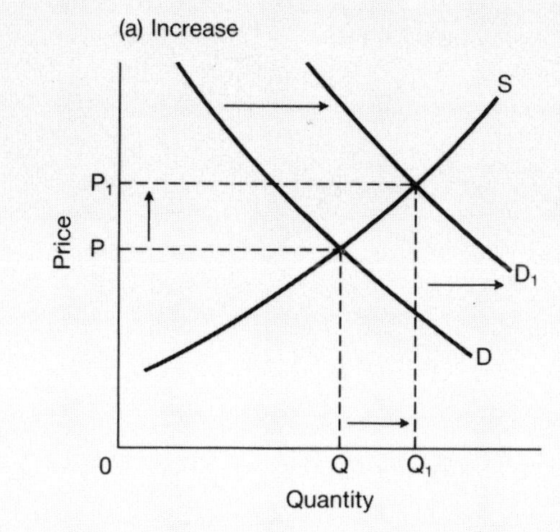

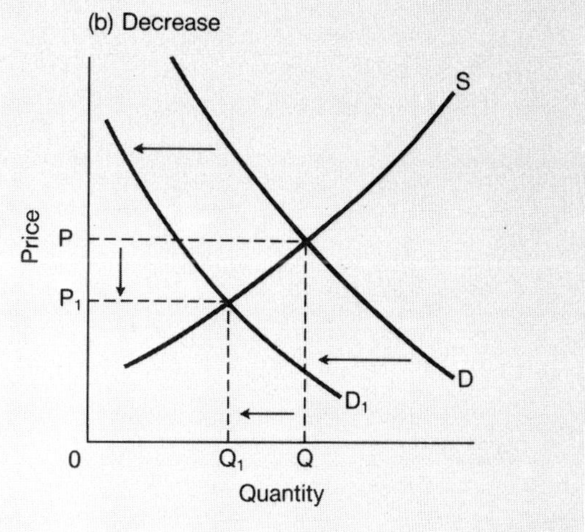

Fig. 8.6 Changes in demand

1 Effect of changes in demand

We now consider what happens if the demand for a product changes for any of the reasons given. For example, suppose that demand has increased because of a basic change in people's tastes. The product is now bought in larger quantities, and this would occur at any price. Thus an increase in demand is shown by a movement of the curve to the right.

The effect of an increase in demand is illustrated in Fig. 8.6a. The adjustment to a new equilibrium involves three distinct movements indicated by the arrows:

i) The demand curve shifts to the right from D to D_1.
ii) Increased demand causes the price to rise from OP to OP_1.
iii) At the higher price, the quantity supplied expands from OQ to OQ_1.

It should be noted that there is no shift in the supply curve but simply a movement along the curve as firms respond to the higher price. Thus, through the rise in price, the quantity supplied adjusts to the extra demand and equilibrium is restored.

If demand decreases, the process of adjustment is exactly reversed. The three movements are shown in Fig. 8.6b starting this time with a shift of the demand curve to the left.

Conclusions about market equilibrium are sometimes called the laws of demand and supply. One such law can now be stated. *An increase in demand normally causes the price to rise and the quantity supplied to expand to a new equilibrium. Conversely, a decrease in demand causes the price to fall and the quantity supplied to contract to a new equilibrium.*

2 Effect of changes in supply

A change in equilibrium may also be brought about by a shift in the supply curve. Such a shift could be caused by any of the given influences on the supply of a product. Thus, anything that improved the efficiency or reduced the costs of firms would stimulate production and so increase supply at any given price. Conversely, a rise in costs would discourage production and decrease supply at any price.

Remember that an increase in quantity is always shown as a movement to the right. An increase in supply would therefore shift the supply curve to the right. A decrease would shift it to the left. Fig. 8.7 shows how equilibrium is restored in each case.

Note that there are again three main movements:

i) a shift in the supply curve;
ii) a movement of price to the new equilibrium;
iii) an adjustment of the quantity demanded to the new equilibrium. The arrows help to distinguish the movements on each diagram.

Another law of demand and supply can now be noted. *An increase in supply normally causes the price to fall and the quantity demanded to expand*

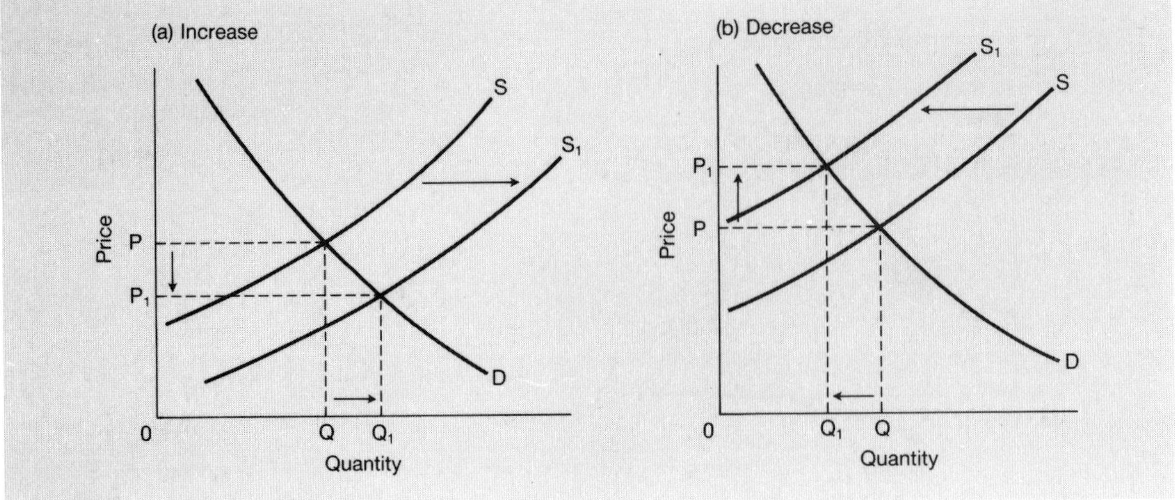

Fig. 8.7 Changes in supply

to a new equilibrium. Conversely, a decrease in supply causes the price to rise and the quantity demanded to contract to a new equilibrium.

At this stage we can point to a further conclusion applying to changes due to both demand and supply influences. We have seen that, in each case, equilibrium is restored by means of a change in price which brings the quantities demanded and supplied back into equality. If demand and supply are very inelastic, it would need a larger price change to bring about the necessary degree of adjustment. The price change resulting from any change in demand or supply will be smaller if demand and supply are more elastic. This conclusion can be demonstrated by comparing diagrams using curves of different elasticities (slopes).

1 Explain precisely what is meant by the equilibrium price in a market. Show the equilibrium price and quantity on the demand and supply diagram you have drawn (Exercise 2, p.85). What would happen in a competitive market if the price was (a) below, (b) above its equilibrium level?

2 Draw rough diagrams to illustrate the effect on price and quantity of the following changes in a market: (a) an increase in demand; (b) a decrease in demand; (c) an increase in supply; (d) a decrease in supply. (Refer to Figs. 8.6 and 8.7 to check your diagrams.)

8.4 The market economy

In every society there must be some way of deciding how to use the productive resources of the community. For example, decisions have to be made about what goods and services to produce and in what quantities. In communist societies these decisions are entirely controlled by governments. In so-called capitalist economies many such decisions are left to private enterprise—that is, to the businessmen who own and control a large part of industry. The major influences on businessmen are the forces of the market and the price system that we have outlined. Economies based on private enterprise are thus described as market economies.

Role of the price system

Special importance is attached to the part played by prices in the market economy. We have seen how prices act as the link between demand and supply in the market. Two particular functions of the price system are essential to the working of the economy.

1 Consumer satisfaction

The price system directs the economy towards the satisfaction of consumer demand. Price levels in the various markets guide firms into the production of those goods and services that people want most. For instance, if tastes change so that we want more of one product rather than another, the change in

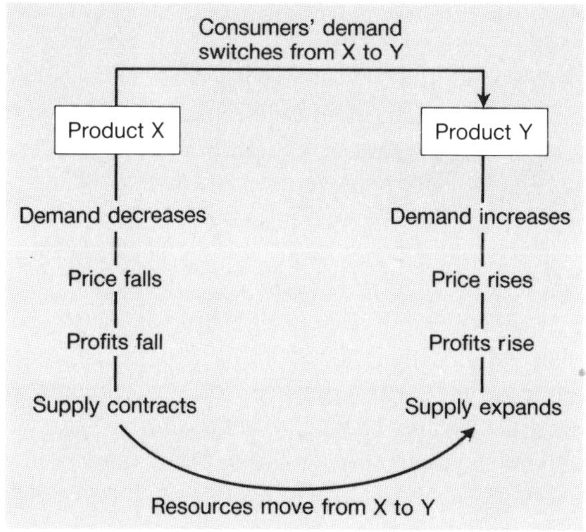

Fig. 8.8 Economic response to demand

demand will be indicated by market price movements (as described in the early part of the chapter) and the quantity supplied will be adjusted to the new situation in each market. This is illustrated in Fig. 8.8 which shows what happens in two markets when demand switches from product X to product Y.

Movements of resources are assisted by changes in their own prices. Industries in which demand is expanding and prices rising can afford to pay higher wages for labour, higher prices for materials, and so on. They consequently attract resources from other industries where demand is falling. The resources of the economy are thus drawn into the industries where people want them to be employed.

The tendency of market economies to respond to demand is summed up by the saying that 'the consumer is king'. This is the basis of the *laissez-faire* economic theory which emphasizes the virtues of private enterprise and is used to resist government interference in the working of the economy. The theory will be examined critically when we consider the limitations of the market economy.

2 Rationing supply

Price restricts the quantity demanded to the available supply. There are never enough productive resources to satisfy all the wants of people, and shortages of products occur in every economic system. The price system then provides a solution by rationing out the supply of scarce products.

Price acts as a rationing instrument simply because when a product becomes scarce – due either to increased demand or diminished supply – its price automatically rises. The rise will continue until the quantity demanded is reduced to the supply available. The market shortage then disappears, and equilibrium is restored. Rationing is thus achieved by the simple device of making the product too expensive for some people to buy.

An alternative method of rationing is illustrated by the ration cards and coupons used to share out limited supplies of essential foods in wartime. Such methods of rationing were then necessary because prices were controlled by law and could not perform their normal function. Wartime rationing required many civil servants and was costly to administer. It also led to the growth of 'black markets' – that is illegal sales of rationed goods at excessive prices. Nevertheless, in the case of basic foods and other essential goods, it was considered preferable to rationing by price.

Limitations of the market economy

The advantages of the market economy should be apparent from the explanation of how it works. Through the price system it automatically tends to satisfy consumer demand. Moreover, it requires no machinery of government control and consequently involves no cost to the taxpayer. On what grounds, then, do governments increasingly interfere with the working of the economy?

1 Unrealistic assumptions

In the first place, it should be noted that the system we have described is an ideal one that has probably never existed in practice. For example, resources do not move easily from one industry to another in response to demand. In particular, the mobility of labour is hindered by many social obstacles such as family ties and housing shortages (see Chapter 3).

A major assumption is that markets are competitive. Thus, it is assumed that competing firms will always produce more in response to an increase in demand. But if there is only one firm in the market, it may find it profitable to restrict supply in order to force the price up as high as possible at the expense of consumers. This is the case of monopoly which we consider in the next part of the chapter. In practice, many markets today are closer to monopoly than to competition. The economy does not therefore adjust itself to demand as smoothly as the theory implies.

Governments have tried to improve the working of market economies in various ways. The movement of labour is encouraged by job centres, training schemes, housing policies, and so on. In considering the problem of monopoly, we shall see that there are elaborate policies to control their power and to promote competition.

2 *Problem of inequality*

Even if the market economy worked ideally, governments would still find it necessary to intervene for social reasons. We have seen that the market demand for a product is the *effective demand*—that is, demand backed by money. Consequently, the richest people with most spending power have the greatest pull on the resources of the economy. Others who lack spending power may go without the basic essentials of life. Demand is related to wealth and not need.

The tendency of market economies to provide for the rich and neglect the poor would be softened if wealth were more equally divided between members of the community. If everyone had exactly the same spending power, they would have an equal pull on the productive resources of the economy. However, the profit incentive which is an essential feature of production in market economies has generally led to greater inequalities of income and wealth. The system has thus tended to increase rather than diminish the contrast between wealth and poverty. This largely explains the growth of socialist ideas. It is also the main reason why governments have become concerned with economic and social affairs.

Governments try to reduce inequalities of wealth and relieve poverty through taxation and social policies. Certain taxes are designed to fall most heavily on the rich, so cutting down their effective demand. A large part of the money raised from taxes is redistributed to poorer people through pensions and other benefits or used to pay for social services such as health and education (see Chapter 13). Price controls and rationing, as adopted in wartime, are also methods of protecting poorer people from the harshness of the market system.

3 *Social needs*

Market economies are organized to supply what people are willing and able to pay for in the markets. But there are important requirements of society as a whole that cannot be bought in markets and can only be provided by governments. Obvious examples are defence, police, and law courts, which have to be provided by governments in every kind of society. These are called *public goods*.

In most modern societies governments also provide certain goods and services which market forces alone would not supply in sufficient quantities perhaps because people, as consumers, do not appreciate their full benefits. For example, not everyone is able and willing to spend enough on educating their children or providing for pensions in old age. These are called *merit goods*.

Even in parts of the economy where the market system works efficiently, governments have found it necessary to protect members of society from some of its effects. In nineteenth-century Britain, for example, market forces led to the exploitation of labour, including the employment of very young children, in industries such as cotton and mining. Parliament was forced to pass Factory Acts to deal with this problem. A modern illustration is the concern over pollution, resulting from industrial production. In Chapter 1 we saw that firms, supplying goods in markets, consider their own (private) costs and revenues but do not normally take into account all the *social costs and benefits* of their actions.

4 *National problems*

Market forces have sometimes led to heavy unemployment or to inflationary situations when prices have risen at an alarming rate. Furthermore, since foreign as well as home-produced goods are available in many markets, serious problems have sometimes arisen in connection with international trade and the balance of payments. Governments have to seek remedies for such important economic problems. We shall return to them in later chapters.

1 What is meant by the market economy?

2 Explain how the price system helps (a) to satisfy consumer demand, (b) to overcome shortages in supply.

3 For what reasons do governments interfere with the working of the market economy?

8.5 Monopoly

We have assumed throughout the chapter that markets are competitive. This means, in particular, that products are supplied by a large number of competing firms. But we know from experience that such a situation does not always exist in practice. Industries are often dominated by a few giant firms, and even when there are a lot of firms competition between them may not be effective.

The opposite extreme to perfect competition is pure monopoly. *Monopoly occurs when the supply of a product is controlled by one firm or group of firms acting together.* As in the case of perfect competition, complete monopoly is rare in practice, but the theory of monopoly helps economists and governments to understand and deal with tendencies in industry towards monopoly.

Reasons for monopoly

1 Legal protection

Monopolies can be granted by law. Thus, inventors are given rights known as patents allowing them complete control of the production and sale of their products over a given period of time. Copyrights similarly cover the field of literature and music.

A form of monopoly power protected by law can also be obtained by the manufacturers of branded products – that is, products distinguished by their own registered brand names. Common examples are among soap powders and processed foods, but the advertisements are full of many others. Each producer has a monopoly of his own product though it may be almost identical in quality to other brands and sell in a very competitive market.

2 Industries unsuited for competition

Industries such as gas, electricity, and water supply naturally develop into monopoly organizations because competition between individual firms would be absurdly wasteful. For example, imagine the effect of a number of firms competing to supply gas to houses in your own area. Similarly, public transport such as railways and local bus services are invariably monopolies. Such industries are sometimes called *natural monopolies*. They generally provide essential public services and are usually under some form of government control.

In some industries competition is limited because of financial reasons. Steel is an example of an industry in which huge capital expenditure is required for a firm to enter. Only very large firms can survive in such industries, and new firms are discouraged from competing by the high cost of setting up.

3 Restricted sources of supply

Control over the supply of a product may come about because it is only found in certain areas of the world. This applies to certain raw materials and minerals such as diamonds and nickel. A similar kind of monopoly also occurs when a firm has technical knowledge which it keeps to itself.

The supply of a product may be restricted to a particular area or locality because transport difficulties exclude outside firms from the market. Examples are to be found among heavy or bulky goods which cost too much to transport long distances. Governments themselves also sometimes encourage monopoly in their home markets by using import duties or other methods to restrict competition from foreign suppliers.

4 Action by firms to reduce competition

Firms themselves set out on policies intended to establish control over the production or sale of their products. The motive for such policies may be to increase profits or simply to avoid the uncertainties of competition. The methods used by firms to achieve monopoly power take a variety of forms indicated below.

Forms of monopoly organization

1 Manufacturers' associations

Firms in the same industry may originally form an association merely to exchange information and look after the interests of their industry in general. However, such co-operation has often led to arrangements of a monopolistic kind. These may take the form of agreements to sell their products at a common price or to divide the market among themselves so that each firm has a certain share of the total sales. Manufacturers have sometimes also forced retailers to sell their products at fixed prices by collectively refusing to supply those who do not obey. Such methods are known as *restrictive practices*. In Britain, they are generally forbidden by law.

2 *Cartels*

Agreements to restrict supply and fix prices are liable to break down unless they are well organized. In forming a cartel, the firms set up a central selling agency. Each firm retains independent control over its own production but sells its products through the central organization. The cartel can also determine how much each of its member firms produces and it distributes the profits to them.

The difficulty of maintaining a cartel is that ambitious firms begin to feel that it restricts their sales too much and so break away. To remove this temptation, tighter organizations are formed.

3 *Mergers*

A merger takes place when independent firms are combined together under the control of one management. The firms may retain their old names and their former managers may still exercise some degree of control over operations on the factory floor but, in effect, they become a single firm with a unified overall policy.

Mergers come about in different ways. Each firm may voluntarily agree to merge or one powerful firm may forcibly swallow up the others. A common method is the *takeover bid* through which a firm seeks to gain control over others simply by buying enough of their shares.

A typical form of merger is the *holding company* which uses its own capital to buy controlling interests in other companies called subsidiaries. In this way a few people owning a comparatively small amount of capital can control an enormous amount of industrial wealth. Huge pyramid organizations are built up in the process. Company A controls B, C, and D, each of which controls further subsidiaries, and so A finally controls the whole structure. Since most shareholders are not organized, control of a company can be established with considerably less than 50 per cent of the voting shares. Thus, those who control the holding company at the apex of the pyramid can wield power over far more capital than they themselves possess.

Governments naturally become concerned over the concentration of so much economic power in the hands of small groups of people. But the power is sometimes concealed because subsidiary companies continue to trade under their own names.

Effects of monopoly

Monopoly power makes it possible to increase profits by restricting the supply of the product and fixing a higher price than would be charged by firms in competition with each other. The consumer thus pays more and does not obtain the quantities that would be available to buy in a competitive market. Furthermore, lack of competition from other firms may affect the drive for efficiency on the part of a monopoly firm. This could lead in turn to higher costs and prices, and might also result in products of inferior quality.

However, monopoly can bring advantages as well as disadvantages. A monopoly organization may achieve economies of scale that would not be possible if the market were divided between small competing firms. It may be able to concentrate production in fewer factories working at full stretch rather than a larger number producing less than their capacity. With higher profits and a more secure market, a monopolist may also be in a better position to undertake the expensive research and investment necessary for efficiency in some industries.

Control of monopoly

1 *Methods of control*

Since the advantages of monopoly could outweigh its disadvantages in certain circumstances, governments have sometimes left it alone and at times even encouraged it. But the possible drawbacks to consumers have generally forced politicians to watch the use of monopoly power and to exercise some form of control over it. The methods of control available are indicated below.

i) Monopolies and mergers may be generally declared illegal and forced to break up.

ii) Monopolies may be investigated by a government agency to see whether their continuance is in the public interest. This approach recognizes that certain benefits may come from monopolies and weighs the advantages and drawbacks in each case. The investigating body can also inquire into the effects of a proposed merger or takeover bid and so prevent a monopoly from coming into existence.

iii) A court or tribunal may be set up to judge particular restrictive practices such as common pricing. If they are found to be against the public interest, the firms concerned can then be forced to abandon them.

iv) In certain cases the government may nationalize a firm or industry, or use the threat of nationalization to discourage the exercise of monopoly power. Short of nationalization, it is also possible for governments to control excessive prices or profits.

2 Britain's monopoly policy

The first method above is the traditional policy of the United States. The British approach has generally been more cautious, on the lines of the second and third methods. There are two main bodies investigating monopoly practices in Britain.

The Monopolies and Mergers Commission investigates and reports on monopolies referred to it by the Director-General of Fair Trading or the Secretary of State for Trade and Industry. A monopoly is defined as a firm or group of firms controlling a quarter or more of the market supply. If the Commission finds that the monopoly is working against the public interest, the Department of Trade and Industry has powers to intervene. The Commission can also investigate the supply of services such as banking.

In addition, the Secretary of State can ask the Commission to look into a merger or proposed merger where it strengthens or creates a monopoly situation or where the value of assets taken over exceeds £30 million. The Secretary of State can consequently dissolve or prohibit the merger.

The Restrictive Practices Court was set up in 1956. The Director-General of Fair Trading is required to keep a register of agreements made between firms and is responsible for bringing such agreements before the Court where they must be justified. The Court has generally been strict in its judgements and many agreements have consequently been ended.

1 Define monopoly. Why do monopolies occur and in what forms?

2 Explain how the formation of a monopoly can bring either drawbacks or benefits.

3 How are monopolies controlled in Britain?

8.6 Further theory

In this section, we pursue a little further some aspects of the demand and supply theory dealt with in the first part of the chapter.

Measurements of elasticity

1 Elasticity of demand

By elasticity of demand we normally mean the relationship between changes in price and changes in the quantity demanded. The larger is the change in the quantity demanded caused by any given change in price, the greater is the elasticity of demand. The following formula is thus used to measure elasticity between two prices:

$$\text{Elasticity of demand} = \frac{\text{Percentage change in quantity demanded}}{\text{Percentage change in price}}$$

Elasticity can be measured in connection with either a fall in price (causing the quantity demanded to expand) or a rise in price (causing the quantity demanded to contract). Let us measure the elasticity of demand when the price falls from 4p to 3p on the simple demand schedule below. The price has fallen by ¼ (25 per cent) of its original level. The quantity demanded has consequently increased from 100 to 120, that is, by ⅕ (20 per cent) of its former level. The elasticity of demand is $\frac{1}{5} \div \frac{1}{4} = \frac{4}{5}$ (or 0·8 expressed as a decimal).

Price (pence)	*Demand*
4	100
3	120
2	200
1	250

If the quantity demanded changes by a larger percentage than the price change, elasticity is greater than 1 and the demand is said to be elastic. If it changes by a smaller percentage than the price change, elasticity is less than 1 and it is said to be inelastic. Elasticity is exactly 1 or unity when the quantity demanded changes by the same percentage as price – for example, if a 10 per cent fall in price causes a 10 per cent increase in quantity.

If the quantity demanded increases by the same percentage as the fall in price, it follows that there should be no significant change in the total amount spent on the commodity. This points to a simple alternative way of estimating demand elasticity –

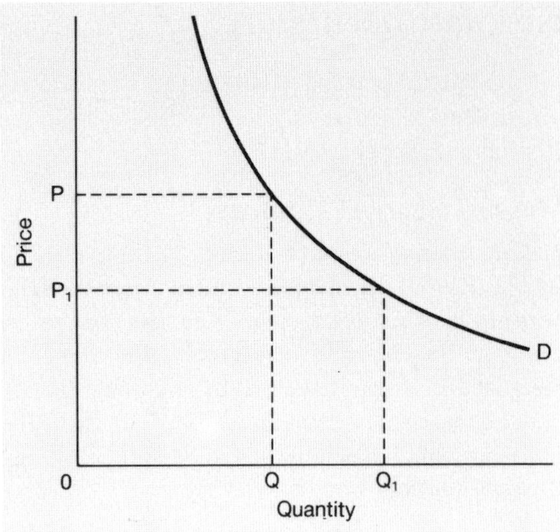

Fig. 8.9 Demand curve of unit elasticity

by reference to the effect of a price change on the total amount spent or, in other words, the *total revenue* of the sellers.

The total revenue at any price is that price multiplied by the quantity demanded. Returning to our simple demand schedule, the total revenue from 100 units sold at a price of 4p is 400p. If the price is reduced to 3p, the total revenue falls to 360p. It falls because the increase in quantity is proportionately smaller than the reduction in price. Clearly, when total revenue decreases as a result of a fall in price, the elasticity is less than 1 and demand is inelastic. Between 3p and 2p total revenue increases from 360 to 400, indicating that demand is elastic (greater than 1) between these two prices.

The following propositions should be apparent from the total revenue figures:

i) Demand is elastic if a fall in price increases total revenue or a rise in price decreases total revenue.

ii) Demand is inelastic if a fall in price decreases total revenue or a rise in price increases total revenue.

If a change in price (up or down) does not change total revenue, the elasticity is 1 or unity. Fig. 8.9 illustrates the special case of a demand curve of unit elasticity at every price. It is drawn to make total revenue (the area OP×OQ) the same at every point on the demand curve.

2 *Elasticity of supply*

The total revenue method cannot be used for supply elasticity but it can be measured, in a similar way to demand, by the formula:

$$\text{Elasticity of supply} = \frac{\text{Percentage change in quantity supplied}}{\text{Percentage change in price}}$$

If the quantity changes by a larger percentage than the price, the elasticity is greater than 1 and the supply is said to be elastic. If it changes by a smaller percentage than price, the elasticity is less than 1 and it is said to be inelastic. If the quantity changes by the same percentage as the price, the elasticity of supply is exactly 1 or unity.

Price (pence)	*Supply*
3	300
2	250
1	50

In the supply schedule above, a fall in price from 3p to 2p reduces the quantity supplied from 300 to 250. The price falls by ⅓ and the supply by ⅙. The elasticity of supply is ⅙÷⅓ = ½ (or 0·5).

3 *Income elasticity of demand*

Changes in income play an important part in affecting the demand for different goods and services. *The extent to which a change in income leads to a change in the demand for any product is known as its income elasticity of demand.*

$$\text{Income elasticity of demand} = \frac{\text{Percentage change in demand}}{\text{Percentage change in income}}$$

Thus, if a 10 per cent rise in income leads to a 20 per cent increase in the demand for a product, its income elasticity of demand would be 2.

4 *Cross elasticity of demand*

Cross elasticity occurs when the demand for two products is related so that a change in the price of one leads to a change in the demand for the other. It can be measured by the formula:

$$\text{Cross elasticity of demand for X} = \frac{\text{Percentage change in the demand for X}}{\text{Percentage change in the price of Y}}$$

For example, if a 5 per cent rise in the price of beef leads to a 10 per cent increase in the demand for mutton, the cross elasticity of demand for mutton would be 2.

Cross elasticity shows how markets and prices are frequently linked. The links can be of several kinds.

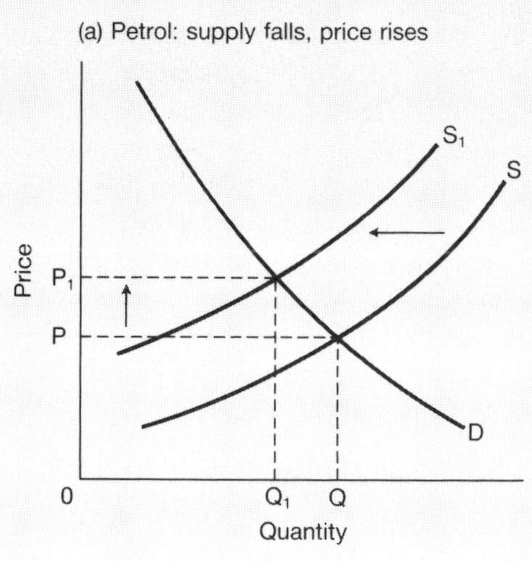

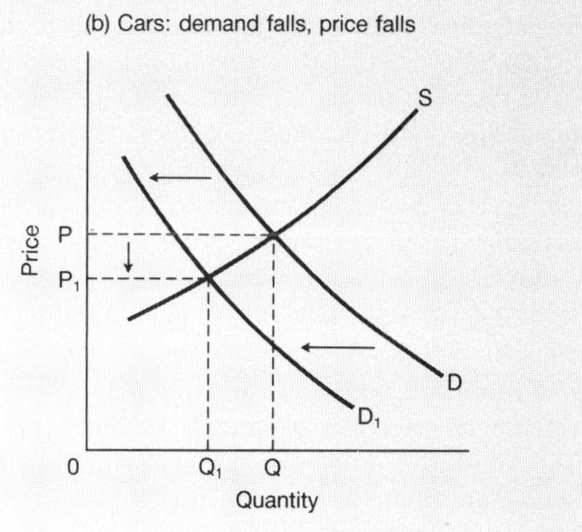

Fig. 8.10 Joint demand

i) *Joint demand.* A demand for cars means a demand for petrol and a demand for fish is likely to be accompanied by a demand for chips. Products related in this way are known as *complementary goods*. Such relationships can be illustrated by movements of the demand and supply curves (Fig. 8.10). Suppose that an interruption of oil supplies creates a shortage of petrol. Two particular consequences may follow: (a) the reduction in supply causes its price to rise; (b) this reduces the demand for cars and leads to price cuts in showrooms.

ii) *Competitive demand* occurs when goods are close substitutes for each other such as coffee and tea. A rise in the price of one is likely to cause an increase in demand for the other and consequently also a rise in its price.

iii) *Composite demand* is a feature of the demand for products which have several distinct uses. An increase, for example, in the demand for steel plate for cars would affect not only the price of steel plate but also the supply and price of steel tubes used in the building and construction industries.

Price controls

We have seen that the price, in a free market, will settle at the level at which demand and supply are equal in quantity. However, in certain circumstances, a government may consider that this equilibrium is either too high or too low. It might then control the price by imposing either a maximum or minimum level enforceable by law.

1 A maximum price

Common examples are rent controls and the wartime controls applying to basic food prices. In both cases prices would have risen to very high levels, in a free market, due to acute shortages of supply.

A maximum price above the equilibrium level is not effective because demand and supply forces can still operate. Below the equilibrium, a maximum price is difficult to maintain because it obstructs those forces. This is illustrated in Fig. 8.11. At the controlled price of OP, the quantity demanded (OQ_d)

Fig. 8.11 Effect of a maximum price

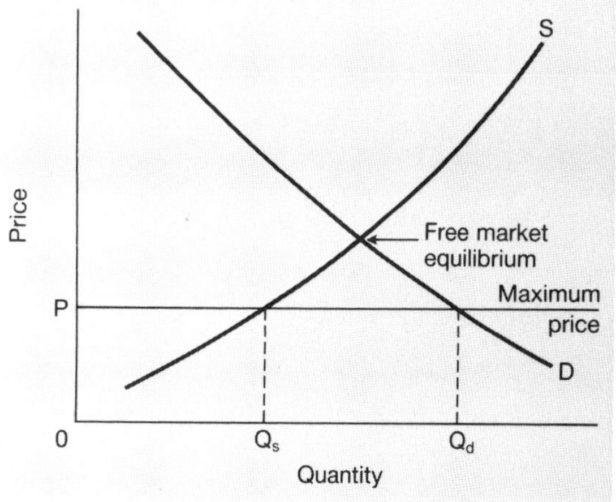

exceeds the quantity supplied (OQ_s). There is consequent pressure to force the price up above the legal maximum towards equilibrium.

The symptoms of such a situation are queues or waiting lists for the scarce product and also 'black markets' in which goods are sold illegally above the fixed price. To avoid these effects it may be necessary for the government to take steps either to reduce demand or increase supply. The former can be done by a system of rationing, as in wartime, and the latter by giving subsidies to producers.

*2 **A minimum price***

A minimum price may be introduced to help particular groups of producers such as farmers. Such a minimum would have no effect if it were fixed below the free market equilibrium, but above equilibrium it causes excess supply in the market. There would obviously be a tendency for firms to sell their surpluses at lower prices unless steps were taken to reduce supply – for example, by buying surplus products. This method is used in the EEC to maintain farm prices at guaranteed levels.

Taxes on spending

Taxes on goods or services are normally paid, in the first place, by producers or sellers. Taxes such as those on tobacco and petrol are charged at a uniform rate on each unit – for example, each packet of cigarettes or gallon of petrol. The effect is to increase the cost of supplying those goods and so to raise by that amount the price at which each unit will be supplied. This is shown in Fig. 8.12. Note that the supply curve has moved upwards by the amount of the tax. (A subsidy would have the opposite effect, moving the supply curve downwards.)

Fig. 8.12 Effect of a tax

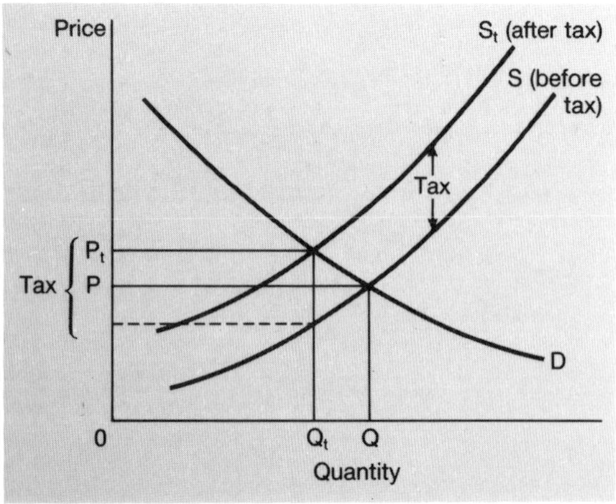

If you examine the diagram you will notice that the rise in the equilibrium price, from OP to OP_t, is not by the full amount of the tax. An obvious reason is that demand is elastic and so a large price increase would cause sales to fall substantially. The producers consequently pay part of the tax out of their own profits.

Output of a firm

Supply depends on the outputs of firms. But how does a firm decide how much to produce?

We assume that a firm is in business to make as much profit as possible. It achieves this aim by producing that level of output at which its total revenue from sales exceeds its total costs of production by the greatest possible amount. Let us first look at some figures representing the costs of a firm (Table 8.3).

Fixed costs do not change with output. They include such items as the upkeep of factory buildings and machines, rents and rates, and managerial salaries. They are sometimes called *overhead costs*.

Variable costs increase as output increases. They include the cost of raw materials, fuel and power, and also wages since more output generally requires more labour.

Total costs are made up of both fixed and variable costs added together.

Average costs are total costs divided by output giving the average cost per unit of output.

Marginal cost is the addition to total costs of producing an extra unit of output. The marginal cost of, say, the fifth unit of output is thus the total cost of 5 units minus the total cost of 4 units.

To calculate profit, it is necessary to compare costs with sales revenue at different levels of output. This is shown in Table 8.4.

Total revenue is simply the number of units produced and sold multiplied by the price at which they sell. Our figures assume that all output is sold at a market price of £10 a unit and so total revenue rises by steps of that amount.

Profit is the difference between total revenue and

Table 8.3 Costs of production

Units of output	Fixed costs £	Variable costs £	Total costs £	Average costs £	Marginal costs £
1	6	2	8	8	8
2	6	8	14	7	6
3	6	12	18	6	4
4	6	14	20	5	2
5	6	24	30	6	10
6	6	36	42	7	12
7	6	50	56	8	14

Table 8.4 Calculation of profit

Units of output	Total costs £	Total revenue £	Profit £	Marginal cost £	Marginal revenue £
1	8	10	2	8	10
2	14	20	6	6	10
3	18	30	12	4	10
4	20	40	20	2	10
5	30	50	20	10	10
6	42	60	18	12	10
7	56	70	14	14	10

total costs at any level of output. You can see that profit reaches a maximum when output reaches 4 units.

Another way to showing the most profitable output is by looking at marginal costs and marginal revenue. Most decisions on output are marginal in the sense that the firm is deciding whether it is profitable to increase or decrease production by comparatively small (marginal) amounts.

Marginal revenue is the addition to total revenue from selling one more unit. In Table 8.4 the marginal revenue is equal to the price of £10 at all levels of output because we assume that units of output are always sold at that constant price. Now note that the fifth unit adds nothing to profit: its marginal revenue of £10 just covers the marginal cost of producing it.

This point, where marginal revenue is equal to marginal cost, is significant. It shows the level beyond which a firm should not expand its output because the extra (marginal) revenue would be less than the extra (marginal) costs of production and so profit would be reduced.

The law of diminishing returns

The above account of how a profit-maximizing firm determines its output depends on the assumption that marginal costs rise with output, and consequently additional units of output, above a certain level, become unprofitable to produce. The basic explanation of rising marginal costs stems from one of the most widely quoted principles of economics – the so-called law of diminishing returns.

Marginal costs are essentially the variable costs of additional factors, particularly labour, employed by a firm to obtain extra output. By contrast, a firm's capital (buildings and machinery) is usually fixed in quantity and cannot be increased in a short period of time. Thus, in the short run, changes in output are normally achieved by changing the quantity of labour employed in conjunction with a fixed quantity of capital.

Let us suppose that a firm expands output by employing more labour. Up to a point, increasing its labour force can enable higher productivity per worker – for example, by providing scope for division of labour and better use of capital. In the language of economics, the marginal product of labour rises and marginal costs correspondingly fall. But with a given quantity of capital, there is a limit to the number of workers that can be efficiently employed. As this limit is approached, the marginal product of labour begins to fall causing the marginal cost of production to rise. Diminishing returns is then said to operate. This is illustrated by the figures (Table 8.5) which show diminishing returns commencing with the fourth worker. Note that both marginal and average product (per worker) then begin to fall.

Table 8.5 Diminishing returns

Number of workers	Total product (units of output)	Average product	Marginal product
1	8	8	8
2	20	10	12
3	36	12	16
4	48	12	12
5	55	11	7
6	60	10	5

The law can now be stated in general terms: *as successive units of a variable factor are combined with a fixed factor, the marginal product of the variable factor must eventually fall.* This causes costs to rise and limits the output of firms at least in the short run. In the long run all factors are variable, and capital can also be expanded. Such expansion amounts to an increase in the overall size of the firm and may bring cost-reducing economies of scale.

1 Note the formula for measuring elasticity of demand. Refer to the demand schedule on page 93 and calculate the elasticity of demand when the price falls from 2p to 1p. Say whether demand is elastic or inelastic between those prices and explain your answer.

2 Note the formula for measuring elasticity of supply. Refer to the supply schedule on page 94 and calculate the elasticity of supply when the price falls from 2p to 1p.

3 Define income elasticity of demand. Suggest examples of products with high and low income elasticity.

Define cross elasticity of demand. Distinguish between complementary and competitive goods.

5 Draw diagrams to illustrate the effects of government intervention in a market to fix (a) a maximum price below the equilibrium level, (b) a minimum price above the equilibrium level.

6 Draw demand and supply curves to illustrate the effects of a tax on cigarettes.

7 Distinguish between fixed and variable costs. Define marginal cost and explain how it determines the output at which a firm achieves maximum profit.

8 State the law of diminishing returns. Illustrate it by plotting a graph from figures in Table 8.5. (Show marginal product on the vertical axis and the number of workers on the horizontal axis.)

Multiple choice

1 The demand curve for a product would normally shift to the right as a result of
- **A** a fall in its price
- **B** a fall in its supply
- **C** a rise in the incomes of its consumers
- **D** a fall in the price of a close substitute
- **E** a rise in the price of a complementary good

2 Which of the following will not cause a shift in the supply curve of shoes?
- **A** a rise in wages in the shoe-manufacturing industry
- **B** a tax on the production of shoes
- **C** a rise in the price of shoes
- **D** greater efficiency in shoe-manufacturing
- **E** a fall in the cost of materials used in shoe-manufacturing

3 The market for shoes is in equilibrium. A change occurs which leads to a new equilibrium with a lower price and a smaller quantity sold. This could be due to
- **A** an increase in demand
- **B** a decrease in demand
- **C** an increase in supply
- **D** a decrease in supply
- **E** none of the above

4 In a free market economy the use of productive resources is determined by
- **A** consumer needs
- **B** consumers' effective demand
- **C** government decisions
- **D** trade union pressures
- **E** employers' preferences

5 If the price of a product falls from 10p to 9p and the quantity demanded increases from 100 to 120 units, the elasticity of demand is
- **A** ¼
- **B** ½
- **C** 1
- **D** 2
- **E** 5

6 Which of the following makes legal judgements on registered agreements between firms?
- **A** the Monopolies and Mergers Commission
- **B** the Director-General of Fair Trading
- **C** the Restrictive Practices Court
- **D** the High Court of Justice
- **E** the Secretary of State for Trade and Industry

7

Units of output	Variable costs
1	£2
2	£8
3	£13
4	£14

The above figures represent the variable costs of a firm. Its fixed costs are £8. What is the average cost of producing 3 units of output?
A £3
B £5
C £7
D £13
E £21

8 A shift in the supply curve of a good could be caused by a change in
1 consumers' incomes
2 the price of the good
3 the wages of workers producing the good

A 1 only is correct
B 1 and 2 only are correct
C 1, 2 and 3 are correct
D 2 and 3 only are correct
E 3 only is correct

9 Cross elasticity of demand is a measure of the reponsiveness of the demand for a product to changes in
A its price
B its supply
C consumers' incomes
D the price of another product
E the demand for another product

10 The law of diminishing returns is said to operate if a firm with fixed capital employs additional workers and as a result
A the total cost of production falls
B the fixed cost of production falls
C the fixed cost of production rises
D the marginal cost of production falls
E the marginal product of labour falls

Essays

1 Discuss the view that, through the price mechanism, a market economy always serves the best interests of consumers and therefore governments should not interfere.

2 With the aid of demand and supply diagrams, explain how the price of video tapes is likely to be affected by (a) a rise in the incomes of consumers, (b) a fall in the cost of producing video tapes, (c) a fall in the price of video recorders.

3 Distinguish between price elasticity, income elasticity, and cross elasticity of demand. Consider whether the demand for petrol is elastic or inelastic in respect of each type of elasticity and give reasons for your opinion.

4 Why do fluctuations occur in the market price of cucumbers? Use demand and supply diagrams to show what is likely to happen in the market if the government (a) imposed a tax on cucumbers, (b) passed a law preventing sellers from raising the price.

Data response

Demand and supply schedules for record players in a competitive market

Price £	Demand (thousands)	Supply (thousands)
15	5	22
14	8	20
13	12	18
12	15	15
11	20	10
10	25	0

1 Draw the demand and supply curves.

2 What is the equilibrium price, and why? How many record players will be sold?

3 What would be the effect in the market if a maximum price of £11 was fixed by law?

4 Assume that demand increases by 50 per cent at every price. Draw the new demand curve on your diagram. What is the new equilibrium price and quantity?

5 What movements would take place in the demand or supply curves and what would happen to the price in each of the following circumstances?

(a) A wage rise for workers in the industry
(b) Records become less popular
(c) The price of records rises substantially
(d) The price of tape recorders falls substantially
(e) A large increase in the rate of income tax
(f) A large increase in the rate of VAT on record players

Chapter 9

Wages and trade unions

9.1 Payment for work

In return for their work, people receive incomes in the form of wages or salaries. *Wages* are normally paid weekly in notes and coins – the pay packet. *Salaries*, on the other hand, are paid monthly by cheque or directly into a bank account.

Salaried workers are usually in 'white-collar' (as distinct from manual) occupations, and their positions are generally considered more permanent than those of wage-earners. Thus, if a salaried employee is dismissed it is customary for the firm to give him a longer period of notice. However, wage-earners are now often paid as much as the salaried staff of a firm, and the distinction between them is disappearing. Economists generally use the term wages to include all forms of payment for work.

Methods of payment

Wages can be related either to a period of time or to a measured quantity of output produced by the worker. These are called time rates and piece rates respectively. There are various modifications of each method, and many wages are a mixture of the two.

1 Time rates

Wages may be paid on an hourly, weekly, or monthly basis, or for each shift of a given length of time. Most industrial workers 'clock' on and off, and receive higher overtime payments for additional time. In the case of salaried employees, the working time may be more flexible and there may be no extra payment for overtime. Indeed, salaries are often stated as an annual amount.

Time rates must obviously be used in jobs where the output of the worker cannot be measured or where the quality of the product could be seriously affected if workers rushed their jobs to earn more money. The output of nurses and teachers, for example, cannot be measured. Road-safety problems could arise if bus drivers were paid according to the mileage covered or number of passengers picked up.

The disadvantages of time rates are that they do not distinguish between efficient and inefficient or lazy workers, they provide no incentive for workers to exert themselves, and supervision may be necessary to ensure that a reasonable amount of work is being done in the time available. Piece rates are adopted to overcome these drawbacks.

2 Piece rates

Under a system of piece rates or piece-work, the worker is paid according to his output – the number of units produced, items assembled, or processes performed over a given period. Where work involves close co-operation between a number of people, the system is sometimes operated on a group basis with the payment shared on an agreed scale. The piece-work principle also applies to bonus systems which reward workers for exceeding a standard output or finishing within a standard time allowed for the job.

All wage systems based on piece-work are designed to provide an incentive to work by rewarding faster and more efficient workers. They also reduce the need for supervision since slack workers automatically lose money.

Nevertheless, there are objections to piece rates from both employers and workers. They could produce fast but shoddy work and are consequently unsuitable for jobs where the emphasis is on quality rather than quantity. They may lead to overstrain on the part of workers. Wages become unstable from week to week, depending perhaps on the health of the worker. Individual differences sometimes cause discontent among workers.

In practice, it is often difficult to work out a satisfactory piece-work system. Furthermore, the introduction of new machines or new methods of production require adjustments to the system from time to time. Piece rates have consequently caused numerous disputes between workers and their employers or among workers themselves, and such disputes have sometimes led to strikes. In a number of cases, firms have abandoned piece rates because of the trouble arising from them.

3 *Profit-sharing*

The idea of profit-sharing has been put forward as a solution to the problem of conflict between management and labour. One method is to give the workers shares in the firm, entitling them to a share of the profits in addition to their normal wages. Such schemes sometimes include a share in management, for example, through the appointment of workers' representatives on the board of directors.

The intention is to strengthen loyalty to the firm. But profit-sharing can also cause discontent when trade is bad and profits fall, particularly when workers become reliant on the distribution of profit. Not surprisingly, the idea is generally regarded with suspicion by trade unions, and ambitious arrangements are known to have quickly broken down.

Wage rates and earnings

There can be a significant difference between the official wage rate and the actual earnings of workers in an occupation. The wage rate – sometimes referred to as the *basic rate* – is the pay a worker would receive for a normal week's work without deductions for tax, national insurance, and pensions.

Earnings are frequently higher than wage rates because they are boosted by overtime, night work, shift payments, bonus payments, and possibly other additions to the basic rate. Indeed, the basic rate of some workers can be a relatively small part of their total earnings.

The tendency for earnings to rise substantially above wage rates is known as *wage drift*. This has occurred on a large scale in some occupations and explains why certain groups of workers are so much better off than others. It also accounts for sharp differences between areas of the country. In areas of labour shortage, such as south-east England, earnings have been inflated by overtime and workers have often obtained special bonus payments or other supplements to nationally agreed wage rates. Wage drift of this kind has obviously added to inflationary pressures in the economy.

Nominal and real wages

A person's nominal wage is simply his wage expressed in money in the usual way – say £80 a week. A worker may obtain an increase in his nominal wage over a period of time without becoming any better off because the prices of the products he buys have risen as fast as the amount of money in his pay packet. In that case, his real wage has not risen. Real wages rather than nominal or money wages determine the standard of living.

A person's real wage is the actual purchasing power, in goods and services, of the money in his pay packet. It clearly depends not only on the amount of money he receives but also on the prices of the things he buys with that money. If wage rates rise faster than prices, real wages rise; but if prices rise faster than wage rates, real wages fall. To judge what is happening to real wages (and the standard of living), it is necessary to compare changes in the level of wages with changes in the level of prices. Measurements of these changes are made by using a statistical method called *index numbers* (see page 119).

Rising prices (or inflation) obviously hold back real wages. In some industries there have been schemes to protect workers from the effect of rising prices by linking their wage rates to the index of retail prices. Thus, if retail prices rise by more than a certain percentage over a given period, the wage rate is automatically adjusted to compensate for the rise. Such schemes are sometimes called *threshold agreements* because employers undertake to increase wages if prices rise above the agreed limit or threshold.

Causes of wage differences

To the worker, his wage is an income on which he lives. To the employer, it is the price he has to pay for labour required by his firm. From the latter point of view, wages can be treated like other prices.

The wage paid in any occupation depends basically on demand and supply – the employers' demand for that type of labour and the supply of it available. To explain differences in the wages of particular

Table 9.1 The levelling effect of labour flow on wages

Spam workers	Sausage workers
Weekly wage £30	Weekly wage £30
Spam consumption rises	Sausage consumption stable
Increased demand for labour	Stable demand for labour
Wages rise to £40	Wages still £30
Inflow or workers	Loss of workers
Surplus of labour	Shortage of labour
Wage rise checked	Wages rise sharply
Weekly wage £40	Weekly wage £40

groups of workers we must first look at the demand and supply influences and then at other factors that might affect particular wage rates.

1 Demand influences

Workers in an industry or occupation would obviously be in a strong position to obtain high wages if the demand for their labour were strong and firms had many job vacancies that could not be filled. This is most likely to happen in an expanding industry requiring certain kinds of skilled labour. Wages would then have to rise to attract the necessary labour from other industries or to persuade more people to train for the occupations concerned. Wage increases would be much more difficult to obtain in an occupation where demand was slack and there were more workers than jobs for them to fill.

It is a big advantage to any group of workers if their labour is in great demand, but the advantage would only be temporary unless supply influences were also favourable to them. This is because a high wage rate due to demand should in time attract more workers into that occupation. The extra workers are likely to come from the ranks of the unemployed, school leavers, and workers from other industries attracted by the high wages. The flow of workers from low-paid to high-paid jobs tends to even out wage rates in the long run. This is illustrated in Table 9.1.

2 Supply influences

If labour could always move freely between jobs, supply would continuously adjust itself to changes in demand, and wages would remain roughly equal for all groups. That some wages remain much higher than others is because the supply of labour into well-paid occupations is restricted in certain ways.

i) The work requires a standard of natural ability or skill that comparatively few people possess.

ii) New workers are deterred by the need for a long training or apprenticeship during which the wage or salary is very low. In some cases, the training itself is expensive and may require financial help from parents.

iii) Trade unions or professional organizations make it difficult to enter the occupation by imposing special conditions or restrictions.

iv) Entry into the occupations involves geographical movement which is hindered by obstacles such as a shortage of housing in the area.

Film stars, top athletes, lawyers, printing workers, and deep sea divers provide examples of occupations in which high earnings may be due to supply restrictions such as those outlined above.

3 Relative attractiveness

Even if labour could move freely from one occupation to another, there would still be wage differences due to differences in the attractiveness of occupations. People have to be paid more to persuade them to undertake less agreeable jobs. They are often willing to work for comparatively low pay in jobs that are pleasant, interesting, or possess particular advantages not connected with money.

The attractiveness of an occupation depends on many factors other than the wage. Any of the following considerations could be important in weighing up the advantages of a job: security of employment; prestige or status associated with the job; promotion opportunities; pension arrangements; fringe benefits such as the use of a car or cheap housing; any physical danger or risk of illness involved in the work; dirtiness, noise, or other disagreeable features; shift work or night duties attached to the job; holidays, hours, and the conditions of work in general.

Such non-monetary considerations clearly help to explain pay differences. It is easy to see, for example, why astronauts earn more than bank clerks or coal miners earn more than farm workers.

4 Other influences

The basic influences on wages are demand and supply, and the relative attractiveness of occupations.

However, a number of other factors can affect the bargaining strength of the two sides when a wage claim is being negotiated. These may include the strength and unity of the trade union, the timing of negotiations, the effect of a strike on the industry and the community, and the attitude of the government and the general public towards particular wage claims. These influences are considered later in the chapter.

1 Distinguish between time rates and piece rates. What are the advantages of piece-work? Why are many workers still paid time rates?

2 What is meant by profit-sharing and why is it not widely used?

3 Explain the difference between (a) wage rates and earnings, (b) nominal and real wages.

4 Explain how an increased demand for workers in a particular industry is likely to affect their wages (a) in the short run, and (b) over a longer period.

5 Some occupations are higher paid than others because of (a) restrictions on the supply of labour or (b) differences in attractiveness of jobs. Explain each of these influences on relative wages and give examples of occupations in which high pay may be due to such influences.

9.2 Trade unions

A trade union is defined as any organization of workers whose principle aim is to represent its members in relation to their employers. Such organizations can be found as far back as the Middle Ages, but modern unions emerged as a result of industrialization and the spread of the factory system in Britain in the nineteenth century. The gathering together of workers in factories made the development of unions inevitable.

Types of trade union

There are about 400 recognized trade unions in the United Kingdom with a total membership of about 10 million. This works out at a rough average of one trade union member to nearly every family in the country. The unions vary greatly in size, ranging from the giant Transport and General Workers' Union with over 1 million members to small unions with memberships of only a few hundred. Although small unions greatly outnumber large ones, they are much less important in terms of total membership (Fig 9.1).

Existing British trade unions can be classified into the broad types illustrated in Fig. 9.2, but there is

This is the headquarters of a large trade union. Can you name the union?

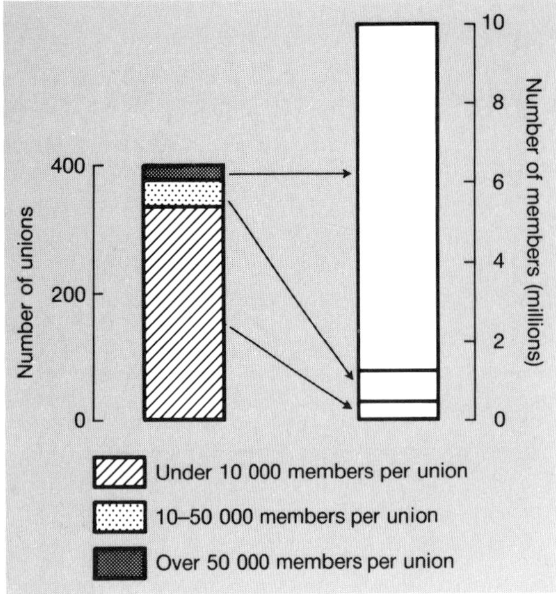

Fig. 9.1 Size and membership of trade unions

no uniform pattern and some unions do not fall neatly into one type. For example, some craft unions now admit comparatively unskilled workers, and office workers are not confined to white-collar unions.

1 Craft unions

The earliest unions formed in Britain usually represented skilled crafts or trades. Thus, the rapid development of unions in the middle of the nineteenth century was entirely among skilled workers who could afford to pay membership subscriptions and were the first to realize the advantages of organization. Their descendants include the Amalgamated Union of Engineering Workers and the Associated Society of Locomotive Engineers and Firemen. Such unions of craftsmen continue to be characteristic of Britain though the trade union movement now covers a much wider social class.

Although many skilled workers still feel that their individual interests are best protected by an independent union, it is usually accepted that craft unions are not good for industry or for the trade union movement as a whole. The Trades Union Congress (TUC) itself encourages the formation of larger industrial unions, and there has been a trend in that direction over a number of years. The Electrical, Electronic, Telecommunications, and Plumbing Union, for example, is clearly an amalgamation of crafts. The following criticisms are made of craft unions.

i) By dividing workers into small groups, craft unions reduce their collective bargaining power and weaken the influence of the trade union movement as a whole.

ii) Craft divisions lead to disputes between unions themselves over relative wage levels or over the allocation of jobs between groups of workers. Wage differences or *differentials* are jealously guarded by some better-paid crafts and this is a cause of frequent conflict. Disputes over the allocation of work or 'who does what'—for instance, between carpenters and electricians over who should make the holes for cables on a building site—are called *demarcation disputes*. The latter have sometimes led to strikes or stoppages that seem irresponsible to outsiders but raise serious issues affecting the employment and livelihoods of those concerned.

iii) Negotiations between management and workers are complicated and delayed because the management has to deal with several unions. Some large companies have to negotiate with as many as fifteen or twenty separate unions.

2 Industrial unions

The aim of industrial unions is to bring all types of workers in the same industry under a single union umbrella. This is the established practice in other countries, such as the United States and Germany, where all the car workers or steel workers, for example, are grouped in a single union.

In the United Kingdom, with craft traditions remaining strong, industrial unions are rare. The National Union of Mineworkers and the Union of Post Office Workers have been quoted as examples, but the industrial unity of the coal miners was ended by strike failure and the formation of a rival union in 1985.

We have already indicated the advantages of industrial unions in criticizing the traditional craft divisions of the British structure. A single union simplifies negotiations between management and workers. It avoids inter-union disputes and enables differences of interest between occupational groups to be settled more easily. It can act more effectively on behalf of the workers by showing a united front to management.

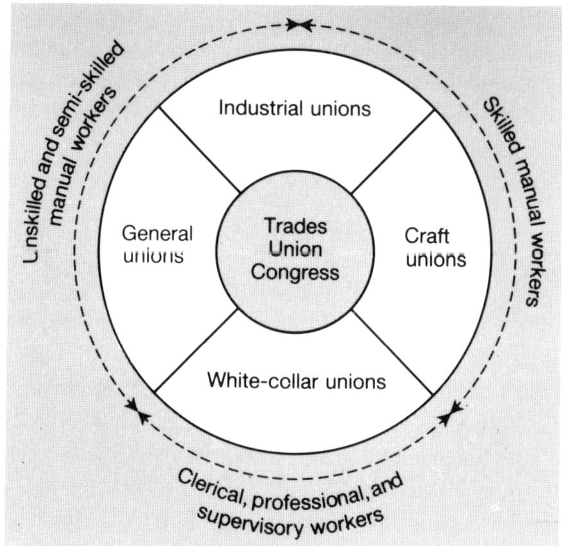

Fig. 9.2 Types of British trade union

3 *General unions*

The craft unions which developed in Britain from the middle of the nineteenth century did not cater for semi-skilled or unskilled workers. Comparatively unskilled workers such as dockers and agricultural labourers began to organize towards the end of the century. But union organization was difficult for many unskilled workers because they were widely scattered in so many different industries. This explains the formation and growth of general unions.

Since general unions do not confine themselves to one industry or one occupation, they usually contain members with widely different aims and interests. This can create problems because the union seems remote from the members and sometimes finds it difficult to control them and hold them together. However, the sheer size of unions such as the giant Transport and General Workers' Union makes them powerful, and they exercise a strong influence on TUC policy.

4 *White-collar unions*

A feature of recent trade union development in Britain has been the growth of trade union membership among groups such as clerical, supervisory, and professional workers who used to show a certain distrust of the trade union movement. Prominent examples are the National and Local Government Officers' Association, the National Union of Teachers, and the Association of Scientific, Technical and Managerial Staffs. Indeed, the growth of so-called white-collar unions has sometimes led to conflict with other unions which saw valued members being drawn away.

The change of attitude among white-collar workers can be explained in several ways.

i) The success of some trade unions in obtaining wage increases and the narrowing of their own advantage in wages over manual occupations convinced many white-collar workers of the gains to be obtained from union organization.

ii) The growing concentration of white-collar workers in large offices or office blocks has created a more factory-like atmosphere and encouraged union development.

iii) Educational progress has enabled people to enter jobs such as teaching from a much wider social background. Consequently, many of the workers in these occupations now come from families with a tradition of union membership.

Evidence of the growth of white-collar unionism is found not only in the rising memberships of the unions concerned. It is also seen in greater militancy on the part of those unions and greater willingness to co-operate with the trade union movement as a whole. These developments have been particularly noticeable in groups such as civil servants, teachers, and bank clerks.

The Trades Union Congress

The main policies of the TUC are decided during the week in each year when delegates from the individual trade unions meet together at the annual conference or Congress. Since the great majority of British trade unions are members of the TUC, the annual Congress represents virtually the whole of the country's trade union movement.

The Congress debates important political and social issues as well as industrial matters of direct concern to the unions. Each union votes according to the number of its members and so the block votes of large unions such as the Transport and General Workers greatly influence the policies.

The Congress elects a General Council of about forty members who are responsible for carrying out TUC policies. However, the Council members are all full-time officials of individual unions, and the day-to-day work of the TUC is in the hands of a General Secretary assisted by the headquarters staff of about a hundred. It is the General Secretary who normally acts as the spokesman for the trade union movement and puts its views to the government, press, radio and television.

The annual Congress and meetings of the General Council provide opportunities for unions to consult together and work out common policies. But the TUC has no direct power over individual unions and relies on persuasion in dealing with them. In the last resort it could expel a union but this power is rarely used.

Functions of trade unions

Trade unions are concerned with anything that affects the material well-being of their members. This clearly includes all matters relating to wages, terms of employment, hours of work, holidays, protection from unfair dismissal, and conditions of work generally. Unions are also active in protecting workers and their families from hardship due to retirement, unemployment, sickness, and injury at work. Since these matters are largely within the scope of the government, the unions have become closely involved in politics. But some also provide their own welfare services for their members.

1 Social and welfare functions

It is not uncommon for unions to organize social activities such as clubs and outings. They may also look after the welfare of their members by providing facilities such as rest centres, making payments to cover sickness or injury, and giving legal advice and assistance on matters connected with employment.

However, the need for such services has diminished in recent years. Society now provides more leisure and recreational opportunities for people in general while the welfare state deals with most cases of personal hardship. Unions therefore concentrate on improving social services by influencing the government. Nevertheless, many continue to provide their own services and, of course, their funds are used to support members during an official strike.

What could this meeting of the national executive of a trade union be discussing?

2 Political activities

Trade unions have realized for a long time that some of their aims can best be achieved by influencing the decisions of the government and Parliament. In this way, they try to ensure that national policies are favourable to their members and resist policies that they consider harmful to their interests.

To promote their political aims, trade unions are closely linked to the Labour party and make large contributions to its funds. Most of this money comes from the 'political levy' which each trade union member normally pays as part of his union subscription, unless he deliberately withdraws from the payment. The trade union movement is thus in a strong position to influence Labour party policies. Indeed, the party was originally founded by trade unions to represent their interests in Parliament. A number of large trade unions also sponsor individual Labour MPs and pay towards their expenses at elections and in the House of Commons.

Apart from its special relationship with the Labour party, the importance of the movement makes it necessary for any government to keep in close touch with the TUC and consult with it on all matters affecting union interests. Unions are concerned with many problems in the field of government. It is in their interest, for example, that employment should be kept at a high level, that prices do not rise too quickly, and that the national economy should expand steadily.

In addition to direct contacts with government departments and ministers, trade unions co-operate with the government in many ways. An important example is the National Economic Development Council (NEDC) in which discussions on economic policies regularly take place between representatives of the government, the unions, and employers.

3 Co-operation with employers

Relations between unions and employers do not always involve conflict. Unions recognize that firms can afford to pay higher wages if they are more efficient, and they are consequently willing to co-operate in methods of increasing production or reducing costs. Indeed, wage settlements have often been combined with 'productivity agreements' designed to increase efficiency.

Co-operation with managements may be achieved by including union representatives on the boards of directors of firms. However, this can create problems, particularly for workers' representatives who find it hard to balance their union function with that of helping to manage company affairs. In the eyes of the workers, union representatives could become identified with the management and so lose their trust. This danger is reduced when consultation is through works committees rather than direct representation in management.

At the highest level of co-operation, there are discussions between the TUC and the corresponding organization of employers – the Confederation of British Industry (CBI). We have seen how the government can be involved in such co-operation as in the meetings of the National Economic Development Council.

4 Collective bargaining

The trade union function to which most importance is attached is that of negotiating with employers on wages and conditions of work. The process of negotiation is called collective bargaining because each union tries to get the best possible terms for its members as a group and the employers' side may also consist of an association representing all the firms in the industry.

The bargaining process normally begins with a union wage claim, possibly accompanied by some additional demands such as improvements in holidays or hours of work. Employers nearly always come back with an offer that is somewhat less that the union's claim. Bargaining then takes place with the object of closing the gap between the two sides. If agreement is reached, a wage settlement can be drawn up (Fig. 9.3).

If negotiations break down or reach a deadlock, there may be several consequences. In an extreme situation, the union may call for strike action to force further concessions from the employers' side. The corresponding weapon available to employers is a 'lock-out' – barring the workers from their jobs – but this is rarely used. Such extremes may be avoided if the two sides accept *arbitration* by an impartial tribunal or board, sometimes through the intervention of the government.

The Secretary of State for Employment may refer a dispute to an independent arbitrator or arbitration

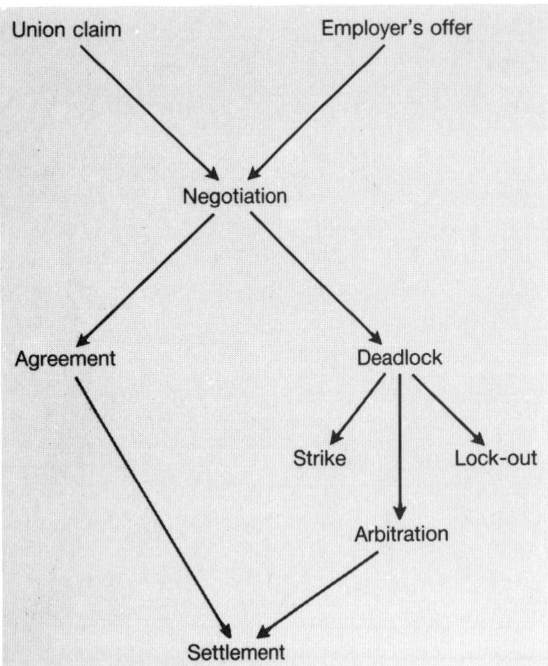

Fig. 9.3 The bargaining process

board, with the consent of both sides, if normal negotiation fails. There is now a regular Advisory, Conciliation and Arbitration Service (ACAS). Arbitration awards are not legally binding but are usually accepted on a voluntary basis. An alternative to arbitration is *conciliation*. The function of a conciliator is to talk with both sides and help them to reach an agreed settlement.

Influences on wage bargaining

The ability of trade unions to obtain higher wages for their members depends on a variety of circumstances affecting the bargaining process.

1 The demand and supply situation

The importance of demand and supply influences on particular wage rates was emphasized at the beginning of the chapter. Clearly, the union bargaining position in, say, the car industry is strongest when there is a large demand for cars and firms are short of workers. Employers are also more likely to give wage increases if the demand for their product is inelastic so that any wage increase could be added to the price of the product without losing sales. (If this is not clear, refer back to the explanation of elasticity of demand in Chapter 8.) But the union position will be relatively weak in an industry where machines can easily do the work of men so that firms are less dependent on their workers.

2 Union strength and solidarity

The bargaining power of a union depends partly on influences concerned with its own organization. These obviously include its size, the proportion of the workers in the industry or occupation who belong to it, the loyalty of its members, and its financial ability to support its members with strike pay.

3 Economic and political conditions

General economic conditions can greatly affect attitudes to wage increases, and so the timing of wage claims or strikes is sometimes very important. Claims are generally strongest in a period of inflation when the cost of living is rising rapidly, but they are likely to be weaker in a period of high unemployment when the emphasis is on jobs rather than pay.

The attitudes of the government and the public can influence negotiations. Employers resist union demands more strongly if the government is urging wage restraint as part of a policy on prices and incomes. In such circumstances, wage rises are hardest to obtain in occupations where the government is itself the employer or exercises direct control – for instance, in the civil service, teaching, or the nationalized industries. On the other hand, unions usually press their claims more strongly if public opinion is in sympathy with their members.

Industrial action

As ultimate bargaining weapons, workers resort to strikes or other forms of industrial action. Their purpose is to force employers to accept or at least move towards workers' demands.

1 Strikes

Strikes occur when workers collectively withdraw their labour. They are called *official* if backed by the union and *unofficial* if done without union support. Most strikes last for an indefinite period but workers sometimes stage a *token* strike of one day or even less to draw attention to their grievances. There are also occasional *sympathetic* strikes when

Pickets at a power station during the miners' strike in 1984. Are they breaking the law?

workers come out to support groups other than themselves.

The effectiveness of a strike depends greatly on the support of the workers concerned. Members of a union who continue to work during a strike are known as *blacklegs*. To discourage blacklegs, some strikers may be stationed as pickets outside the factory gates and try to persuade them not to enter. *Peaceful picketing* is allowed by law, but it is illegal to use force of any kind.

Strikes are often blamed for Britain's economic difficulties. But comparisons with the strike records of other countries do not generally show Britain at a disadvantage apart from exceptional years such as 1972 and 1984 when industry was disrupted by prolonged stoppages in the coal mines (Fig. 9.4). The peak of 1979 was associated with the breakdown of the Labour government's policy of pay restraint. In normal years illness is a far greater cause of absenteeism.

In judging the effects of strikes, it should be remembered that lost production may be made up to some extent by overtime on return to work. In any case, a certain number of strikes are inevitable in a society that believes in free bargaining and the right of each person to withhold his own labour.

However, strikes do mean less production for the firms and lost wages for the workers. Compared with strikes in other countries, strikes in Britain are more often unofficial and appear more damaging. They occur frequently in vital industries where stoppages have wide effects on the economy. Thus, strikes in docks, transport, and the power supply industries are most likely to affect exports, throw people out of work, hit production in other industries, and cause hardship to the general public.

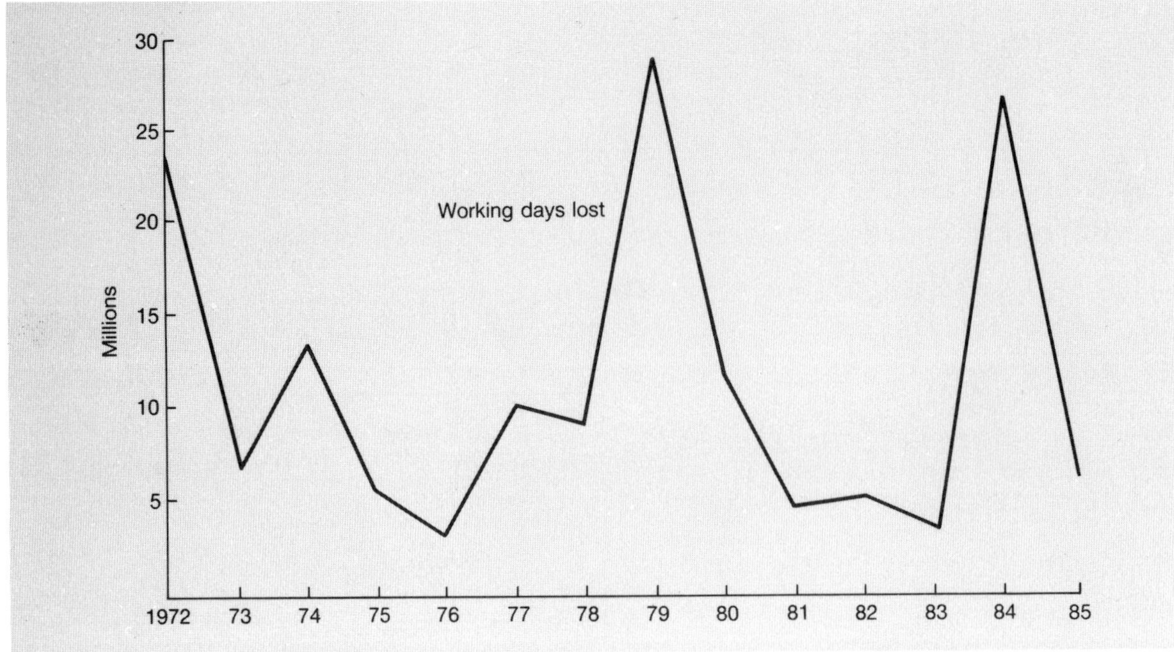

Fig. 9.4 Britain's strike record

2 Other types of industrial action

A strike is not the only means by which workers can put pressure on their employers. Here are some other methods that have been used to create production difficulties in certain industries.

i) *Banning overtime* is obviously an effective weapon in an industry that is short of labour. Many industries rely on overtime to meet periods of peak demand.

ii) *Working to rule* means that workers of an industry stick strictly to the rules and regulations governing their work. Such rules are sometimes detailed and complicated and intended as guidelines rather than for strict observance. The effect can be similar to that of a 'go slow'.

iii) *A go slow* occurs when workers openly slow down their operations as an indication of their discontent.

iv) *Blacking* is a method by which workers act against other firms (not their own employers) by refusing to handle their goods or co-operate with them in any way. It can obviously be used to support other groups of workers.

All the above types of action can be used without total loss of wages (as in a strike) and may be extremely effective in certain circumstances.

Trade union organization

Unions are generally organized in a pyramid fashion as illustrated in Fig. 9.5. A common criticism is that trade union leaders cannot control their own members, but this does not take account of the fact that union organization makes the leaders dependent on their members, through a democratic system of election, starting with the shop stewards at the base of the pyramid.

1 Shop stewards and local bargaining

The shop steward is an ordinary worker and union member elected by other members of his own work group. He is in continuous contact with the workers on the factory or 'shop' floor and acts as their spokesman in negotiations with the management. He also has duties to his trade union—collecting subscriptions, dealing with inquiries, passing on information, and recruiting new members.

In a large factory, there would be a number of shop stewards, perhaps from different unions, who meet together on a shop stewards' committee. Such a committee may elect a leader known as a convenor who becomes the representative of all the firm's employees.

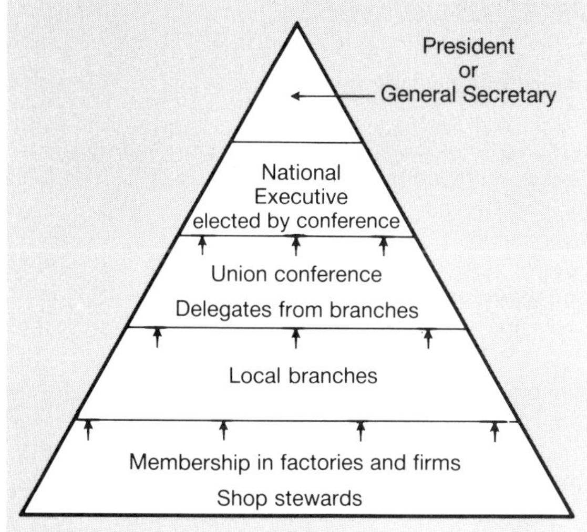

Fig. 9.5 The structure of a trade union

Though national negotiations between unions and employers' associations settle such questions as the basic or minimum wage rates throughout an industry, there is also a less formal system of bargaining between local managers and shop stewards. These negotiations at factory or workshop level deal with such issues as who does what in the factory, the length of tea breaks, the level of overtime rates and bonus payments, and other matters affecting both earnings and conditions of work.

Workers may feel that the local bargaining affects them more closely than the remote activities of their leaders at a national level. Indeed, a strong case can be made for encouraging the movement toward local bargaining as a more realistic system. The growing importance of the shop stewards has also come to be recognized by many employers who allow them time to perform their union duties during working hours.

2 Local and national organization

The local unit of a union is known as the branch. This is likely to draw members from a number of different factories or firms in the area covered. *Branch meetings* deal with local issues and also elect delegates to attend national conferences of the union. In the case of large unions, local branches may also be grouped into district or regional committees.

Union conferences are held every one or two years and enable the rank-and-file delegates to make their views known to the leadership. The conference is supposed to determine the policy of the union but, as it meets so infrequently, most of the practical decisions are taken by the *National Executive* and full-time leaders. The National Executive is elected by the conference, meets regularly, and reports to the conference. Its most powerful figure is normally the General Secretary or the President of the union.

Trade union reform

There has been growing criticism of trade unions in recent years. They are accused of being either too powerful or out of touch with their ordinary members. Such views are strongly held in the Conservative party and, in the early 1980s, trade union powers were curbed by Acts of Parliament. Some of their main provisions can be listed:

i) Protection for individual workers against *closed shops*—that is, compulsory union membership.
ii) Banning of *secondary picketing*—that is, at premises other than the pickets' own place of work.
iii) Modification of *immunities* that formerly protected union funds from legal actions for damages.
iv) Requirement of *ballots* before strikes.
v) Requirement of ballots to confirm union political affiliations and contributions, mainly affecting the Labour party.

1 Describe the main types of trade union and give examples of each.

2 What changes have been taking place in Britain's trade union structure? Why is it generally agreed that industry would benefit from the substitution of industrial unions for the traditional craft unions?

3 Explain briefly each of the functions performed by trade unions.

4 What is the TUC and why is it important?

5 What factors determine the bargaining strength of a trade union? In the light of those factors, comment on the bargaining power of the union in any topical pay claim or dispute.

6 Define each of the following terms used in industrial relations: unofficial strike, sympathetic strike, blackleg, picketing, lock-out, working to rule, blacking.

7 Describe the typical organization of a trade union by briefly indicating the function performed at each level shown in Fig. 9.5.

Multiple choice

1 The total payments (including bonus payments, overtime, etc.) shown on a pay packet, calculated before tax deductions, is known as the worker's
- **A** nominal wage
- **B** real wage
- **C** basic wage
- **D** earnings
- **E** take-home pay

2 Types of industrial action available to trade unions include
1 working to rule
2 banning overtime
3 a lock-out
- **A** 1 only is correct
- **B** 1 and 2 only are correct
- **C** 1, 2 and 3 are correct
- **D** 2 and 3 only are correct
- **E** 3 only is correct

3 A person appointed to try and bring both sides together in an industrial dispute with the aim of achieving an agreed settlement is called
- **A** a conciliator
- **B** an arbitrator
- **C** a justice of the peace
- **D** a registrar
- **E** a commissioner

4 Which of the following would NOT strengthen the position of a trade union in bargaining for higher wages?
- **A** a closed shop
- **B** high unemployment in the industry concerned
- **C** high labour productivity in the industry concerned
- **D** large profits in the industry
- **E** labour shortages in the industry

5 Acts of Parliament make it unlawful for a trade union to
1 strike without a ballot of its members
2 organize picketing by striking members
3 ballot its members before calling a strike
- **A** 1 only is correct
- **B** 1 and 2 only are correct
- **C** 1, 2 and 3 are correct
- **D** 2 and 3 only are correct
- **E** 3 only is correct

Data response

Trade union membership

	1971	*1981*
Number of trade unions	525	421
Numbers according to membership:		
Under 1000 members	289	227
Between 1000 and 100 000 members	203	169
Over 100 000 members	23	25
Total trade union membership (000s)	11 135	12 182
Males	8 382	8 406
Females	2 753	3 776

1 What trend in the number and size of trade unions is indicated by a comparison of the two years? Why is the number falling?

2 Distinguish between craft, white-collar, industrial, and general unions. In the light of that classification suggest why most British trade unions are quite small but a few are very large.

3 What are the advantages and disadvantages (if any) of belonging to a large trade union?

4 Calculate the approximate percentage of women in the total membership of trade unions for each of the two years. Suggest reasons for (a) the comparatively small percentage, (b) the change in that percentage.

5 The total membership of trade unions has actually fallen since 1981. Suggest possible reasons.

Essays

1 Why do accountants earn more than coal miners?

2 What factors determine the success of a trade union in securing wage increases for its members and why are some unions more successful than others?

3 Do we need trade unions? Why do workers join them? Should Parliament pass laws to restrict their powers?

Chapter 10

Money and prices

10.1 The nature of money

Problems of barter

Primitive farming communities have been able to work without money of any kind. In such societies, each family supplies most of its own needs from the produce that it grows itself. Since the family is independent, it does not rely on obtaining goods from outsiders. If it occasionally wants things produced by other people, these may be obtained by giving some of its own products in exchange.

The direct swopping or exchanging of goods without the use of money is called barter. The practice remains familiar to schoolboys, but it suffers from drawbacks and problems that make it quite unsuitable for normal use in advanced societies.

1 Finding the other person

In the first place, you can only exchange by barter if you find someone whose intentions exactly match your own. For instance, if you want to exchange a spade for wheat you must find someone who not only has wheat to spare but is also willing to exchange it for a spade. If no such person can be found, your purpose could only be achieved by a roundabout series of swops – for example, your spade for a bucket, the bucket for potatoes, and perhaps eventually the potatoes for wheat. Barter is thus said to require a *double coincidence of wants*.

2 Settling the terms

Even when you find the right person your troubles are not necessarily over. The next problem is to reach agreement on how much wheat the spade is worth. In a society without money, the value of goods can only be measured in terms of other goods. But it is not possible to fix the value of an article in relation to all the other things for which it might be exchanged. The two sides must consequently haggle over the terms whenever an exchange takes place.

In settling the terms of a barter deal, a further obstacle may arise because many goods cannot be split into smaller units or quantities. The problem did not arise in our previous example because one of the products, wheat, can be divided into any suitable quantities. But if both goods are indivisible, a fair exchange may be very difficult to arrange. For example, how does one exchange a spade for a goat unless they happen to be considered of equal value?

3 The problem of saving

Difficulties also arise when people want to save or accumulate wealth in a society without money. It is of course possible to build up stocks of goods but these can deteriorate or lose value and may take up a lot of space. Think how much more convenient it is to hold and store wealth in modern forms of money such as notes or bank deposits.

Functions of money

Barter would not serve the needs of modern industrial societies. A feature of such societies is the system known as division of labour described in Chapter 3. Under this system, each person concentrates on a single job or trade while relying on the work of others for most of the goods and services he consumes.

Money plays an essential part in such a system. Each person works at his own job to earn an income in money and then exchanges the money for the things he wants. Without money the system would break down. Barter would be much too slow and clumsy a way to carry out all the exchange dealings undertaken in modern societies based on division of labour.

We define money as any kind of material or object

that has come to be accepted within a society as a normal means by which people pay for their purchases of goods or services. When a material becomes accepted as money it begins to fulfil the functions outlined below. In doing so it solves the problems we associated with barter.

1 A medium of exchange

With money, exchange is no longer limited to people whose requirements exactly match. The problem is solved by splitting the exchange process into two distinct transactions: you first sell what you have got in return for money and then use the money to buy what you want. Moreover, since money can be divided into small units such as pence it can be exchanged for goods of any value.

Acting as a medium of exchange is the primary function of money. Its other functions depend on its recognition as a medium of exchange. If it ceases to fulfil this function, it would stop being money and could no longer perform the other functions.

2 A unit of account

When a housewife in Britain does her shopping, she does not have to bargain with the shopkeeper over how much each article is worth because she pays in money and the value of each article is already fixed in units of money. Pounds and pence are thus used to measure value just as metres, centimetres, and millimetres measure length, and kilograms and grams measure weight. The price of anything is simply its valuc in money.

Through the price system, money provides a common standard by which all values can be measured. It therefore avoids the time-wasting process of bargaining which usually accompanies barter transactions. It also makes it easier for people and firms to keep accounts since all transactions can be recorded in money.

3 A standard for deferred payments

A great deal of modern business depends on borrowing and lending. For example, we can obtain things now and pay for them over a period of time in the future by means of a bank loan or hire-purchase. Money serves as a measure of loans and debts. You can imagine how difficult it would be to arrange such transactions in a society without money.

4 A store of value

We referred earlier to the difficulties of saving or accumulating wealth for future use if goods themselves had to be put into storage. Money is generally convenient and cheap to store – for example, in a bank. It is always wanted by people and so unlikely to lose its value suddenly. Holding your wealth in money also has the special advantage of enabling you to buy anything you want without delay or difficulty at any time, now or in the future.

The ease with which money can be used to buy other things is the quality that really distinguishes it from other forms of wealth. In modern societies, wealth may be held in many forms. People store large amounts of wealth in stocks and shares, land and buildings, art treasures, precious jewels, and so on. These forms of wealth may be profitable or satisfying to hold. But if the owners wanted to change them for other things, they would probably first have to sell them for money.

Forms of wealth are sometimes called assets. Money is an asset that everyone wants to hold, at least in some quantity, and the only one that is acceptable over any shop counter. This special ability to be exchanged for all other things is called *liquidity*. People invariably hold some of their wealth in money because it is the most liquid asset (Fig. 10.1).

Fig. 10.1 An assets liquidity scale

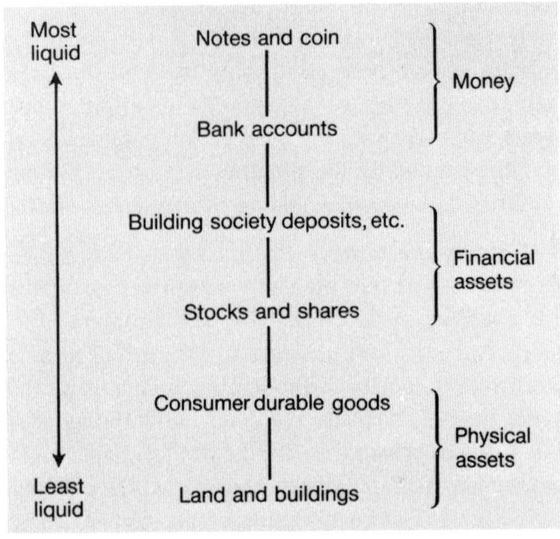

The development of money

The problems of barter and the functions of money explain why some form of money appeared in most societies at an early stage in their development. But early forms of money were crude and inefficient compared with modern money. Three broad stages can be distinguished in the evolution of modern money.

1 Commodity money

The earliest forms of money consisted of particular commodities or materials that were widely valued' by the members of a society and so came to be generally accepted as a means of payment. Shells, axe-heads, salt, and even cattle, are all examples of commodities that were used as money in primitive communities.

Such forms of commodity money had obvious drawbacks due to weight, bulk, perishability, inconsistent quality, or other failings. But the fact that they were accepted in the community – just as Bank of England notes are accepted in Britain – enabled them to carry out the functions of money, however inefficiently.

2 Precious metals

If money grew on trees and we could freely pluck it ourselves we would not accept it as a payment from others. To serve as money, a material must be rare enough to be valued but plentiful enough to go round. Other useful qualities are that it should be convenient to store, easy to carry about, and capable of being divided into small recognizable units. It is consequently not surprising that metals such as gold and silver came to be widely used as money – either in the form of bullion that could be weighed or as coins into which they could be melted and shaped.

3 Paper money

During the sixteenth century in England, people who owned gold commonly deposited it for safe keeping in the vaults or safes of goldsmiths – the craftsmen who worked with gold and so maintained places for safe storage. By accepting such deposits, the goldsmiths had in fact started to become bankers.

The goldsmiths acknowledged the deposits by issuing receipts undertaking to repay the gold to its owners when required. The owners could use the receipts to reclaim their gold or, alternatively, make payments to other people simply by handing over their receipts and so transferring the ownership of their deposits. It is thus easy to see how the goldsmiths' receipts, representing a stated amount of gold, could themselves circulate as money. An obvious further development was to divide the receipts into convenient units such as £1. In this way, the modern bank note came into existence. Look at the wording on a note and you will see how it originated as a promise to pay a given sum of money deposited in the bank.

As explained above, notes were originally accepted as money because they were backed by gold of recognized value. This sytem came to be known as the gold standard. It clearly required that note-issuing banks should hold enough gold to meet all possible claims for repayment. But since there was only a limited supply of gold, this severely restricted the issue of notes.

Some early forms of money: are all of them coins like we have today?

Britain abandoned the gold standard in 1931. The Bank of England – now the only note-issuing bank in England and Wales – does not possess gold to back even a tiny fraction of the notes issued. We accept notes simply because they are recognized by the law (as legal tender) and we know that they are similarly accepted by all other people throughout the country. In the same way, we accept coins, manufactured by the Royal Mint, at a face value (stamped on them) far greater than their intrinsic value (in metal).

Types of money

The money now used in Britain and most other countries consists of notes, coins, and bank deposits.

1 Notes and coins

Notes are printed by the Bank of England and some other banks in Scotland and Northern Ireland. Coins are manufactured by the Royal Mint. Both notes and coin are known as token money because the material in them is worth far less than the value stated on them. The quantities issued are controlled by the Bank of England and adjusted from time to time according to the needs of the community. The note issue is consequently increased every year in periods of heavy spending such as Christmas.

Bank of England notes and coins are *legal tender* – that is, money which the law requires people throughout the country to accept as a means of payment. Thus, a shopkeeper may refuse a cheque but cannot refuse notes in payment for goods on display. Coins are legal tender up to limited amounts – copper up to 20p in total value and silver up to £5 (or £20 in 50p pieces). Larger amounts of small change may of course be accepted but the law gives the right to refuse. Bank of England notes are unlimited legal tender and must be accepted in any quantities.

2 Bank deposits

Though not legal tender, cheques based on bank deposits are accepted throughout the community as the normal means of making large payments. Bank deposits therefore come within the definition of money. A narrow definition excludes deposit accounts which cannot be transferred by cheque but the more widely used definition includes both current and deposit accounts. We need not distinguish between them for the time being.

In defining money, a distinction must be made between bank deposits or accounts and the cheques drawn upon them. A *cheque* is an instruction to a bank to pay a stated sum of money out of a deposit in cash or transfer it into the deposit of another person named on the cheque (Fig. 10.2). The cheque itself is not money but represents a sum of money in a bank deposit and is a means by which ownership of that money is transferred from one depositor to another.

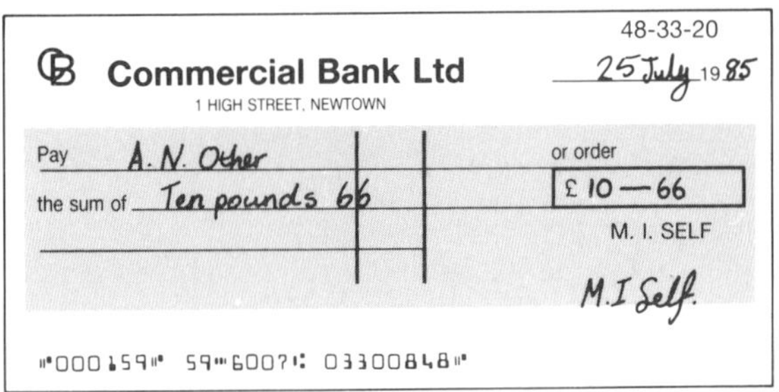

Fig. 10.2 A crossed cheque

In an advanced society with a developed banking system, bank deposits are the main form of money. They are convenient to hold and, through cheques, can be easily and safely transferred in quantities of any size. For example, they avoid the expense and risk of robbery involved in large movements of notes. The advantage of making wage payments by cheque explains why many large firms encourage their employees to hold bank accounts.

Banks themselves have also been active in attracting customers among workers who did not traditionally use banking services. The volume of bank deposits has expanded rapidly, and about 90 per cent of the value of all money transactions in the United Kingdom are now settled by cheque.

If you are unfamiliar with cheques, look at Fig. 10.2. As a precautionary measure it is common practice for a cheque to be *crossed* (with two parallel lines) requiring it to be paid into a bank account and not cashed directly over the counter.

1 Define barter and list its defects as a method of exchange.

2 Note the definition of money and briefly explain each of its four functions.

3 The essential quality of money is liquidity. Explain what this means and compare other financial assets such as shares or securities.

4 Describe the types of money now in use. Which types are legal tender and what does this mean?

5 Why are bank deposits recognized as money but not cheques?

10.2 The value of money

In describing the functions of money, we saw it is used to measure value just as other units are used to measure length, weight, and so on. There is, however, one important difference between money and most other units of measurement. Units of length or weight, for example, are fixed and do not change. Units of money themselves change in value as the prices of goods and services change.

The value of a unit of money is its purchasing power – that is, the quantity of goods and services it is capable of buying at existing prices. The higher the level of prices, the lower will be the purchasing power or value of each unit of money. The value of money moves in the opposite direction to the general level of prices.

There are of course many prices, and they do not all move together. But periods occur when the trend of prices in general is clearly and strongly upwards or (much less frequently) downwards. Such periods are linked with inflation or deflation.

Inflation

Inflation occurs when prices are generally rising and the value of money is correspondingly falling. The causes are complicated but can be explained by two kinds of forces affecting the price level. These forces are sometimes distinguished by the terms 'demand-pull' and 'cost-push' (Fig. 10.3).

1 Demand-pull

The demand for a country's products results from the spending of individuals, firms, the government, and also foreigners who buy its exports. As long as their combined spending can be matched by production there should be no shortage of goods and so no strong pull of demand on prices. But there is a limit to how much industry is capable of producing at any time and, if spending continually rises, shortages of certain goods must occur sooner or later. With supply then unable to satisfy the demand,

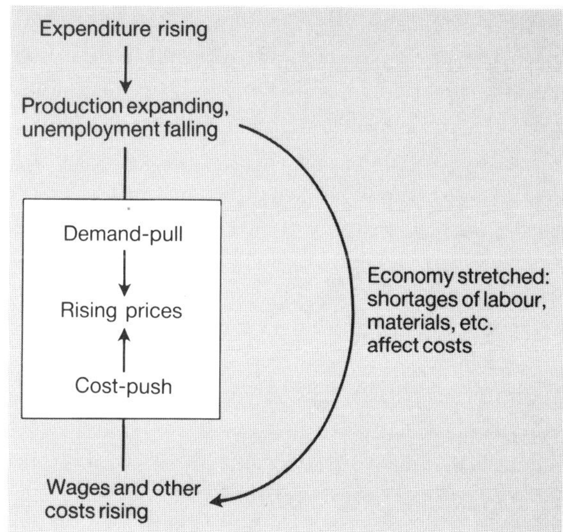

Fig. 10.3 Forces of inflation

there is a strong tendency for prices to rise. This is the situation of inflation due to demand-pull.

Economists judge how close industry is to the limit of its productive capacity by the level of unemployment in the country. A high level of unemployment usually means that factory space and machines as well as the country's labour force are not being fully used. Prices are likely to rise most rapidly when unemployment is low and industry does not have spare capacity to meet an expanding demand for its products.

Demand-pull inflation obviously occurs when people have plenty of money and spend it at a rapid rate. This kind of situation has been described as 'too much money chasing too few goods'. We shall see later how the Bank of England tries to check such inflation by restricting the quantity of money in the economy. In Chapter 13, we see how governments can also influence the level of spending in the economy by their own taxation and expenditure policies.

2 Cost-push

If goods cost more to produce, the profits of firms must fall unless they offset the extra costs by charging higher prices for their products. A general increase in wages, the costs of raw materials, or other production costs can thus lead to widespread increases in prices. In effect, rising costs are pushing up prices.

Although demand-pull and cost-push are two distinct forces, they are most likely to occur together. We saw that demand-pull is strongest when people are spending a lot of money and industry lacks the spare capacity to satisfy the demand for its products. In this situation, firms usually find their costs rising rapidly for a number of reasons:

i) With unemployment low and firms short of labour, trade unions are in a strong position to obtain wage increases for their members.

ii) Many firms can only meet the rising demand for their products by overtime working which involves high rates of pay.

iii) Production costs may also be forced up by other factors such as shortages of materials causing their prices to rise or mechanical failures when machines are being worked intensively.

Effects of inflation

Why should there be so much concern about inflation? If rising prices are accompanied by rising wages, there is no reason why wage-earners should be worse off. Indeed, during periods of inflation, many people are able to increase their earnings faster than prices so that they are really better off. In so far as inflation is accompanied by an expanding volume of demand in the economy there should also be more jobs and a rising level of production which generally means a higher standard of living. However, if inflation goes too far any such benefits are likely to be overshadowed by social and economic drawbacks.

1 Social injustice

Inflation causes injustice between sections of society, some gaining and some losing. The effects are complicated but a number of points are listed below. It can be seen that, in general, the poorest in the community are most likely to suffer hardship because they are least able to protect themselves against rising prices.

i) Wage-earners may gain or lose according to their ability to obtain pay increases. Those in strong trade unions or otherwise strong bargaining positions can usually secure pay rises that outweigh price rises and so raise their real incomes. Others with weak bargaining power are likely to fall behind as the cost of living rises.

ii) People dependent on fixed incomes such as fixed company pensions or investment interest are inevitably poorer. State pensioners and others reliant on social security are now normally protected by the government practice of annually raising social benefits in line with inflation – a process known as *indexation*. However, inflation can still leave them worse off relatively to other sections of society.

iii) People who owe or borrow money generally gain because the money they pay back is worth less than when it was borrowed and spent. Conversely, lenders are liable to lose from inflation.

iv) Savers are likely to lose because the value of their money falls as prices rise. Interest earned on savings may not be sufficient to compensate for the fall in value. Inflation could consequently have the effect of discouraging saving and encouraging spending – which itself adds to inflation. It is particularly harsh on the small savers. Wealthy people with large savings can usually protect themselves by buying property or shares that rise in value as prices rise.

2 Economic drawbacks and dangers

i) *Adverse effects on trade*. Inflation can have serious consequences in a country that relies heavily on its foreign trade. This clearly applies to the United Kingdom. A rise in the price of British products makes them more expensive for overseas buyers as well as our own inhabitants. Exports are therefore liable to decline. At the same time, imports will probably increase because inflation usually means more spending and also foreign goods become cheaper in comparison with home products – assuming that prices have not risen as much in other competing countries. With exports falling and imports rising, inflation often brings problems connected with the balance of payments (Chapter 15).

ii) *Runaway inflation*. With demand-pull and cost-push both working together, it is easy to see how inflation can get out of control. The most extreme danger is that with prices rising rapidly (and the value of money falling) people will lose confidence in money itself. In this situation, they are no longer willing to hold money and so exchange it immediately for paintings, jewellery, cigarettes, chocolates, or any other products whose values are rising in relation to money. The rise in spending and prices may then accelerate out of control.

Britain has never experienced inflation of a runaway type. A classic example occurred in Germany in 1923 when the value of the mark fell to almost nothing while prices were multiplied by billions. Economists refer to this as *hyperinflation*.
iii) *The danger of slump*. History has shown that inflation is frequently followed by the reverse conditions of economic slump and unemployment. This is likely to happen nowadays because the measures taken by governments to curb inflation include restraints on spending. There is then a real danger that the reduction in demand will be too great, leading to deflation.

Deflation

Deflation is caused by falling demand and is in some respects the reverse of inflation. But its effect is not necessarily falling prices. The main symptoms are slackening output, fewer jobs, and (for many people) lower living standards. Deflation is thus associated with periods of so-called economic depression, slump, or recession.

The most severe deflation of modern times occurred in the early 1930s when unemployment in Britain rose to over 3 million. That figure has again been exceeded as a consequence of the slump of the early 1980s. In the decades following the Second World War the economy was generally under strong pressure of demand due to both private and government spending, and the problems were usually concerned with inflation rather than deflation. Movements of the British economy since the 1970s are described in Chapter 16.

Policies for inflation and deflation

The aim must be to steer a course that avoids the extremes of inflation and deflation. This generally means keeping spending at a level high enough to avoid unnecessary unemployment but not so high that it causes prices to rise excessively. Three main forms of control have been used by governments.

1 Fiscal policy

This involves control of government expenditure and taxation (influencing private spending) operating largely through the annual budget. We deal with it in Chapter 13.

2 Monetary policy

Recent government policy has been strongly influenced by a number of economists (known as *monetarists*) who believe that the root cause of inflation is excessive money circulating in the economy. Their solution is to control the supply of money by methods available to the Bank of England which we examine in the next chapter.

3 Incomes policy

Successive governments have tried to check inflation by policies aimed at restraining pay increases, either by gaining voluntary co-operation from employers and trade unions or through direct intervention in wage bargaining. Pay restraint, if effective, could curb both demand-pull and cost-push inflationary pressures. We return to it in Chapter 16.

1 What is meant by the value of money and how is it related to prices?
2 Define inflation. Distinguish clearly between the demand-pull and cost-push forces that cause inflation.
3 Why are both kinds of inflation most likely to occur when there is little or no unemployment in the economy?
4 Note the groups of people most likely to suffer from inflation and explain why in each case. Who gains from inflation?
5 Explain why inflation usually weakens the country's trading position.
6 What do economists mean by hyperinflation and how does it come about?
7 What is deflation and what is its main consequence?

10.3 Price index numbers

Policies to deal with inflation or unemployment must be based on how the economy is behaving. For example, it is important to know as accurately as possible what is happening to production, employment, and prices.

The difficulty of measuring general movements of prices is that there are so many goods and services with different prices that do not all move together. Even in a period of acute inflation when most prices are rising rapidly there are likely to be some that are stable or falling. How then is it possible to calculate a general trend from all these different movements in the prices of individual items? The answer lies in the use of index numbers.

Index numbers provide a statistical method of measuring general changes in the price level of an assortment of items. Figures are regularly published for wholesale prices, stock exchange share prices, export and import prices, and so on. One of the best known series in Britain is the index of retail prices to which we refer below.

Method of calculation

The method can be simply explained by assuming that the index covers only two items – say, bread and cheese. It would of course be easy to take a simple average of their price changes over any period, but this would not give a true indication of the change in their combined cost to consumers unless household expenditure on each commodity happened to be the same. For instance, if the price of bread rose by 70 per cent and cheese by 10 per cent the average increase would be 40 per cent. But their combined cost would not rise by exactly that average if consumers spend more on, say, bread than cheese.

To take account of the different significance of items in the index, a system of *weights* is adopted. In a retail price index each item is weighted according to its relative importance in the average family budget. Thus, if out of every 100p spent each week on bread and cheese 80p goes on bread and 20p on cheese, the ratio of 80 to 20 reflects their relative importance and these figures represent their respective weights out of a total of 100. By using the weights, our index takes account of the fact that consumers spend four times as much on bread as on cheese.

Let us now calculate the weighted index on the original assumption that the price of bread rose by 70 per cent and cheese by 10 per cent. First, it is customary to express percentage price changes in an index by calling all prices 100 on the starting (or base) date. The percentage increases for bread and cheese are thus represented by the numbers 170 and 110 respectively. (If a price fell by, say, 10 per cent, the number would become 90.) The index number for each item is then multiplied by its weight. The resulting products are next added together and the total finally divided by the sum of the weights as illustrated in Table 10.1.

Table 10.1 Index number calculation

Item	*Price change per cent*	*Index number*		*Weight*		*Product*
Bread	+70	170	×	80	=	13 600
Cheese	+10	110	×	20	=	2 200
Total				100		15 800

Weighted index = 15 800 ÷ 100 = 158

The weighted index figure of 158 shows a combined price increase of 58 per cent instead of a 40 per cent increase using an unweighted average. The difference arises because the larger price increase was for bread on which our consumers spend more.

Index of retail prices

The index has its origins in a very narrow cost of living index which began in 1914. This was designed to measure changes in the prices of a small group of necessities – mainly food, clothing, fuel and rent – which largely determined the cost of living of the working class at that time. Since the Second World War it has been extended to include the prices of a very wide range of goods and services which cover the bulk of consumer spending. Prices are obtained from centres scattered throughout the coun-

Table 10.2 Index of retail prices (July 1985)

Items	*Weights*	*Index numbers (Jan 1974 = 100)*
Food	190	335·3
Alcoholic drink	75	412·5
Tobacco	37	539·6
Housing	153	465·8
Fuel and light	65	501·5
Household durables	65	263·0
Clothing and footwear	75	221·4
Transport and vehicles	156	396·7
Miscellaneous goods	77	394·3
Services	62	383·2
Meals out	45	414·6
All items	1000	375·7

Which items classified in the retail price index are represented by these two photographs?

try and the resulting index figures are published monthly.

The present scope of the index is indicated by Table 10.2 showing its main groups. Groups such as food and clothing are each divided into a large number of individual items. The group of household durables includes television sets and the whole range of modern electrical appliances as well as furniture, hardware, etc. Transport and vehicles cover the various items entering into the cost of private motoring in addition to public transport fares. Services include such varied items as postage, entertainments, and laundering.

Clearly, the scope of the index now goes far beyond the cost of living in the sense of subsistence. The items and weights are obtained from annual surveys of family expenditure which exclude only the poorest (pensioner) households and, at the other end of the scale, those in which the head of the household earns more than double the national average. A separate index is prepared for old age pensioners.

Limitations of price index numbers

The index of retail prices is widely used as a standard for wage claims and settlements. Wages are sometimes even tied to the index through arrangements for an automatic rise when the index figure has risen by an agreed amount. Under the name of *indexation*, it is now normal practice for pensions and other social security payments to be raised annually in line with the index to offset inflation. However, in making such practical use of the index, it is important to be aware of its problems and limitations.

1 Problems of structure

An initial problem is the choice of items to be included and the weights attached to them. In the case of an index of retail prices, the question is essentially one of deciding the range of households to which the index should apply. Clearly, the patterns of consumer spending largely depend on income so that different commodities and weights should be used for households on different income levels. Thus, an index based on the expenditure of an average family is not a suitable guide to the cost of living of pensioners. For instance, they are less likely to be affected by changes in the index due to motoring costs or hotel meal charges.

2 Problems of price measurement

Obvious difficulties arise in recording price changes over such a vast range of items. There are likely to be local variations in the prices of some goods and services. However, this difficulty is met to some extent by calculating an average of prices taken from different parts of the country. More difficult to overcome is the fact that price changes may be concealed by changes in the character of the products themselves. Thus, small reductions in the weight, size, or quality of products amount to effective increases in prices which may go unnoticed.

3 Problems of change

In a rapidly changing economy, the structure of any index is liable to become seriously out of date unless there is frequent revision of items and weights. New products coming on to the market may have to be added to the list of items or substituted for other items no longer in demand. Television sets, for example, were not a candidate for inclusion in a retail price index before the Second World War.

Table 10.3 Retail index: changes in weights of selected items

	1962	*1972*	*1979*	*1985*
Food	319	251	232	190
Housing	102	121	120	153
Transport and vehicles	92	139	143	156
Meals out	—	46	51	45

Even if the products themselves do not alter, changing tastes or fashions require periodic revision of the weights. Above all, in an expanding economy, a rising standard of living is certain to be accompanied by changes in the pattern of spending. Thus, in the index of retail prices, an increasing proportion of the total weights has had to be allocated to luxury forms of spending while the food category as a whole has been proportionately reduced (Table 10.3).

1 What is the purpose of index numbers? Why are they usually weighted? What determines the weights given to items in an index measuring retail prices?

2 Refer to Table 10.1. Assuming that the weights of bread and cheese remain 80 and 20 as given, calculate the index figure when (a) the price of bread rises by 10 per cent and cheese by 70 per cent, (b) the price of bread rises by 10 per cent and cheese falls by 10 per cent. Show your method of calculation.

3 Write a brief description of the government's index of retail prices. What points should you bear in mind when using the index as a measure of change in the cost of living?

Multiple choice

1 A person borrows £1000 from a bank. This is an example of money performing its function as a
- **A** medium of exchange
- **B** unit of account
- **C** measure of value
- **D** standard for deferred payment
- **E** store of value

2 Which of the following is included in most modern definitions of money?
1 bills of exchange
2 bank current accounts
3 building society deposits
- **A** 1 only is correct
- **B** 2 only is correct
- **C** 1 and 2 only are correct
- **D** 2 and 3 only are correct
- **E** 1, 2 and 3 are correct

3 Inflation always causes loss to people
1 on fixed incomes
2 who borrow money
3 who save money
- **A** 1 only is correct
- **B** 1 and 2 only are correct
- **C** 2 and 3 only are correct
- **D** 1, 2 and 3 are correct
- **E** 3 only is correct

4 Bank of England notes are
- **A** not legal tender
- **B** limited legal tender
- **C** unlimited legal tender
- **D** manufactured by the Royal Mint
- **E** backed by gold

5 The most likely consequence of inflation is an increase in
- **A** the value of money
- **B** the liquidity of money
- **C** employment
- **D** exports
- **E** imports

6 All the following statements are correct EXCEPT
- **A** Exchange can take place without money.
- **B** Modern division of labour depends on money.
- **C** More money in the economy must make us better off.
- **D** Liquidity is an essential quality of money.
- **E** Societies have existed without money.

7

Item	*Year 1 index number*	*Year 2 index number*	*Weight*
X	100	150	70
Y	100	110	30

From the above information, the weighted price index for Year 2 is
- **A** 120
- **B** 124
- **C** 130
- **D** 138
- **E** 160

Data response

	1980	*1981*	*1982*	*1983*	*1984*
Retail price index	100	112	121	127	133
Average earnings	100	118	131	143	153

1 Draw graphs of the movements of prices and earnings (on a single diagram with the time scale on the horizontal axis).

2 Between which two years were prices rising most rapidly? Calculate that rate of inflation, i.e. the percentage increase in the price index.

3 What do the graphs tell you about changes in the standard of living (or real incomes) over the period covered?

4 What policies could have been adopted by the government to reduce the rate of inflation?

Essays

1 Consider whether modern forms of money efficiently perform the functions required of money in the economy.

2 Why and by what means do governments try to check inflation?

3 How can inflation be measured and how reliable is the measure?

Chapter 11

The banking system

11.1 The money market

It will help us to understand the British banking system if we look first at the activities of a group of firms, centred in London, forming a financial network known as the money market. The Bank of England and ordinary banks are part of this network. Also prominent in it are firms called discount houses and accepting houses.

The principal function of the money market is to lend money to private firms and the government for short periods of time, normally up to three months. This lending is done to a large extent through the purchase of securities which mature – that is, the money must be repaid – within short periods such as three months. Such short-dated securities are called bills. The bills concerned are of two kinds – commercial bills of exchange (drawn up by firms) and Treasury bills (issued by the government).

Bills of exchange

Bills of exchange were widely used during the nineteenth century to finance both home and foreign trade. Their importance in home trade declined rapidly with the development of banking and payment by cheque. They continue to be used to finance international trade though banks have increasingly taken over this field as well.

The advantage of a bill of exchange as a method of financing trade is that it gives the purchaser of goods time to pay while enabling the seller to obtain his money immediately. In international trade, for example, an importing firm often needs time to sell the imported goods in its own country before it is in a position to pay. A bill of exchange enables it to do this without forcing the exporting firm to wait for the money which it may want urgently in order to carry on its own business.

Fig. 11.1 illustrates the movements of a bill of exchange in a simplified way, and the main steps involved are further outlined below.

i) The exporter (seller) draws up the bill making it due for payment on an agreed date. It is then sent off with other export documents.

ii) The importer (buyer) accepts the bill by signing it or – to make it still more reliable – arranges for its acceptance by a bank or accepting house (merchant bank). The latter will charge a small commission for its service. The accepted bill is then returned to the exporter.

Fig. 11.1 A bill of exchange in international trade

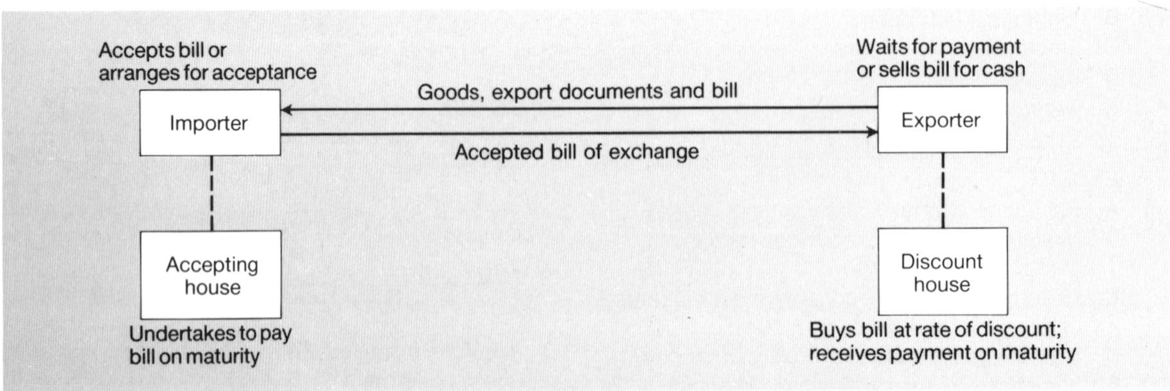

iii) If the exporter is unwilling to wait for payment he can sell the bill for cash to a discount house. However, the discount house will pay a lower price for the bill than its face value. The difference is equivalent to a rate of interest, called the rate of discount, earned by the discount house for lending the money until the bill is due for payment.

For example, if a discount house pays £980 for a £1000 bill with three months to maturity the rate of discount is about 2 per cent for three months or 8 per cent per annum. (To be accurate, the rate would be somewhat higher calculated as a percentage of the £980 paid by the discount house.) The rate of discount depends on how long the bill has to run, the reliability of the acceptor, and also general conditions in the money market.

Treasury bills

The declining importance of bills of exchange, particularly during the First World War and the trade depression of the 1930s, stimulated the discount houses to find other profitable uses for their funds. Government borrowing through the issue of Treasury bills provided them with a convenient alternative.

Treasury bills normally entitle the purchasers to repayment at the end of three months. This kind of borrowing is useful to the government because its revenue from taxes comes in unevenly. Thus, it can meet a temporary shortage of funds by issuing more bills.

The bills are sold weekly by the Bank of England (on behalf of the government) in amounts of £5000 upwards and so are mainly bought by firms with large amounts of money to invest in this way. The purchasers include merchant banks and other financial concerns, but a large portion of the weekly issue is always taken up by the discount houses, offering rates of discount which give them a fair return on their investment. The ordinary banks do not themselves compete for the weekly issue but are involved in ways that we shall consider later.

Discount houses

Specialist discount houses are peculiar to Britain. They developed in the nineteenth century largely because British banks preferred to avoid the risks of discounting bills and concentrated on other kinds of banking business. Dealing in bills is a major activity of the money market and the term discount market is used to refer to the same network of firms.

We have seen how the discount houses lend to the government and private business by discounting Treasury bills and bills of exchange. Their funds are in fact obtained mainly by borrowing from banks at rates of interest low enough to give the discount houses a margin of profit compared with the rates of discount at which they lend. Banks are willing to lend at such low rates on the condition that the money will be repaid on demand or almost immediately if required. These *loans at call* are of great importance to the banks as a means of raising cash quickly when they are running short.

If the banks are short of cash and recall their loans to discount houses, the latter can always obtain help from the Bank of England. For example, the Bank of England will supply the discount houses with cash by buying or rediscounting their bills. It is then said to be acting as 'the lender of last resort'. The relationship between the banks, discount houses, and Bank of England is illustrated in Fig. 11.2 and has a special significance to which we return later.

Accepting houses

We noted how the growth of trade was assisted by firms which put their names on bills of exchange as a guarantee of payment. These firms were usually private merchant banks with international reputations that made it possible for them to become

Fig. 11.2 The discount market

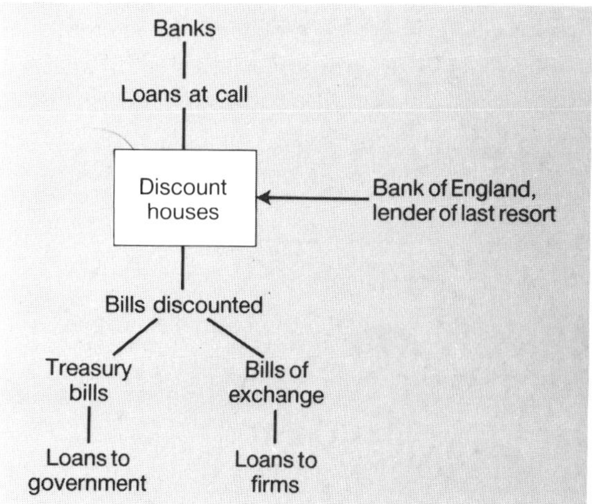

specialists in this kind of business. Not surprisingly, they include such widely known banking names as Rothschild and Baring.

Acceptance business diminished with the declining use of bills of exchange. The accepting houses have survived by extending their interests in many fields of banking while still making use of their overseas connections. For example, they act as financial advisers to large companies, handle issues of new shares, lend to discount houses, and buy Treasury bills on their own account.

1 What type of lending takes place in the money market? How are the loans normally made and who are the borrowers?

2 Explain the process by which a bill of exchange is used to finance trade, and indicate the services performed by accepting houses and discount houses.

3 Explain the relationship between the discount houses and (a) the banks, (b) the Bank of England.

11.2 Commercial banks

The bulk of ordinary banking business in England and Wales is carried out by a small number of commercial banks dominated by the 'big four'–Barclays, Lloyds, Midland, and National Westminster. These are public companies owned by shareholders and sometimes referred to as the joint-stock banks.

The concentration of British banking in a small number of very large banks came about through a series of amalgamations beginning in the nineteenth century. The typical British bank is consequently one that operates through a network of local branches in towns and villages throughout the country. Its size and resources enable it to achieve economies of scale and also help to ensure reliability. Britain has experienced bankruptcies among large firms but not among the commercial banks.

Functions of commercial banks

1 Taking deposits

This is the basic function of commercial banks and makes all their other activities possible. From the customers' point of view, bank deposits are a safe and convenient form in which to hold money. The two main kinds of deposits are called current and deposit accounts.

Current accounts enable depositors to withdraw their money on demand over the bank counter or to make payments by cheque to other people. It is mainly for the convenience of a current account that most people leave money in banks. Banks may charge customers for the service of handling their current accounts and making payments by cheque. Since customers receive no interest on their money in current accounts, they usually do not deposit more than they require to meet their needs from day to day. Surplus money is more likely to be left in deposit accounts.

Deposit accounts are a form of saving which earn interest for the depositors. The rate of interest is linked to and somewhat below the bank's 'base rate' to which we refer later. Cheques cannot be drawn on deposit accounts and seven days' notice is normally required for withdrawals.

2 Making payments

Most business transactions and many payments between individuals are made by cheques drawn on bank accounts. Through the banks' arrangements for cheque 'clearing' (described below) these payments are settled simply by entries in bank registers without any physical movements of money. In addition, the banks co-operate to provide a 'giro' service similar to the Post Office's National Giro. This enables people to make or receive payments at any bank even if they do not themselves have accounts.

The *Clearing House* provides an efficient system of dealing with payments by cheques that have to be settled between different banks. If two people have accounts with the same bank, it is easy to see how a cheque paid by one to the other can be settled (or cleared) by a simple process of adjustment in the registers of that bank. Thus, if Smith receives a cheque from Jones, the bank merely increases Smith's deposit and reduces Jones's deposit by the amount of the cheque. But if their accounts are at different banks, arrangements must be made for money to be transferred from one bank to the other.

Until the eighteenth century, each bank employed clerks to carry cheques and collect the money due from other banks. The Clearing House was developed by the banks themselves as a central meeting place where their representatives could settle all such payments.

Suggest three possible purposes of the customer at the counter of this commercial bank.

At the daily clearings, each bank totals up its accounts in relation to every other bank. For example, if Barclays has cheques worth £5 million payable by Lloyds while Lloyds has £6 million payable by Barclays, then the balance of £1 million owed by Barclays to Lloyds is cleared off. Moreover, since each bank has an account with the Bank of England (also represented at the Clearing House), the process is completed by transferring £1 million from Barclays' account to Lloyds' account in the books of the Bank of England. In fact, there is no need for cash to be handled at any stage, even in the Clearing House. Banks that are not members of the Clearing House arrange for their cheques to be cleared through one of the 'clearing banks'.

3 Various services to customers

Apart from their main banking functions, the commercial banks make various extra services available to their customers. These include providing credit card facilities, making standing-order payments, executing wills, supplying travellers' cheques and foreign currencies, giving financial advice, and handling investments in stocks and shares.

4 The business of lending

Banks make a profit for their shareholders by using money deposited with them to lend out at profitable rates of interest. Bank loans are of great economic importance because they are used to finance a lot of spending and the nation's business depends on them to a considerable extent. To understand the lending activities of banks, we must look first at the structure of a bank balance sheet and the way in which they arrange their assets.

The balance sheet

Table 11.1 shows the main items in a commercial bank's balance sheet and an approximate percentage share of each item in the total. The deposits of customers are called *liabilities* because banks, in effect, owe that money to their depositors and are liable to pay when required. A bank's liabilities also include capital invested by shareholders but this item need not concern us here. The economic significance of banks lies in the use made of money deposited. This is shown on the *assets* side of the balance sheet. A proportion is retained in notes and coin to meet

Table 11.1 *Example of a bank balance sheet*

Liabilities	*Per cent*	*Assets*	*Per cent*
Sterling deposits:		Notes and coin	1·5
Current accounts	25	Balances with the Bank of England	0·5
Deposit accounts	40	Money at call	3·0
Other currency deposits	20	Bills	3·0
Capital and other liabilities	15	Market loans	12·0
	100	Advances	50·0
		Investments	10·0
		Other assets	20·0
			100.0

the cash demands of customers. It can be seen that the bulk of assets consists of loans and investments of various kinds.

Distribution of assets

In arranging their assets, banks are governed by two dominating motives, liquidity and profit.

Liquidity is essential to banks because they must always be prepared to meet the demands of their customers to withdraw deposits in cash. Failure to do so would lead to loss of confidence, a consequent rush of customers to withdraw their money, and the probable collapse of the bank. Such failures were common in the early history of banking in this country but are most unlikely today. First, the existence of large nationwide banks enables one branch to draw on others if faced by a heavy local demand for cash. Secondly, the banks are not only careful to keep adequate cash reserves but also ensure that a safe proportion of other assets (loans) can be turned quickly into cash should the need arise.

Particular attention has always been given to the percentage of cash and other liquid assets held by banks. The Bank of England used to require banks to maintain a prescribed minimum percentage of certain liquid (or reserve) assets. Thus, from 1971 to 1981, banks had to maintain a *reserve assets ratio* of at least 12½ per cent. This practice was ended in 1981, allowing banks greater flexibility of assets distribution. But liquidity remains an essential condition of sound banking and the Bank of England continues to exercise supervision.

The *profit* motive of banks conflicts with their need for liquidity. This is because higher rates of interest are generally earned by lending for longer periods and sacrificing liquidity. The most profitable assets are advances and investments but these are also the least liquid (Fig. 11.3). Starting with cash reserves (which earn no interest) the assets are listed in the balance sheet in descending order of liquidity but increasing profitability. We go on to explain them in that order.

1 Notes and coin

Enough instant cash must be kept in the safes and tills of branches to meet withdrawals and carry on business from day to day.

2 Balances with the Bank of England

Each bank holds a small but important portion of assets in an account at the Bank of England. These *bankers' deposits* are counted as cash by the banks because the money can be withdrawn in notes and coin if required just as people draw on their own current accounts at commercial banks themselves.

Fig. 11.3 A bank's assets structure

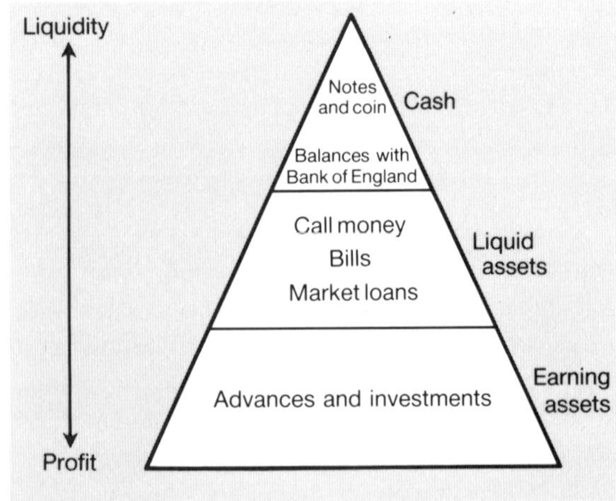

We have already seen how banks use their deposits with the Bank of England to settle their accounts in the Clearing House.

Bankers' deposits together with notes and coin form the cash reserves of banks. They earn no interest and banks consequently hold no more than is required for day-to-day purposes. The rest of their funds can be used for profitable lending.

3 Money at call

Bank loans on call to discount houses have already been mentioned in connection with the operation of the money market. These loans earn comparatively low rates of interest but can be recalled immediately if banks find themselves short of cash. They are regarded as next in liquidity to cash itself.

4 Bills

The bills held by banks include Treasury bills, local authority bills, and commercial bills of exchange. As explained at the beginning of the chapter, they are short-term securities that can always be sold for cash in the money market and therefore count as a liquid asset.

5 Market loans

Banks lend to each other and to other borrowers seeking cash in the money market. These market loans are generally short-term and classified as a liquid asset.

6 Investments

Commercial banks have always used some of their funds for investment in long-term securities, mainly government stocks described as *gilt-edged*. Such investments earn high rates of interest and the motive is profit, not liquidity. If necessary the securities may be sold for cash in the Stock Exchange, but substantial sales would depress their prices and so involve the banks in heavy losses.

7 Advances

Advances to their customers are the largest and most profitable part of bank lending. But they are considered the least liquid of bank assets because borrowers cannot be relied upon to pay back when the cash is needed.

The advances are made to personal customers (for cars, household improvements, etc.) and to businesses. British banks traditionally prefer to lend for fairly short periods (months rather than years) and their typical advances to firms are to provide 'working capital'—for example, to manufacturers for the purchase of raw materials, to farmers for seeds, and to merchants or retailers to buy stocks of goods or pay for new equipment. In recent years, however, banks have shown willingness to lend for longer periods to assist industrial investment. They have also entered into competition with building societies in providing mortgage loans for house purchase.

Each bank fixes its interest rates in relation to an announced *base rate* that can vary with changes in general market rates of interest. But the rate of interest charged on any loan also depends on an estimate of the risk involved. Thus, a large reliable company may pay only 1½ per cent above the base rate while a personal borrower is charged as much as 3½ per cent above. Some form of security, such as stocks and shares or an insurance policy with a value in cash, is also normally required, particularly from a personal borrower.

The most common form of bank advance is an *overdraft*. This gives the customer the right to overdraw his account up to an agreed limit. Interest is then only charged on the amount actually overdrawn. The date of repayment is usually flexible and overdrafts are sometimes renewed again and again. An ordinary *loan* is usually repayable by instalments, with interest, over a fixed period.

Credit creation

Bank lending is important not only because it finances a great deal of spending but also because it adds to the country's stock of money in the form of bank deposits. Bank deposits are obviously created when customers pay money into their accounts. Less obviously, banks themselves cause deposits to be created by their own lending activities. The process by which bank loans create deposits is known as credit creation. It is in fact the main way in which the country's supply of money has grown.

The process of credit creation depends on a few simple facts: first, money deposited in banks is mostly lent out; secondly, money lent is spent by the borrowers; thirdly, money spent is received by shops or other businesses and will sooner or later be put back into bank accounts as new deposits. These new deposits begin a further round of lending, spending, more deposits, and so on.

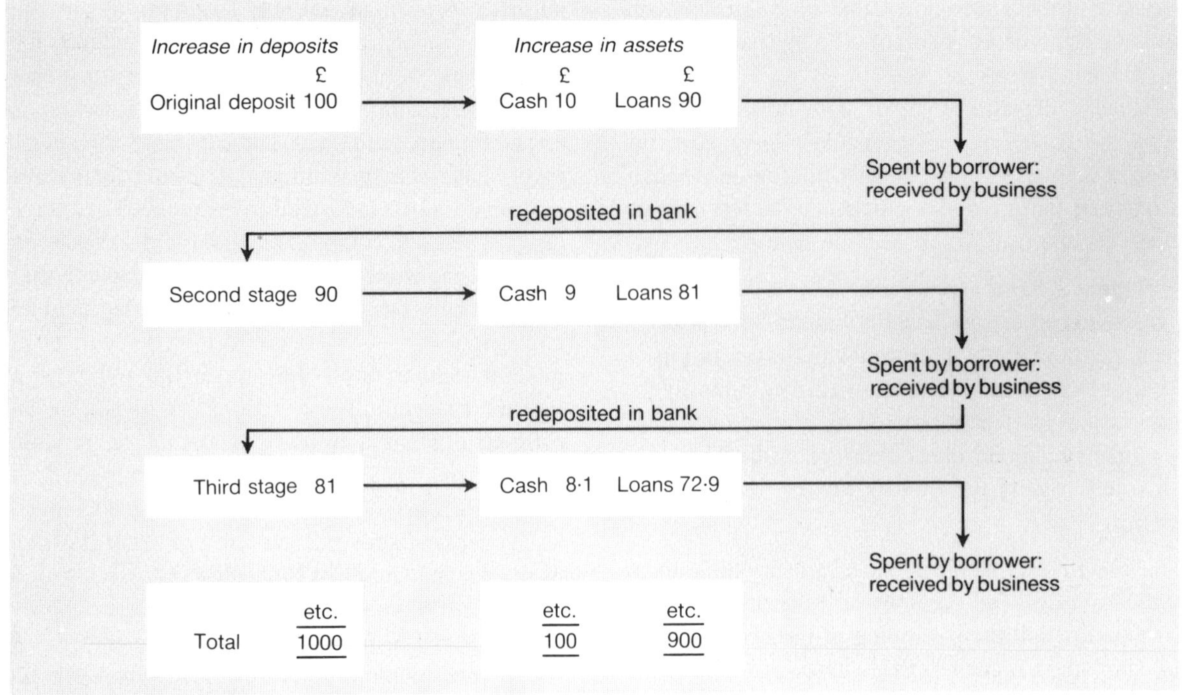

Fig. 11.4 The process of credit creation

Follow the stages of the process illustrated in Fig. 11.4. It starts with the assumption that extra cash of £100 (not previously taken out of a bank account) is put into a bank deposit. It further assumes that banks maintain a reserve ratio of 10 per cent of their deposits, held entirely in cash. 90 per cent of money deposited is thus lent out at each stage, but this finds its way back into bank accounts after being spent.

Note that the process eventually comes to an end because a proportion of deposits (10 per cent in the example) is retained as cash reserves at each stage, and the amount available for lending consequently diminishes until there is nothing left to continue the process. Fig. 11.4 shows only the first three stages. Remember that there are further stages before the process works itself out and the final totals are reached.

The final effects are shown by the totals at the bottom of the diagram. Note that total deposits have risen by £1000 or ten times the extra cash deposited, so maintaining the 10 per cent reserve ratio. If the ratio were 20 per cent (one-fifth of deposits), the multiple of credit expansion would be 5 and total deposits would increase by 500 in the example.

In practice, however, deposits do not expand to this extent for several reasons. First, banks cannot always find enough borrowers to whom they can safely lend. Secondly, the money lent by banks may not all come back into the banking system since some members of the public may decide to hold more cash personally or put more into other financial institutions such as building societies. Moreover, if there is concern over inflation, the Bank of England may take steps to restrict bank lending. We next consider the Bank of England and its policies.

1 Note each of the functions of a commercial bank. Distinguish between current and deposit accounts.

2 Note the two main motives of commercial banks. Why do these motives conflict and how do the banks strike a balance between them?

3 Name the assets that banks regard as cash and two other liquid assets.

4 Name the two most profitable bank assets. For what purposes and in what ways do banks make advances to their customers?

5 Explain the process of credit creation. What limits the ability of banks to create credit?

The Bank of England in the City of London. Who are its customers?

11.3 The Bank of England

The Bank was founded in 1694 to carry on ordinary banking business but, from the beginning, it has also acted as the banker to the government. During the nineteenth century, it came to be recognized as the *central bank* of the country, and its commercial banking activities became less important. It ceased to deal with the general public and its main customers today are the British government, UK banks, and overseas banks and governments. In 1946 the Bank was nationalized, but this made little difference to its role since it was long accustomed to working with the government rather than seeking profit.

Functions of the Bank of England

1 The note issue

The Bank of England has the sole right to issue notes in England and Wales, though other banks continue to issue notes in Scotland and Northern Ireland. At one time, the quantity of notes issued depended on the gold reserves held by the Bank. But since the abandonment of the gold standard in 1931, the note issue has become entirely *fiduciary*—that is, not backed by gold. An increase in the issue requires the approval of the Treasury and Parliament (if it is to be permanent), but this is now largely a formality and the Bank really controls the quantity of legal tender money.

Notes and coins go out into circulation through the commercial banks which draw on their deposits at the Bank of England in order to meet the demands of their customers for cash. The quantities issued are thus related to the needs of the public. Increases normally occur at the peak spending periods of Christmas, Easter, and the summer holidays, with reductions at other times when the demand for cash falls. However, an expanding economy uses more and more money, and the general trend of the note issue is strongly upwards.

2 The government's bank

The Bank of England acts as banker to the government in much the same way as commercial banks act as bankers to private customers. Under the heading of *public deposits* it holds the accounts or bank balances of the government. Revenue from taxation is paid into these accounts and expenditure on the various government services is drawn out of them.

With its financial experience and knowledge, the Bank is well qualified to act as an expert adviser to the government. It is in constant contact with the

Treasury, the department mainly reponsible for government financial and economic policies. It issues Treasury bills and other government securities, and generally manages the National Debt – that is, the total borrowing of the government.

3 External business

Its responsibility for the country's currency means that the Bank has important functions connected with international finance. In a fund known as the *Exchange Equalization Account*, it holds the national reserves of gold and foreign currencies. These reserves can be drawn upon to pay for imports from other countries and are sometimes used to keep the exchange value of the pound steady against other currencies by methods to be explained later.

Any controls required by the government over foreign exchange transactions – that is, the exchange of pounds for other currencies – are administered by the Bank of England. It also co-operates with the central banks of other countries and represents Britain in organizations such as the *International Monetary Fund*. We return to these external functions of the Bank in Chapter 15.

4 The bankers' bank

Nearly all banks and related institutions such as discount houses keep accounts at the Bank of England. We have seen how these accounts (called bankers' deposits) are used to make payments between banks in the Clearing House.

Payments to and from the government are also settled through bankers' deposits and the government's accounts (public deposits) at the Bank of England. Thus, when private firms or individuals pay taxes to the government by cheque, bankers' deposits fall and public deposits rise at the Bank of England. Conversely, payments made by the government are settled by transfers from public deposits to bankers' deposits.

Fluctuations in bankers' deposits are particularly important because they form part of the cash reserves of the banking system. We shall see later how the Bank of England can influence bank lending by controlling the level of bankers' deposits.

5 Monetary policy

As the nation's central bank, the Bank of England controls the monetary system of the country in accordance with the economic policy of the government. For this purpose, it co-operates closely with the Treasury, the department responsible for the government's economic policy as a whole.

The Bank's control over the monetary system is achieved mainly by influencing the lending of other banks and the rates of interest at which they lend. In a period of inflation, its aim is to discourage spending by restricting bank loans and forcing up rates of interest charged to borrowers. Alternatively, in times of heavy unemployment, it may encourage spending by making loans easier to obtain at low rates of interest.

Control of bank lending is particularly important because it largely determines the supply of money in the economy. As we have seen, bank deposits are the main modern form of money, and bank lending adds to deposits through the process of credit creation. Thus, in controlling bank lending the Bank of England is also exercising control over the quantity of money. Money clearly provides the fuel for inflation, and an influential body of economists now believe that inflation can only be held back by strict control of the money supply.

Monetary controls

1 Lending directives

When the Bank of England was nationalized in 1946, it was given power to issue directions to the commercial banks. Backed with this power, it has sometimes put limits or *ceilings* on the level of bank lending or told banks that they should concentrate on certain national *priorities* such as helping exports. Bank managers have then been forced to resist customers' requests for loans for personal spending. However, the Bank now tries to avoid such direct methods of control and prefers to exert its influence in other ways.

2 The reserve ratio

A higher ratio means that banks hold a larger proportion of deposits in the form of cash or liquid assets and so less is available for lending to customers. The Bank of England's power to impose a minimum reserve assets ratio could thus be used to restrict the volume of bank lending and growth of deposits.

3 Special deposits

To restrict their lending, the banks may be required to deposit with the Bank of England – in addition to their normal bankers' deposits – a certain percentage of their total deposits from customers. Interest is paid on special deposits, but banks cannot use the money for lending and it is not counted in their reserve assets. In this way the banks are forced to keep a portion of their funds idle in addition to their normal reserves. When the Bank wants to encourage lending, it can simply release some or all of the special deposits.

4 *Open market operations*

The Bank of England's open market operations take the form of buying or selling either Treasury bills (in the money market) or government stocks (in the Stock Exchange). For the purpose of illustration, let us suppose that the Bank's aim is to stimulate economic activity by encouraging commercial banks to expand their lending. This could be achieved through open market *purchases* – for example, by instructing its broker to buy securities on its behalf in the Stock Exchange. The consequences may be summarized as follows.

i) Sellers of the securities receive Bank of England cheques which they pay into their own bank accounts. Commercial bank deposits thus immediately rise by that amount.

ii) The Bank of England clears its cheques with the commercial banks concerned simply by adding to their bankers' balances in its own accounts.

Fig. 11.5 Effect of open market operations

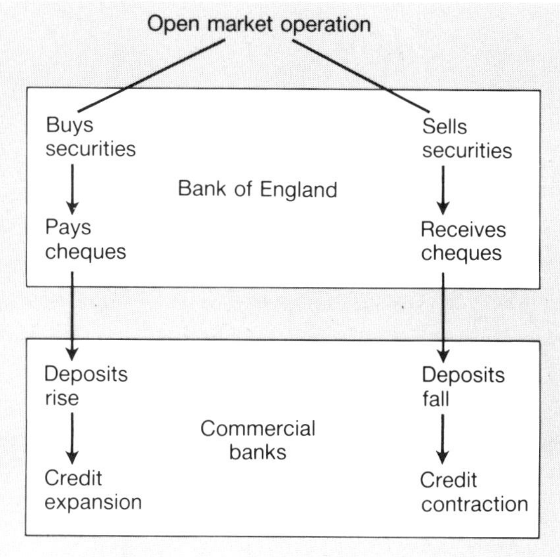

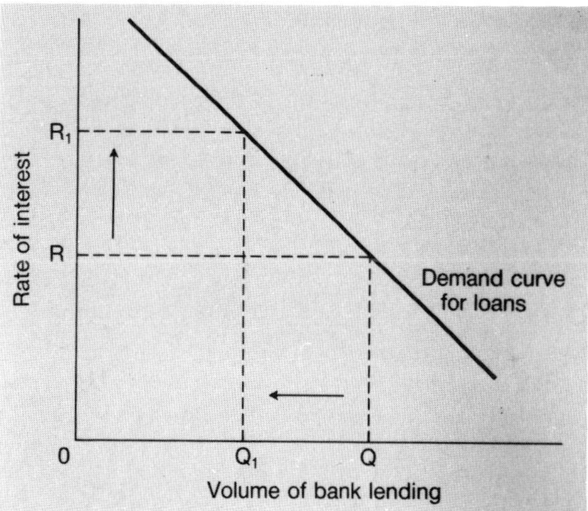

Fig. 11.6 A demand curve for loans

iii) Since those balances form part of their cash reserves, the commercial banks are now in a position to further expand their loans and deposits through the process of credit creation already described.

Open market *sales* of securities would, in effect, reverse the steps outlined above, resulting in credit contraction (Fig. 11.5). In practice, the greatest impact of the Bank's open market operations is likely to be on interest rates – rising in conjunction with credit contraction or falling in response to credit expansion. The influence of the Bank on interest rates is considered next.

5 *Control of interest rates*

Interest rates affect the volume of lending through the demand for loans. In this connection, the rate of interest may be seen as the price of loans, affecting the quantity demanded like any market price. Thus at a higher rate of interest banks are likely to lend less because there are fewer willing borrowers (Fig. 11.6).

Traditionally, the Bank of England influenced the level of interest rates by announcing its own official lending rate – known as *bank rate* or *minimum lending rate* (MLR). A change in MLR could act as a signal to banks and other financial institutions to adjust their rates accordingly. Announcement of MLR ceased in 1981, but the Bank of England continues to influence the level of interest rates by other means.

If the Bank wants interest rates to rise, it may

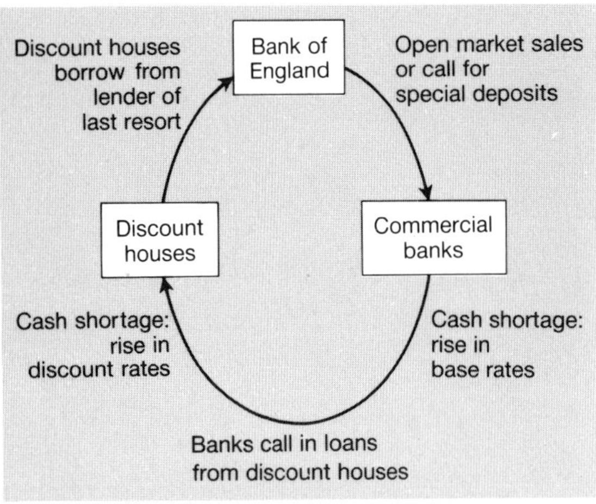

Fig. 11.7 Forcing up interest rates

reduce the cash reserves of banks by open market sales or calling for special deposits. The consequences are likely to be as follows.

i) Faced with a cash shortage, banks are willing to pay higher rates of interest to attract deposits and also charge higher rates for loans. They signal these changes by announcing a rise in their base rates.

ii) Banks may also act to relieve the immediate cash shortage by calling in their loans (money at call) to the discount houses.

iii) The discount houses are forced, in turn, to borrow from the Bank of England. The Bank is then acting as the *lender of last resort* and is able to impose its own intentions with regard to interest rates on the money market.

You should be able to follow the sequence of events in Fig. 11.7, starting and finishing at the Bank of England. In practice, the effects of the Bank's policies are likely to spread even more widely to other financial institutions. For example, a significant increase in bank base rates is usually followed by building societies since they compete with the banks for deposits.

We have illustrated the Bank's influence on interest rates from the viewpoint of a monetary squeeze, causing a shortage of cash in the banking system and so forcing up interest rates. By a reverse policy of monetary expansion, making cash plentiful and encouraging lending, the Bank can also influence interest rates downwards.

6 *Management of government debt*

Credit expansion can be caused by commercial bank lending to the government or public sector of the economy as well as to private customers. Governments have tried to combat inflation by reducing their own borrowing (through fiscal policy) and also financing a larger proportion outside the banking system – in particular, by inducing members of the public to buy government bonds or take up national savings. This again generally involves paying higher interest rates.

1 Describe briefly each of the functions of the Bank of England.

2 Why is it important for the Bank of England to exercise control over the lending of other banks?

3 Show how the Bank of England can restrict bank lending by (a) open market operations, (b) special deposits, (c) issuing directives. What actions could it take to encourage bank lending?

4 Refer to Fig. 11.7 and describe the means by which the Bank of England may force banks and other financial institutions to raise their interest rates. In what circumstances might it want to do this?

Multiple choice

1 Which of the following normally borrow from the Bank of England acting as the lender of last resort?
A stockbrokers
B accepting houses
C public companies
D commercial banks
E discount houses

2 The liquid assets of a commercial bank include
1 special deposits
2 Treasury bills
3 balances with the Bank of England

A 1 only is correct
B 1 and 2 only are correct
C 2 and 3 only are correct
D 1, 2 and 3 are correct
E 3 only is correct

3 The Bank of England is responsible for all the following EXCEPT
A the issue of notes and coin
B the issue of Treasury bills
C the foreign currency reserves
D the bankers' Clearing House
E managing the national debt

4 Assuming the Bank of England set a reserve assets ratio of 20 per cent, what is the maximum increase in total deposits that could result from a new cash deposit of £1000 in a commercial bank?
A £1000
B £2000
C £5000
D £8000
E £10 000

5 The Bank of England is NOT
A the lender of last resort in the money market
B the only note issuing bank in the United Kingdom
C the central bank of the United Kingdom
D a nationalized financial institution
E involved in the working of the bankers' Clearing House

6 Which of the following is one of the 'big four' British commercial banks?
A Abbey National
B National Savings
C Trustee Savings
D Midland
E Co-operative

7 A discount house purchases a £50 000 bill of exchange with 3 months to maturity at a rate of discount of 8 per cent per annum. The purchase price would be in the region of
A £52 000
B £51 000
C £50 000
D £49 000
E £48 000

8 An essential feature of a commercial bank current account is that it entitles the holder to a
A fixed rate of interest
B bank overdraft
C share of the bank's profit
D cheque book
E personal loan

9 The Bank of England can compel or induce commercial banks to cut their lending by any of the following actions EXCEPT
A issuing lending directives
B releasing special deposits
C forcing up interest rates
D open market sales of government securities
E imposing a high reserve assets ratio

10 Which of the following statements provide a valid explanation of the process of credit creation?
1 Banks do not hold all their customers' deposits in the form of cash.
2 Money lent by banks normally returns to banks as new deposits.
3 There is no limit to the volume of bank lending.

A 1 only is correct
B 1 and 2 only are correct
C 2 and 3 only are correct
D 1, 2 and 3 are correct
E 3 only is correct

Data response

An island community is served by a single bank with a balance sheet containing the following items only:

	Currency units (millions)
Cash reserves	2
Other reserve assets	8
Current accounts	20
Deposit accounts	30
Advances	40

1 Distinguish the liabilities and assets and set them out in the form of a conventional bank balance sheet.

2 Calculate (a) the total liabilities, (b) the reserve assets ratio.

3 Suppose that the bank reduces its reserve assets ratio to 10 per cent by granting additional advances to customers while maintaining the same quantity of reserve assets. Calculate (a) the increase in its advances, (b) the resulting total of its liabilities.

4 What would be the motive for the bank's action in Exercise 3 above and why should it be cautious in pursuing it?

5 In what conditions of the island economy might the action be justified?

Essays

1 How do the institutions of the money market help the economy? Explain the role of the money market in the control of the economy.

2 How are the functions and aims of commercial banks reflected in the liabilities and assets listed in their balance sheets?

3 In what respects does the Bank of England both resemble and differ from an ordinary commercial bank?

4 For what reasons and by what methods could the Bank of England act to stimulate spending in the economy?

Chapter 12

The financial network

12.1 The capital market

When firms or the government wish to borrow money for short periods, this is usually done through banks or the money market as described in the preceding chapter. But a loan that has to be paid back quickly is not usually suitable to finance expensive developments such as building new factories or installing costly machines. Businessmen generally meet the cost of such projects either by ploughing back profits they have accumulated in the past or by long-term borrowing through what is called the capital market. The government, local authorities, and nationalized industries are also large borrowers in the market.

New issues

In the case of public joint-stock companies, the normal method of borrowing in the capital market is to issue new stocks or shares for sale to the public. The government can similarly meet the cost of capital projects such as transport developments or power stations by issuing its own stocks. Such new issues should be distinguished from the dealings in 'old' securities which take place in the Stock Exchange.

A company wishing to sell new shares would normally employ the services of a specialist *issuing house* – usually an experienced merchant bank. But first a number of conditions must be met: it would need the approval of the Stock Exchange Council for its shares to be 'quoted'; it would also have to publish a prospectus outlining its financial position and the nature of its business.

When all the conditions are fulfilled, the shares can be advertised for sale by the issuing house. To ensure that all the shares are sold, it may arrange for the issue to be underwritten. This means that it obtains an undertaking from another financial institution to buy up any unsold shares at an agreed price. Alternatively, the issuing house may underwrite the shares itself.

A cheaper method of selling a new issue is by means of a *placing*. Instead of new shares being offered to the public, it is arranged for them to be taken up by a large investor, possibly an institution such as an insurance company, without the formality of a published prospectus. Another fairly common method is to offer new shares to existing shareholders in proportion to the quantity of shares they already hold in the company. This is known as a *rights issue*.

Sources of capital

The funds borrowed in the capital market come from a number of sources including personal investors, the government (when it assists particular firms), the government-backed finance corporations (see page 46), commercial and merchant banks, and a number of financial concerns whose business it is to attract personal savings and mobilize them for profitable investment. The latter group of *institutional investors* are the largest suppliers of funds to the capital markets and they merit further explanation.

1 Investment trusts

Investment trusts are public joint-stock companies whose shares can be bought and sold on the Stock Exchange. With the funds received from their own share issues, they buy a variety of other stocks and shares. They are in fact companies formed not to produce goods themselves but to buy and manage investments in other companies.

Through the trusts, investors with limited funds are able to spread their risks over a wide range of companies. They can also benefit from the expert knowledge of the trust managers who are more likely to know where funds can be put to the most profitable use. Of course, the return obtained from investment trust shares whether in the form of dividends or rising share values depends on the success of its investment policies. Depending on the fortunes of the companies in which the trust invests, shareholders can lose as well as gain.

2 Unit trusts

Though similar to investment trusts, unit trusts are not companies whose shares can be bought and sold in the stock market. They cater for small investors who buy not shares but units of a stated value. The money obtained from the sale of its units is used by the trust to buy stocks and shares in a range of companies. Holders of units can sell them back to the trust at any time for cash. The cash value of units depends on the success of the trust's investments at that time.

3 Insurance companies

These are among the largest suppliers of funds in the capital market. People take out insurance policies to cover themselves financially against risks of many kinds. The main division is into general risks (including fire, theft, accidents, and shipping) and life insurance or assurance. Most companies have policies to cover many types of risks, but some concentrate on life assurance and Lloyds is famous for shipping and general risks. The charge for insurance usually takes the form of a regular payment known as a premium, the size of which obviously depends on a calculation of the risk.

With a regular inflow of premiums, insurance companies are able to accumulate huge funds. As with banks, some of their funds must be held in cash and liquid assets to meet claims on them. However, the bulk is available for investment in stocks and shares, including new issues. The investment policies of the companies are therefore important to the economy and, as shareholders, they are deeply involved in industry and commerce generally. This also applies to the managers of *pension funds* and superannuation schemes holding people's savings for retirement.

4 Building societies

The main business of building societies is to lend to individuals to buy their own houses. They sometimes also lend to firms to buy industrial and commercial premises. Their loans (called mortgages) are generally for long periods of twenty years or more, while their funds come mainly from small savers who can withdraw their money easily when they want it.

People with money in building societies are sometimes called shareholders, but their shares are not dealt with on the Stock Exchange and are much more like deposit accounts with banks. The societies therefore compete with banks for funds and must pay a competitive rate of interest. If banks and other rivals raise their rates, the societies must also pay more to attract and hold their deposits. This forces them to charge higher mortgage rates to their borrowers. By the same reasoning, a general fall in deposit rates should enable them to reduce mortgage rates.

5 Finance houses

Their speciality is to provide hire-purchase finance for sales by shops and other retailers. Thus, when shops make hire-purchase arrangements for their customers, the money is often lent by finance houses. Their funds are obtained largely by issuing shares or attracting deposits, chiefly from other companies including banks. In this way, banks have become involved in hire-purchase business and some large finance houses are owned or controlled by commercial banks.

1 What is the difference between the capital market and the money market?

2 What is a new issue? Note each of the methods that can be used to make such an issue.

3 List the main institutional investors and state how each obtains and uses its funds.

12.2 The Stock Exchange

Stock markets are to be found in a number of provincial centres but the most important by far is the London Stock Exchange. Although a national institution, it is privately owned by its members and controlled by their own elected council.

Members of the Stock Exchange

The membership is traditionally divided into two groups of firms, brokers and jobbers, carrying out distinct functions as outlined below and illustrated in Fig. 12.1. Radical changes, introduced in 1986,

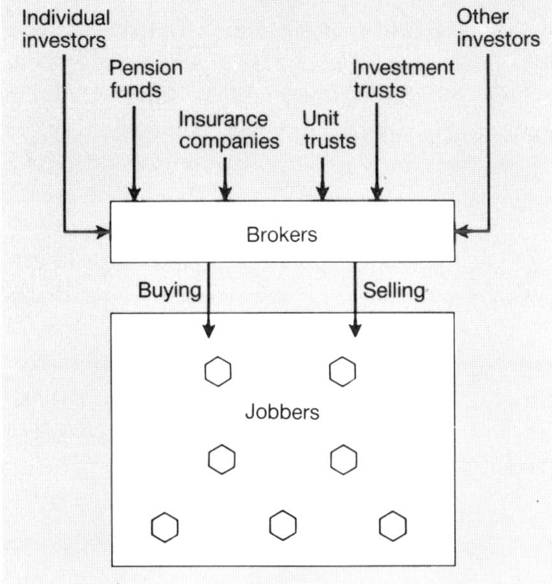

Fig. 12.1 Stock Exchange transactions

include provision for dual capacity, allowing member firms to combine the functions of both brokers and jobbers.

Stockbrokers deal directly with the general public. A person wishing to buy or sell shares on the Stock Exchange cannot do so on his own account. He must obtain the services of a broker who, acting on the instructions of his client, buys from or sells to a jobber. Brokers charge a commission for their services which may include professional advice on what to buy or sell.

Stockjobbers carry out the functions of wholesalers or middlemen, buying shares in order to sell them at a profit. Their selling prices are therefore always higher than their buying prices. The difference between the two prices provides a profit margin known as the jobber's 'turn'. The riskier the share the greater will be this margin. Jobbers tend to specialize in certain types of shares, such as government stock or mining, and they stand in corresponding groups on the floor of the Exchange.

Stock Exchange transactions

Transactions in stocks and shares are undertaken by individual investors, firms such as insurance companies, and institutions such as pension funds (Fig. 12.1). Anyone wishing to buy shares must first contact a broker and instruct him on what he wants, the quantity, and the highest price he is willing to pay. The broker then goes to the group of jobbers who deal in the shares concerned.

Without knowing whether the broker wishes to buy or sell, each jobber will quote two prices, the higher one at which he is prepared to sell and the lower one at which he would buy. The broker is thus able to buy for his client at the lowest price in the market. The process is reversed when a broker sells shares on behalf of his client.

The Stock Exchange provides an example of a perfectly competitive market with professional dealers aiming to get the best possible bargains. Any jobber quoting share prices higher than those of his competitors around him would find himself buying a lot of shares, but not selling them. Becoming overloaded with the shares concerned, he would be forced to bring his prices down to the level of his competitors. This ensures a uniform market price for each share and generally safeguards the interests of Stock Exchange clients.

Stock markets have their own language and those who wish to follow their activities ought to know the terms listed below.

A bull is a person who expects share prices to rise and so tends to buy in the hope of selling later at a profit.

A bear is one who expects share prices to fall and so tends to sell.

Gilt-edged securities are stocks issued by the government, local authorities, and nationalized industries, and therefore regarded as exceptionally reliable investments.

Blue-chips are the shares of large well-known companies which are regarded as sound investments.

Equities are simply the ordinary shares of companies.

Functions of the Stock Exchange

Many millions of securities (stocks and shares) change hands every year as a result of transactions on the Stock Exchange. All leading newspapers publish lists of share prices and their movements are indicated by several index numbers of which the *Financial Times* index is probably the best known. What is achieved by all this activity and how does it help the economy?

Who are these dealers on the floor of the Stock Exchange?

1 A market for securities

The basic function of the Stock Exchange is to provide a market for the purchase and sale of second-hand securities (as distinct from new issues). Anyone who buys company shares or government stock knows that they can be sold for cash at any time in the future. The Stock Exchange thus encourages people to buy stocks and shares, and it brings buyers and sellers together.

Although the Stock Exchange is chiefly a market for second-hand shares, it is possible to introduce a new issue by 'placing' it in the hands of jobbers. Moreover, its activities make it easier for companies to raise funds for expansion through new issues. Individuals and institutions are more willing to take up new issues because they know there is an efficient market where they can be sold for cash at any time. For the same reason, it helps the government and other public authorities to borrow money by issuing stocks.

2 Protection for investors

The value of stocks and shares is affected by the ups and downs of economic life and buying them involves a degree of financial risk. This kind of risk is a part of business and cannot be avoided. But the continuous exchange of money and securities on a large scale also brings the risk of fraud, particularly to small unsuspecting investors, and the Stock Exchange is conscious of its responsibility in this connection. It investigates companies whose shares are quoted, and tries to ensure that the activities of its own members are honest and straightforward. It is also sometimes prepared to compensate the victims of fraud. By providing such safeguards it encourages investors.

3 Stabilization of prices

The constant possibility of large gains or losses on shares makes investors very sensitive to rumours and exaggerations about company prospects. This can result in magnified share price fluctuations as investors rush to buy or sell. Such fluctuations can be disturbing to business confidence and divert funds from where they are most needed. Jobbers who specialize in certain types of shares are less likely to panic over unfounded rumours and so may be prepared to hold shares when others are selling or sell when others are buying. The effect of their actions is then to offset fluctuations and stabilize share prices.

4 An indicator of business prospects

Stock market trends provide a general indication of the health of the economy. They may also reflect the relative strengths of different parts of the economy. In particular, the success of a company is indicated by movements in the price of its shares. A company whose shares are seen to be doing well finds it easier to raise capital through new issues. It is claimed that in this way the Stock Exchange helps to channel funds into the growing areas of the economy.

Criticisms of the Stock Exchange

The functions outlined above are used as arguments to justify the activities of the Stock Exchange. However, not everyone finds them convincing. To some, the concentration on making money appears distasteful and socially unproductive.

A number of specific questions crop up for discussion. Is an organized market for securities really necessary? In view of shady activities exposed from time to time, does the market provide sufficient safeguards against fraud and corruption? To what extent do share price movements reflect all the factors affecting business prospects? Are funds attracted into socially desirable sectors of the economy or rather to where quick profits can be made?

1 Distinguish between the functions of a stockbroker and a stockjobber.

2 Outline the process of buying or selling shares. Explain the distinctions between (a) bull and bear, (b) gilt-edged and blue-chip.

3 Why is the Stock Exchange often given as an example of a perfectly competitive market?

4 The Stock Exchange is chiefly a market in second-hand securities. What does this mean? Why is it important for both industry and the government to have such a market?

5 In what ways does the Stock Exchange seek to serve and safeguard the interests of investors?

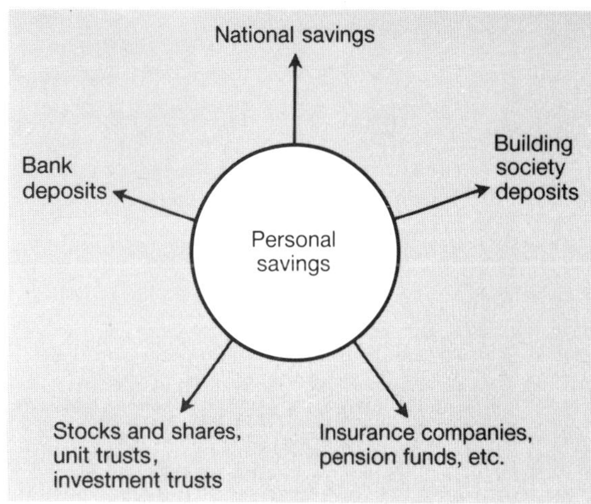

Fig. 12.2 Forms of personal saving

12.3 Personal finance

Saving

The savings of the community come from three main sources: surpluses accumulated by the public sector (that is, the government, local authorities, and nationalized industries); undistributed profits of companies; and the personal savings of individuals. Personal saving has generally accounted for about a quarter of the total.

Encouraging people to save for the future is considered to be good social policy. It also has economic advantages. We have seen how personal saving can be channelled through the various financial institutions into productive investment. In an inflationary period, extra saving also helps to restrain the level of spending. The position is of course reversed in conditions of unemployment when it may be sound economic policy to encourage spending and discourage saving.

The main ways in which people hold their savings are indicated in Fig. 12.2. The difference between bank or building society deposits (earning a fixed rate of interest) and shares or units (affected by business fluctuations) should require no further explanation. There is further information below on life insurance as a form of saving and also the various types of national savings.

Life insurance is a method of regular saving used to give financial protection to one's family or dependants in the event of death. Through an *endowment policy*, it can also be arranged for the sum insured to be paid on reaching a fixed age, so providing a convenient form of saving for later years. Of course, the insurance company charges for taking on the risk of paying on an early death. But it invests the money accumulated from premiums, and it is possible to have a policy with profits whereby a share of the profits from the company's investments is added to the amount due.

National savings comprise various forms of lending to the government, chiefly by small savers. They include deposits with the National Savings Bank (operated through post offices) and Trustee Savings Banks (providing deposit facilities similar to the National Savings Bank), national savings certificates, premium savings bonds (Ernie), index-linked certificates, and the government's Save As You Earn scheme.

By investing in premium bonds, the saver in effect gambles his interest for the chance of a prize. SAYE enables savings to be accumulated through regular deductions from pay packets and offers a high rate

For what purposes might you enter these premises?

of interest if the money is left untouched for five to seven years. The return on index-linked certificates is based on the annual percentage rise in retail prices.

Each form of saving has its own attractions. A person's choice may be influenced by one or more of the following motives: a good rate of interest; avoidance of risk; liquidity or ease of withdrawal in cash; protection against the effect of inflation; other special benefits.

Borrowing

In a society geared to a high level of consumer spending borrowing is undertaken on a large scale by individuals as well as firms. Bank overdrafts, hire-purchase, or other credit facilities are thus widely used to purchase cars, television sets, furniture, and many other consumer durable goods. However, by far the largest personal borrowing transactions are undertaken when people buy houses. With the tendency for both house prices and interest rates to rise, the problems of house purchase have attracted particular attention.

House purchase

1 The price of houses

All prices tend to rise in the long run but house prices have often risen faster and more persistently than prices in general. This trend can be explained by the laws of demand and supply (see Chapter 8.)

The demand for houses has risen steadily with an increasing number of people wishing to own their homes. But the supply of new houses has not kept up with demand due to the limitations of the building industry and the scarcity of building land – particularly in the vicinity of towns where most people work and want to live. Soaring land prices, caused partly by the activities of speculators, have in fact been a large element in the inflation of house prices since the Second World War.

The house buyer is faced with other expenses over and above the price of the house itself. There are solicitors' charges for the legal arrangements, possibly a fee for a surveyor's report on the property, perhaps also the charges of an estate agent, and of course the cost of removal. These are likely to add several hundred pounds to the total expenses.

2 Borrowing the money

House prices are much too high for most people to buy for cash. The normal method is to borrow a large proportion of the purchase price through a loan known as a *mortgage*. The essential feature of a mortgage is that the property itself is the security for the loan and may be forfeited if the loan is not repaid according to the agreement. Repayment of capital and interest is usually by monthly instalments over periods up to thirty years.

A mortgage can sometimes be obtained from a local council. The advantage of a council mortgage is that it might cover the full price of the house and the rate of interest is less likely to be raised when other rates are being put up. Insurance companies and banks also lend for house purchase. But most home owners obtain their mortgage from building societies which specialize in this form of lending.

Insurance

The other major financial institutions with which the average person is likely to come into contact are the insurance companies. We have already referred to them in general terms and also to life insurance as a form of saving. Other types of insurance required by ordinary families include mortgage protection (used to safeguard a family against the loss of the home by covering any mortgage debt outstanding on the death of the bread-winner), household contents (covering loss due to fire or theft), and motor insurance (third party or comprehensive).

1 Assume that you have accumulated savings of £5000. Refer to Fig. 12.2 and say how you would divide the money between the alternatives available. Explain your reasons for selecting or rejecting particular forms of saving.

2 If you decide to buy a house, what steps would you take and what expenses would you expect to meet? Why have house prices generally risen faster than most other prices?

Multiple choice

1 The Stock Exchange is primarily a market in
- **A** new share issues
- **B** bills of exchange
- **C** Treasury bills
- **D** second-hand securities
- **E** foreign currencies

2 Which of the following are recognized functions of a jobber in the Stock Exchange?
1 buying and selling shares
2 quoting prices for shares
3 giving advice to investors
- **A** 1 only is correct
- **B** 1 and 2 only are correct
- **C** 1, 2 and 3 are correct
- **D** 2 and 3 only are correct
- **E** 3 only is correct

3 Which of the following would NOT be claimed as a function of the Stock Exchange?
- **A** providing an effective market for securities
- **B** acting as a barometer of company prospects
- **C** encouraging the public to invest in industry
- **D** protecting investors against fraud
- **E** providing investors with a liquid form of saving

Questions 4-6 refer to the following types of financial institution:
- **A** Finance houses
- **B** Issuing houses
- **C** Unit trusts
- **D** Insurance companies
- **E** Building societies

4 Which institution specializes in hire purchase lending?

5 Which institution caters for small savers wishing to invest in company shares?

6 Which institution provides protection against personal risks?

7 If you want a form of saving that provides both liquidity and regular interest payments, which of the following options would be LEAST attractive?
- **A** national savings certificates
- **B** a bank deposit account
- **C** gilt-edged securities
- **D** a life insurance policy
- **E** company debentures

Data response

Personal financial assets	*Percentage of total*
Life insurance and pension funds	32
Building society shares and deposits	18
Company stocks and shares, etc.	16
Bank deposits	13
National savings and government securities	11
Notes and coin	3
Other	7

1 Draw a chart (e.g. a pie chart) to illustrate the above data.

2 What is the largest component of personal saving? Why do people save in this form?

3 What is the most liquid asset held by the public? Why is it not held in greater quantities?

4 Name two forms of saving particularly attractive to small savers because they combine liquidity with a good rate of interest.

5 Which type of asset would be chosen by someone hoping for a quick profit or capital gain? What are the drawbacks to this use of savings?

6 List the different motives for saving suggested by the preceding questions. Give examples to show how these motives can conflict so that people must determine their priorities in choosing forms of saving.

Essays

1 Outline the institutions that make up the capital market and show how they serve the needs of goverments, firms, and households.

2 Is a stock exchange necessary for the efficient functioning of the economy?

3 The Stock Exchange is often given as an example of a perfectly competitive market, but this is contradicted by its monopoly over share dealings, restricted membership, and divided functions. Examine the operation of the Stock Exchange in the light of this statement.

Chapter 13

Public finance

All those parts of the economy directly controlled by the government are known as the *public sector*. This includes not only the central government in London but also local authorities throughout the country and the nationalized industries. By public finance we mean the financial activities of the public sector. The two main sides of public finance are public expenditure and revenue (chiefly taxation). These two sides are brought together every year in the budget.

13.1 Public expenditure

Growth of public spending

Public expenditure comprises all the spending of central and local government authorities and also government lending to the nationalized industries. The total of public expenditure now accounts for more than 40 per cent of total spending in the economy. This proportion has grown almost continuously since the beginning of the present century when it amounted to about 10 per cent of all spending (Fig. 13.1).

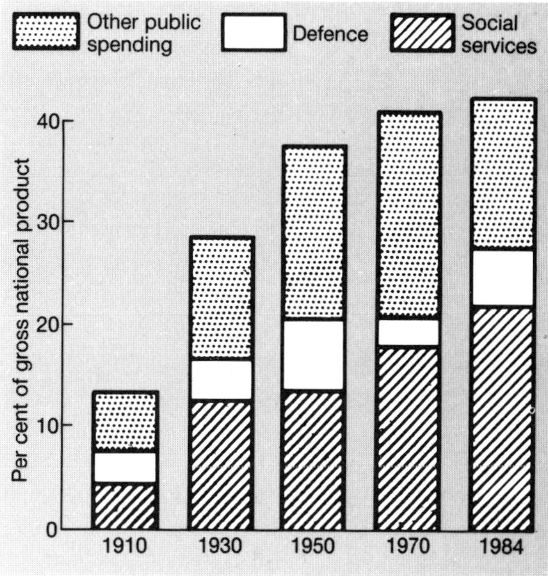

Fig. 13.1 Growth of public spending

The growth of public expenditure is linked with the abandonment of the nineteenth-century doctrine known as *laissez-faire* – the belief that governments should interfere as little as possible in the life of the community apart from maintaining an orderly society and protecting it from foreign aggression. Thus, until about the middle of the last century, government activity was largely restricted to providing a framework of law and justice, conducting foreign relations, administering colonial territories, and providing an adequate army and navy.

Today, the government is held responsible for the general welfare of the people and is expected to concern itself with almost every aspect of their lives. The rapid growth of public expenditure is explained, in particular, by the massive intervention of the government into economic and social affairs.

Classification of public expenditure

A classification useful to economists distinguishes the following broad categories.

i) *Capital spending* on large long-term projects such as the construction of hospitals or motorways. This form of spending is an investment that will benefit future generations. It is commonly financed by borrowing rather than taxation.

ii) *Current spending on goods and services.* This covers the payment of wages or salaries and the cost of materials or supplies necessary to operate existing public services from day to day.

iii) *Transfer expenditure.* This refers to payments such as pensions and unemployment benefits which the government makes out of taxation mainly to those who need special help. Such spending differs fundamentally from the other two categories because it is not 'real' expenditure by the government but rather a method of shifting spending power between members of the community, generally from richer to poorer people. In effect, the government is not itself using productive resources but influencing the private use of resources.

Classification of public services

The main groups of services financed out of public money are outlined below, and the allocation of money between them is indicated in Fig. 13.2.

1 Defence and external relations

Expenditure on external relations includes the cost of maintaining British embassies and consulates in foreign countries, Commonwealth services, aid to developing countries, and contributions to the European Economic Community. However, the bulk of expenditure under this heading is on defence, including the maintenance of equipment of the armed forces and the upkeep of military establishments at home and abroad. Britain's defence spending is high by international standards, accounting for more than 5 per cent of total spending in the economy.

2 Economic services

Governments are nowadays held responsible for the general performance of the economy and the maintenance of full employment. Substantial sums are consequently spent on job creation, grants to agriculture and industry (including assistance to private firms as well as nationalized industries), regional development (particularly in areas of heavy unemployment), industrial research, and so on. Expenditure on some of these items continues to expand though Conservative governments sometimes try to reduce their intervention in the economy.

3 Environmental services

A variety of services can be broadly classified under this heading. They include law and order (including police), fire services, roads and transport, public health services such as sewage and refuse disposal, inspection of foods and drugs and other forms of consumer protection, council housing, and the provision of social amenities such as parks and swimming baths. Many of these community services are provided by local authorities and financed from local rates as well as national taxes.

4 Social services

Expenditure on this category has increased most rapidly since the beginning of the century. Social security, education, health and other personal social services (including care of the old and handicapped) now account for about half of all public spending. Their expansion is connected with the development of the welfare state (see page 156).

Fig. 13.2 Allocation of public money (1984-5)

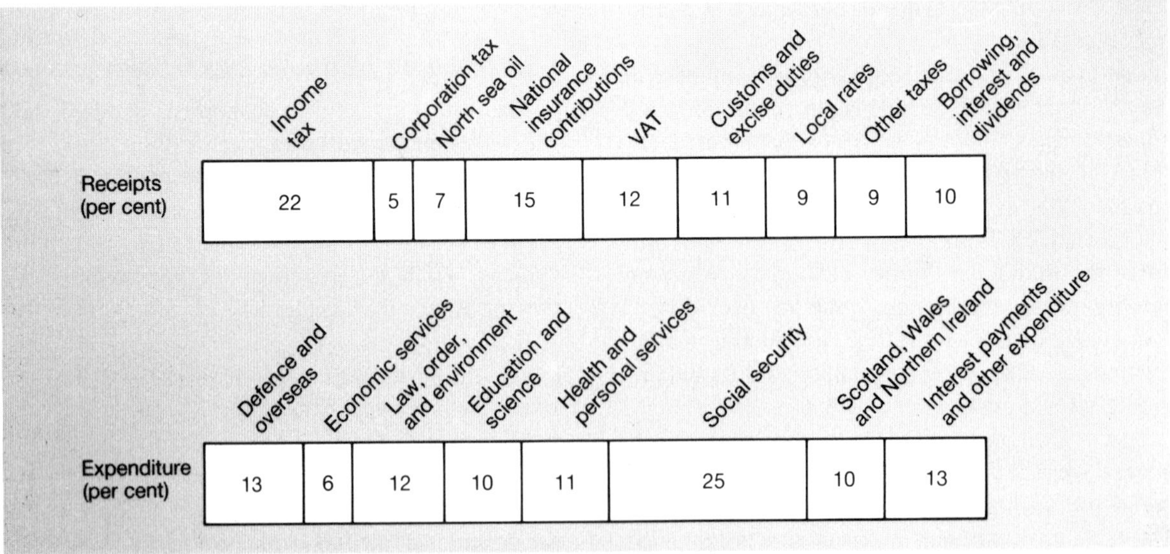

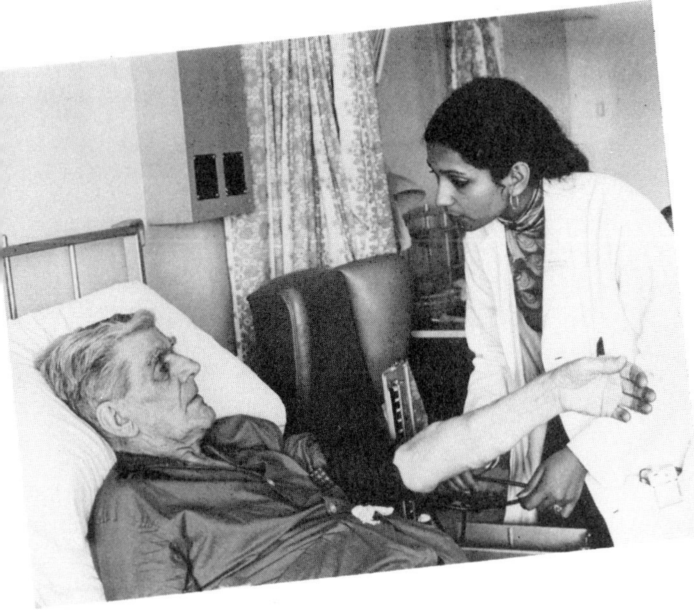

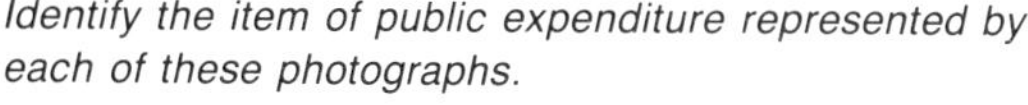

Identify the item of public expenditure represented by each of these photographs.

Control of public spending

There is obviously a limit to the amount that any government can tax and spend. The problems of a government are very largely concerned with determining priorities: how should it allocate the available money between competing claims? Money spent on defence equipment, for instance, means less for schools, hospitals, or roads. The taxpayer wants his money to be used in his best interests. He is also concerned about waste or extravagance.

Plans for public spending are prepared in the first place by the government, but no money can be spent unless it is voted by the House of Commons. Every year, before the budget, the government submits to the Commons detailed estimates of its expenditure for the next twelve months. It also publishes an annual White Paper on public expenditure setting out its programmes for several years ahead.

The Conservative government elected in 1979 pledged itself to reduce the share of the public sector in the economy and cut the total of public spending. Significant reductions were made in a range of programmes including education, housing, transport, and other environmental services. However, defence spending was substantially increased and, with growing unemployment, the cost of social security rose dramatically. In 1985 total public expenditure in *real* terms – that is, allowing for the effect of inflation – was higher than when the government took office.

1 Define public expenditure. Refer to its growth since the beginning of this century and say why it has occurred.

2 Note, with examples, the classification of public expenditure into three economic categories. Explain the difference between current and capital spending and show why it is important to distinguish transfer expenditure from the other two.

3 Note the classification into four main groups of public services, giving examples of each. Refer to Fig. 13.1 and explain the main trends since 1950.

13.2 Taxation

Nearly everyone takes a gloomy interest in taxation because it hits their pockets. But taxation today is more than just a means of extracting money. Before looking at the existing tax structure, we consider some of the motives that influence a Chancellor of the Exchequer in prescribing the tax mixture contained in his budget.

Aims of taxation

1 Financial

Large items of capital expenditure such as new power stations or hospitals are normally financed by borrowing. Some public services are partly financed by particular methods such as the charges for the National Health Service and rents for council houses. But the government relies on taxation for the bulk of its income or revenue.

As public spending has risen so has the need for taxation. In 1984/5 taxation of all kinds (including social security contributions) amounted to about 40 per cent of the gross national product – the total of what we produce and earn as a nation. This puts Britain quite high in international comparisons of taxation.

The first purpose of taxation is clearly financial – to raise the revenue necessary to meet the cost of public services. A hundred years ago, many people would have regarded this as the only purpose. The social and economic possibilities of taxation hardly entered into the calculations of nineteenth-century Chancellors such as Gladstone. Nevertheless, tax changes have always had much more than just financial effects on taxpayers. This fact is recognized by all modern Chancellors in preparing their budgets.

2 Social

Taxation has sometimes been used to discourage the consumption of particular goods because of their harmful effects. A well-known historical example was the tax on gin, originally imposed in the eighteenth century to reduce drunkenness which was then a serious social problem among the working classes. High taxes on tobacco and alcohol are nowadays sometimes justified on similar grounds.

However, taxes on such items are important sources of government revenue, and it is not easy to distinguish social from financial motives. Indeed, Chancellors may be torn between conflicting motives. For instance, a tax that discouraged smoking may be good for the nation's health but not for the government's revenue.

An important modern use of taxation is to achieve a fairer distribution of income and wealth among members of the community. This is done by taxing the rich heavily and using much of the money to help the poor. Such policies are associated with forms of progressive taxation which we examine later.

3 Economic

As we noted earlier, too much spending in the economy can lead to inflation and too little to unemployment. Taxation is a means by which the government can adjust the level of spending. Thus, taxes can be increased if spending is too high or reduced if it is too low. Such policies are explained more fully in connection with the budget at the end of the chapter.

Tax changes are also used to influence particular parts of the economy or achieve particular economic effects. For instance, an industry can be encouraged to invest and expand by means of tax reliefs on its products, protective customs duties, or extra taxes on competing products. Similarly, regional tax concessions are granted as a method of stimulating industry and reducing unemployment in particular areas.

Other specific examples will be given in the following part of the chapter, but economics students should become accustomed to looking at each tax from the point of view of its effects on the economy.

Principles of taxation

In judging taxes, we naturally look at the aims and motives behind them and the extent to which these aims are fulfilled. In addition, there are certain obvious qualities or standards which taxes should achieve as far as possible. As long ago as the eighteenth century, the pioneer economist Adam Smith laid down four canons or principles to which taxes ought to conform. These are still relevant today but must be supplemented by economic considerations which are now important and added as a fifth category below.

1 Certainty

In a democratic society, taxes should be understandable to the taxpayer. There should be clear rules concerning the time, method, and amount of payment. It is a drawback for taxes to be complicated and confusing to those who pay them.

2 Convenience

Taxes should be arranged as conveniently as possible for those who have to pay. This means that the government should take into account the circumstances of the taxpayer. A good example is the system called Pay As You Earn (PAYE) whereby employers deduct income tax weekly or monthly from wages and salaries. There is no trouble in payment and workers cannot run up large tax debts.

3 Economy

A good tax should be easy and cheap to collect. It is obviously wasteful if a large proportion of the revenue from a tax is taken up by the cost of administering and collecting it. Also connected with administration is the principle that a tax should not provide easy loopholes for evasion. This means loss of revenue and injustice to those who pay their due.

4 Equality

The principle that people should be treated equally does not mean that everyone should pay the same amount but that the burden of payment should be equal. The amount a person pays should thus take account of his ability to pay. To Adam Smith, this would be achieved by a proportional tax – one requiring each person to pay the same proportion or percentage of his income. More tax is then paid by those with large incomes. However, attitudes to taxation have changed and most people today would probably not consider that proportional taxation goes far enough towards equalizing the burden at different income levels. We return to this point shortly.

5 Economic effects

Adam Smith was largely concerned with the efficiency and fairness of taxes. Modern economists also look at the effects of different taxes on the economy. From this point of view, two further principles may be added: first, taxes should not damage the economy by discouraging work or production; secondly, it is desirable that taxes should be capable of adjustment to deal with economic problems such as inflation and unemployment. We pursue these aspects further in comparing types of taxation.

Classification of taxes

1 Progressive, regressive, and proportional

Taxes are described as progressive, regressive, or proportional according to whether the rate of tax rises, falls, or remains constant with increases in income or wealth. Table 13.1 illustrates the difference between the three types

With the 10 per cent proportional tax, the poorest of the three taxpayers pays least but would be left with only £900 to spend out of an income of £1000 and is probably deprived of necessities. The burden is thus heavy on low incomes.

Table 13.1 Calculation of different types of taxation

Taxpayer's income	Proportional tax		Progressive tax		Regressive tax	
£	£	%	£	%	£	%
1 000	100	10	100	10	100	10
10 000	1 000	10	2 000	20	500	5
50 000	5 000	10	15 000	30	1 000	2

Progressive taxation is based on the view that, to equalize the burden, richer people should not only pay more but also a larger proportion of their income or wealth in tax.

A tax is said to be regressive when the proportion paid actually falls as wealth or income rises. The table shows that this can occur even if the higher incomes pay more tax. For example, a millionaire cigar smoker may spend more on tobacco and so pay more tobacco tax than the pensioner who rolls his own cigarettes, but the tax will take a smaller proportion of his income and is therefore regressive.

Progressive taxes reduce inequalities of wealth or income while regressive taxes accentuate them. However, in judging the fairness of a tax system one should look at the structure as a whole. The regressive nature of particular taxes may be balanced by the progressive effects of others.

2 *Direct and indirect taxes*

The most common classification of taxes is into these two broad groups (Fig. 13.3).

Direct taxes are charged directly on the taxpayers' income or wealth (capital). They comprise personal income tax, corporation tax (on company profits), capital gains tax, and inheritance tax. A distinguishing feature, in Britain, is that they are all collected by the Board of Inland Revenue.

Indirect taxes are charged on expenditure and normally form part of the prices of goods and services when people buy them. In Britain they are collected by the Customs and Excise Department. They are called indirect because, though they are normally collected from firms, the burden of payment is commonly shifted on to consumers when they make their purchases. The burden of direct taxes cannot usually be shifted to others in this way.

Comparison of direct and indirect taxes

Every tax has its own special advantages and drawbacks but it is useful to make a more general comparison between the two broad categories of direct and indirect taxation. Such a comparison is made in the light of the tax aims and principles already outlined.

1 *Revenue*

Direct taxes are a major source of government revenue in all rich countries with high levels of income. They are not only good for revenue but also the revenue from them is fairly reliable and usually capable of expansion to meet the needs of the government. Thus knowing the level of the national income, the Chancellor can predict with reasonable certainty the amount of money obtainable from any given increase in the rate of income tax.

Indirect taxes can also provide a large revenue but are generally at a disadvantage in this respect. The revenue from a tax on spending depends on how the tax affects the level of spending – in the language of economics, it depends on the elasticity of demand. An increase in the tax on petrol, for example, could actually reduce the revenue if it brought about a large fall in the demand for petrol.

Fig. 13.3 Britain's tax structure

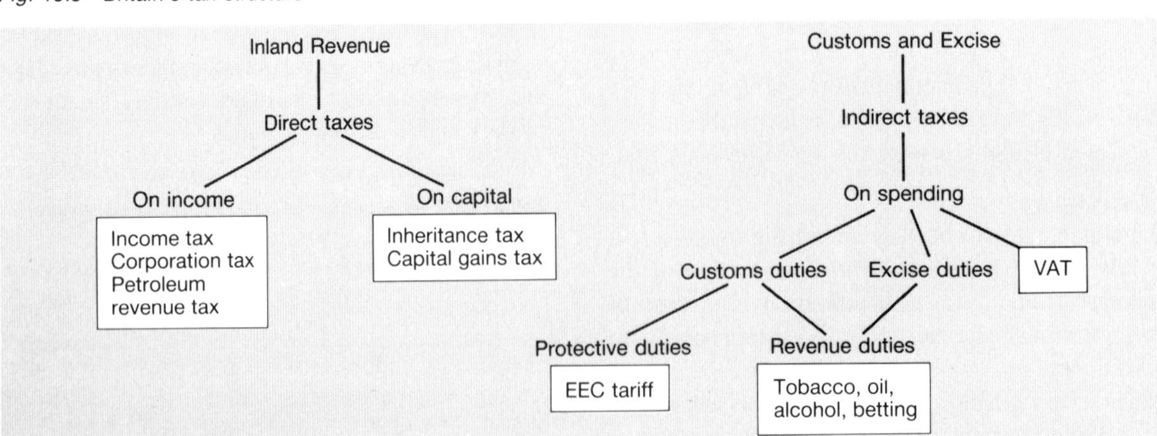

2 Equality

We have seen that direct taxes can be progressive, proportional, or regressive. In Britain, the main direct taxes are clearly progressive. They are designed to equalize the burden of taxation as a whole and bring about a more equal distribution of the national income. Britain's income tax also illustrates how a direct tax can help to equalize burdens by allowing for taxpayers' personal circumstances such as family responsibilities.

Indirect taxes compare unfavourably in this respect. Taxes on spending are likely to be regressive because poorer people necessarily spend a larger proportion (and save a smaller proportion) of household income. In theory, they can be made progressive by concentrating heavily on luxury spending by the rich. But such taxes would not raise much revenue. To raise revenue, the taxes must fall on products that are bought by large numbers of people. A glance at Britain's indirect taxes shows that they are spread widely over products bought by all income groups and so tend to be regressive.

3 Economic aspects

Progressive direct taxes on income and wealth are criticized on the grounds that people are discouraged from working and saving if their earnings from extra work or interest on savings is taxed at a high rate. Similarly, firms may not invest and expand if their profits are heavily taxed. These are called *disincentive* effects. Because of them, it is argued that high direct taxes can hold back production and economic growth.

The disincentive effects of direct taxes may be exaggerated. For instance, it could be argued that if people's earnings are taxed they will work harder or longer in order to avoid a fall in their living standards. However, it is usually believed that very high rates of direct taxation – for example, on overtime earnings – would deter some people from extra work. This could not happen with indirect taxes which hit spending rather than earning or saving.

Economists also look at taxation as a means of controlling our spending, particularly to check inflation. From this point of view, indirect taxes have an important advantage. They can be altered quickly, and their instant effect on prices quickly affects our spending. Changes in direct taxes take longer to bring into operation and do not affect our spending behaviour so rapidly.

However, direct taxes have one great advantage over indirect taxes in dealing with inflation. They do not add to prices and so do not lead to wage demands which aggravate inflation.

4 Administration

Direct taxation tends to be complicated and costly to administer. For example, it often requires elaborate assessments of income or wealth, creating work for both civil servants and taxpayers. In Britain, the collection of income tax is simplified by PAYE but this does not do away with detailed personal assessments. Indirect taxes are usually less complicated and, being collected from firms, cause little inconvenience to taxpayers in general.

Britain's taxes

The main sources of current tax revenue are shown in Fig. 13.3. Nearly every budget brings changes in the structure and rate of taxation. Many taxes need annual adjustment merely to keep revenue in line with inflation and compensate for the falling value of money – a process known as *indexation*. In the pattern outlined below, all tax rates are for the purpose of illustration and subject to annual revision.

1 Income tax

Income tax is a progressive tax on earnings or other incomes above a minimum level or threshold. The threshold is determined by a system of *personal allowances*. In 1986/7, for example, the allowance stood at £3655 for a married couple and £2335 for a single person. Additional allowances could be claimed for dependants and certain other expenses. Taxable income – that is, above the threshold – was taxed at a basic rate of 29 per cent, rising in steps to the maximum of 60 per cent on income levels exceeding £41 200 (Fig. 13.4).

An annual assessment of income is made for every taxpayer. To simplify collection, employers are required to deduct income tax from wages or salaries before payment. This arrangement is called Pay As You Earn (PAYE). The self-employed, and others not subject to PAYE, make their payments direct to the Board of Inland Revenue.

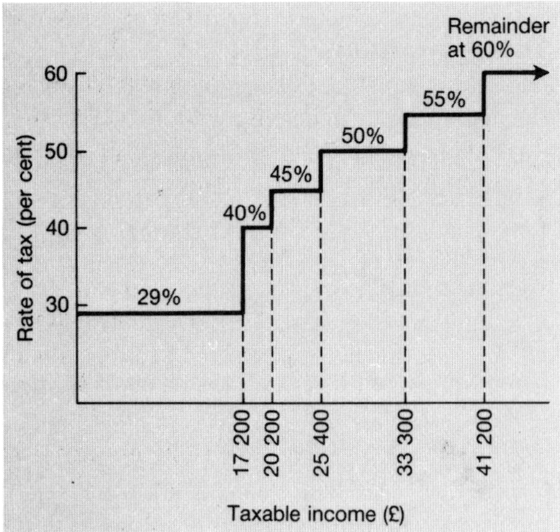

Fig. 13.4 Income tax progression (1986-7)

2 Corporation tax

Companies are taxed at a uniform rate on all profits whether distributed to shareholders or retained as company reserves. The 1984 budget provided for a phased reduction of the standard rate of corporation tax from a current rate of 52 per cent to 35 per cent in 1986. The profits of North Sea oil companies are also subject to a *petroleum revenue tax* which is additional to corporation tax.

3 Inheritance tax

This was introduced in the 1986 budget to replace capital transfer tax which used to be charged on large transfers of personal wealth either at death or during lifetime. Inheritance tax does not apply to lifetime gifts and reverts to an earlier form of estate duty payable at time of death only. It thus becomes a tax that is avoidable by making lifetime transfers of wealth to heirs. The rate of tax rises progressively from 30 to 60 per cent on property valued above an exemption limit of £71 000. Transfers made within seven years of death will be taxed at a diminishing rate.

4 Capital gains tax

This tax is charged at a uniform rate (30 per cent) on profits made from the purchase and sale of stocks and shares and other forms of property excluding owner-occupied houses. Of course, it is also possible to have capital losses but these can be offset against gains to reduce the tax in any year.

5 Customs and excise duties

Customs duties are taxes on imports or goods brought into the country. Excise duties are taxes on goods produced within the country. Both are therefore indirect taxes on spending.

Customs duties are of two kinds: some are *protective* duties designed to shield home industries from foreign competition. During the slump of the 1930s, Britain adopted protective duties (tariffs) for a wide range of industrial products. Membership of the EEC means the removal of such duties against other member countries but brings Britain within the *common external tariff* surrounding the Common Market as a whole. Other customs duties are called *revenue* duties because they have no protective purpose and are merely intended to raise money. They are either on goods not produced at home or balanced by an equal excise duty on the home products.

The principal customs and excise revenue duties are on tobacco, alcoholic drinks, and petrol and other oils. These products are all bought in large quantities and their consumption does not fall significantly when their prices rise—that is, their demand is inelastic. They are consequently reliable sources of government revenue and Chancellors frequently resort to them when they need more money. Excise duties on betting and vehicle licences also provide substantial amounts of revenue.

6 Value added tax

VAT was adopted as an indirect tax throughout the Common Market and introduced in Britain in 1973. It is charged on the value added to products when they pass from one firm to another at successive stages in their production.

Table 13.2 shows three stages in the production of an article and assumes a value added tax of 10 per cent. You should be able to follow the steps by which the tax is passed on in the selling price at each stage until it reaches the consumer in the retail price.

In practice, each firm pays Customs and Excise the full VAT on its output but claims back the tax already paid on its purchases from other firms. Thus, in Table 13.2 the manufacturer pays £40 (output tax) but claims back the £10 (input tax) paid at the primary stage. The consumer, at the end of the line, cannot claim back or pass on the tax and so pays the full 10 per cent on the final product.

Table 13.2 Calculation of VAT

Stage	*Buying price* £	+	*Value added* £	+	*10 per cent VAT* £	=	*Selling price (including VAT)* £
1 Primary producer	0		100		10		110
2 Manufacturer	110		300		30		440
3 Retailer	440		100		10		550
			500*		50†		

*Total value added †Total VAT

VAT applies broadly to most goods and services with exceptions for a limited number of items such as food, fuel, and educational services. Its wide coverage makes it good for revenue, and Chancellors have already found it a useful means of regulating the level of spending in the economy. It was originally charged at a single rate, but a higher rate was later introduced for electrical appliances and other 'less essential' consumer goods. In 1979 it was restored to a single rate fixed at 15 per cent. However VAT is a regressive tax on spending and also puts a heavy load of administration on many businesses.

1 Show, with examples, how taxation is used to achieve financial, social, and economic aims.

2 Note and briefly explain Adam Smith's four principles of taxation. What further principles would now be added by economists?

3 Explain the distinction between (a) progressive, regressive, and proportional taxes, (b) direct and indirect taxes.

4 Compare the merits of direct and indirect taxation from the viewpoints of raising revenue, promoting equality, achieving economic aims, and costs of administration.

5 Under the heading *Britain's taxes*:
   (a) Draw Fig. 13.4.
   (b) Describe the main features of income tax.
   (c) Write a sentence each on corporation tax, capital gains tax, and inheritance tax.
   (d) Describe the features of VAT.
   (e) Explain why the taxes on tobacco, alcohol, and oil are called revenue duties and why these items are particularly selected for taxation.

13.3 The budget

The budget speech

In March or April each year the Chancellor of the Exchequer delivers his budget speech to a crowded House of Commons. The interest of most people is aroused by the possibility of tax changes. But the budget is much more than an announcement of taxes for the year. It provides a statement of the government's financial position for the year ending in March. It indicates the financial and economic prospects for the year beginning in April. It explains the government's social and economic objectives, as well as its proposals for taxation, over the next twelve months.

The budget and the economy

The growth of government spending and taxation has helped to make the budget a key factor influencing the behaviour of the economy. The economic aspects of the budget have thus become increasingly important. The parliamentary debate on the budget has become largely a debate on the government's economic policy, and the Chancellor himself is no longer merely a minister of finance but the minister responsible for the national economy as a whole.

Right up to the Second World War, the main aim of Chancellors in preparing their budgets was to balance the government's revenue with its expenditure. Today, the purpose of the Chancellor is not to balance the government's accounts but to achieve the correct balance of the economy as a whole. This is achieved when total spending (including the government's) is just about equal to the value of the nation's output with all its resources employed. For

What might the Chancellor of the Exchequer, Nigel Lawson, hope to achieve through his budget?

this purpose, he may deliberately avoid a balanced budget and aim at either a surplus or a deficit in the accounts.

A budget surplus is achieved when the revenue from taxation exceeds government expenditure. In effect, the budget is then taking more money out of the economy than it is putting in, and so reducing the total level of spending. This makes sense when too much spending is causing inflation. Reverse the reasoning and you will see why a budget deficit–with the government spending more than it is raising in taxation–is the correct policy in conditions of deflation and unemployment (Fig. 13.5).

The Chancellor's aim must be to achieve a total level of spending high enough to provide jobs for everyone but not so high that it causes serious inflation. This is the elusive goal of full employment combined with stable prices.

Of course, it is difficult to foresee the behaviour of the economy, and the judgement contained in the

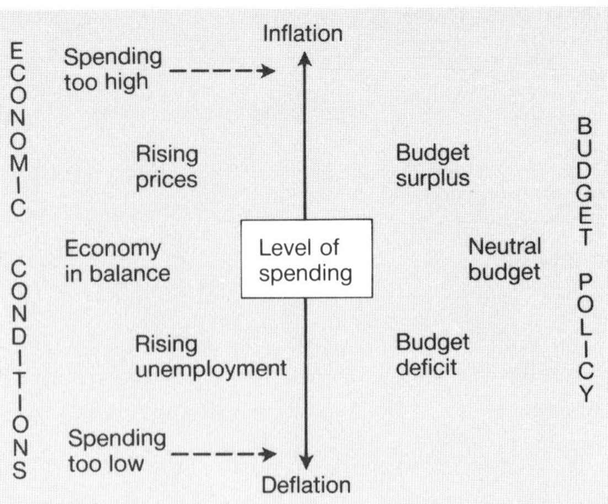

Fig. 13.5 Management of the economy

budget may prove wrong. If serious inflation or unemployment develops between annual budgets, it is possible for the Chancellor to introduce a supplementary budget or mini-budget. He also has the power to alter the rate of VAT and some other indirect taxes between budgets.

Some people believe that tax adjustments should be made whenever required and the ritual of an annual budget is unnecessary. However, it does provide an opportunity for Parliament and the country to focus attention on the government's financial policies and the working of the economy.

1 When and where does the Chancellor of the Exchequer make his main budget speech, and what does it contain?

2 What is (a) a budget surplus, (b) a budget deficit? Explain why the Chancellor may want a deficit at a time of high unemployment but would prefer a surplus to check inflation.

13.4 Local government finance

Local councils are responsible for over a quarter of all public spending, providing major public services such as education, police, roads, and housing. Councils also provide a variety of environmental services (water, drainage, parks, etc.) and personal social services such as the care of old people and the physically handicapped. Fig. 13.6 indicates how money is allocated between the services and where it is obtained.

Sources of local revenue

1 Rates

Rates are the established form of local taxation in Britain and the main independent source of council revenue. We consider them separately below.

2 Government grants

Grants from the central government have grown to be the largest source of local revenue partly because of the inadequacy of rates but also because major local services such as police and education are of national importance and carried out by local authorities as agents of the government. Some of the grants are allocated to *specific* services – for example, a grant of 50 per cent of police expenditure. But the bulk consists of a block grant, called the *rate support grant*, which each local authority can use in the way it chooses.

The rate support grant takes into account the needs and resources of different areas and so poor authorities receive more than the rich. In this way, the central government helps to secure uniform standards throughout the country. Grants are also a means of central control since they can be held back if the government is not satisfied with local policies or standards of service.

3 Other income

Income is obtained from council house rents and a variety of fees or charges which local authorities make for providing facilities such as swimming baths, car parks, public transport, entertainments, and so on. These revenues are generally used up in meeting the cost of the facilities concerned.

4 Loans

Borrowing is the normal method of meeting capital expenditure such as the building of schools and housing estates. Local authorities may borrow from the central government or independently – for example, by issuing their own stocks. But all large capital projects requiring loans must have the approval of the government.

The rating system

The rate is a tax on land and buildings paid by the occupiers of houses and other premises within a local government area. There are exemptions for certain types of property including agricultural land. The determination of the local rate involves a number of distinct steps outlined below.

1 Calculating the rate

i) In the first place, each property is given a *rateable value*. This is based on the estimated annual rent that the property is worth taking into account its size, structure, and location. Properties throughout the country are valued at intervals of five or more years by officials of the Board of Inland Revenue.

ii) From the rateable values of all properties within

Fig. 13.6 Local revenue and spending (1982-3)

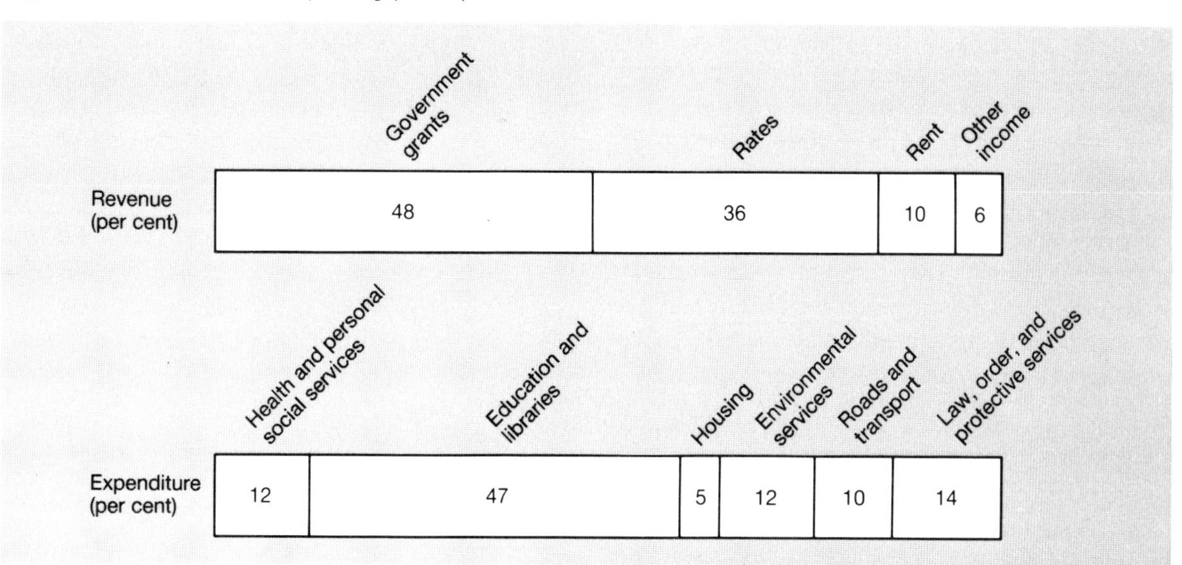

its boundaries, the local authority calculates the total rateable value of the area.
iii) Before each financial year, the authority makes estimates of its total expenditure on services of all kinds. Allowing for government grants and other incomes, it can then estimate the total cost to be met out of rates.
iv) The authority fixes the rate in the pound necessary to raise the required amount of revenue. For example, if the total rateable value of the area is £10 million and it needs to raise £5 million from the rates, a rate of 50p in each pound of rateable value will bring in the required amount. This is called the *rate poundage*. It is charged uniformly on the rateable value of all properties in the area. A property of rateable value £200 will thus pay £100 in rates.

2 Criticisms of rates

As a form of taxation, rates have certain obvious advantages to local authorities. They are easy to collect, difficult to evade, and provide an exceptionally reliable source of income.

Yet rates are among the least popular of all taxes. First, they are regressive: they take a larger proportion of the incomes of poorer households; they bear heavily on large families requiring most accommodation; they tend to be highest in poor areas where rateable values are relatively low and the cost of social services is usually high. Secondly, they discourage home improvements which add to the rateable values. Thirdly, because rateable values are fixed for a period of five years or longer, rate revenue does not expand automatically during periods of inflation and so councils are forced to raise rate poundages almost every year to meet the rising costs of their services.

The criticisms have led to proposals for various alternatives such as a local income tax. But every alternative has its own defects. Meanwhile, the inequalities and hardships created by rates are softened by the system of government grants and also special reliefs available to poor ratepayers.

1 Note the main services on which local councils spend their money, indicating roughly the percentage of their total spending on each (Fig. 13.6).

2 Note the main sources of local government revenue and the approximate percentage of the total from each (Fig. 13.6). In what ways and for what reasons do local councils receive financial aid from central government?

3 Note the definition of the local rate. On what is the rateable value of a property based? Show how the rate is annually determined by calculating (a) the rate poundage fixed in an area where the total rateable value is £50 million and the council requires £40 million revenue from the rates, (b) the payment on a property of £300 rateable value.

4 On what grounds can it be argued that rates should be replaced by a local income tax or some other alternative?

13.5 The welfare state

Development of social services

Until the nineteenth century governments hardly concerned themselves with social matters and the welfare of each individual was seen as his own concern. The extension of voting rights during the nineteenth century brought pressure on governments to carry out social reforms. These included Acts to control working conditions in mines and factories, the introduction of free and compulsory education, and the creation of a public health system. The structure of local government was reorganized at the end of the century for the purpose of administering the new social services.

The growth of modern social services was largely due to two reforming governments, the Liberals before the First World War and Labour following the Second World War. The Liberal reforms included the introduction of pensions and the beginning of the system of national insurance. The main social reforms of the post-war Labour government related to social security, national insurance, and the National Health Service.

These reforms laid the foundations of the welfare state – a society that looked after its citizens 'from the cradle to the grave'. We can judge the accuracy of this description by considering the main areas of social policy.

Social security

The system of social security is designed to provide a safety net of financial support for those members

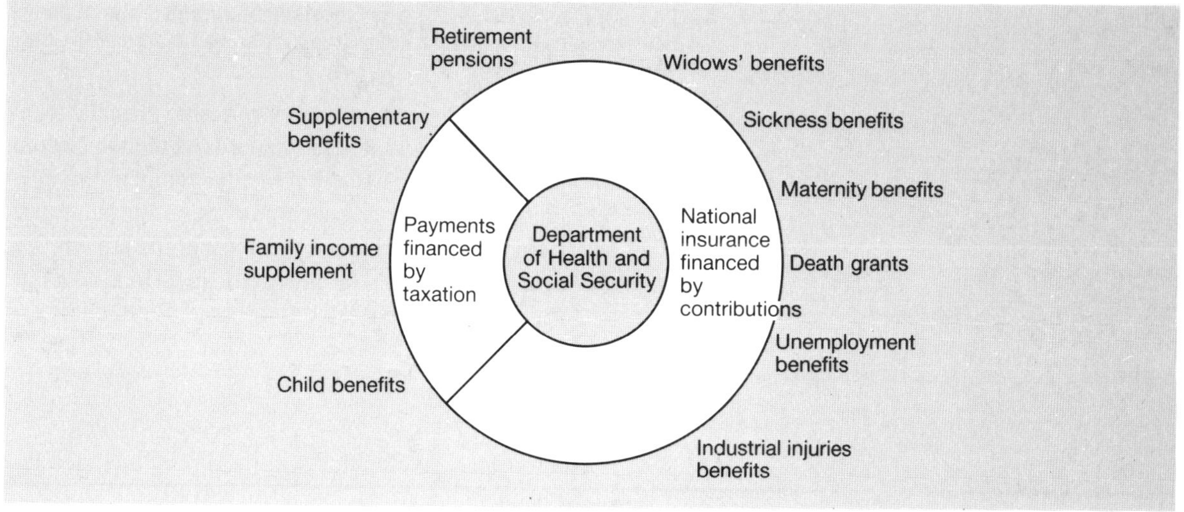

Fig. 13.7 Social security payments

of the community who cannot support themselves. It does this through a comprehensive network of payments or benefits covering the various causes of financial hardship (Fig. 13.7).

A number of the principal benefits come under the scheme of national insurance. This means that the cost is largely met from insurance contributions, and people only qualify to receive the benefits concerned by paying the required contributions. However, other benefits are financed entirely from general taxation and extend to people who are not covered by national insurance.

1 *National insurance*

The National Insurance Acts apply to everyone between school-leaving and retirement ages. The largest group of contributors are employed persons for whom contributions are paid by their employers as well as themselves. Employees' contributions are deducted from earnings, like income tax, at a fixed percentage rate.

The main national insurance benefits cover unemployment, sickness, maternity confinements, industrial injuries (during work), and retirement and widows' pensions. There are also lump sum death grants (to help with burials and cremations) and payments for childbirth. It has become normal practice for the main social security benefits to be annually raised to keep up with inflation.

2 *Other benefits*

Supplementary benefits are paid to people who need financial help and either do not qualify through the national insurance scheme or whose needs are not adequately covered by insurance benefits. A large number of retired persons, for example, rely on supplementary benefits in addition to the basic pension. But the benefits have to be individually claimed and depend on a means test involving a detailed inquiry into personal circumstances. The level of supplementary benefits has come to be regarded as the official 'poverty line'.

Child benefits are paid in respect of children under 16 (and full-time students up to 19). They are paid through post offices and normally go to the mother.

Family income supplement is an additional payment which can be claimed by families whose incomes are below a certain level.

The National Health Service

The creation of the health service in 1946 was a major landmark in the development of the welfare state. Its purpose was to make medical treatment freely available to every person in the country without need for insurance contributions or financial conditions of any kind.

A system of charges was subsequently introduced for prescriptions, dental treatment, spectacles, and

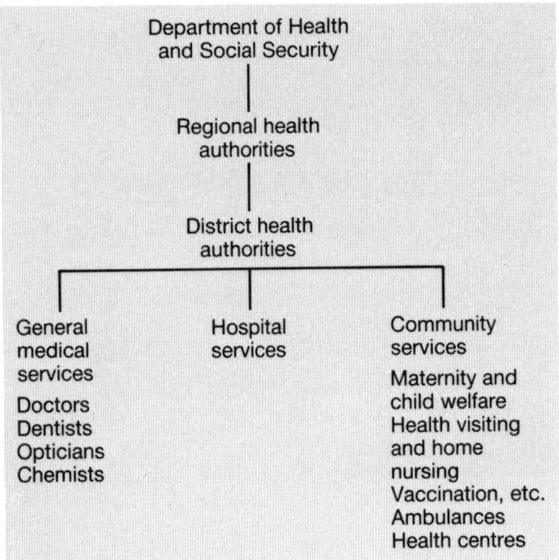

Fig. 13.8 The National Health Service

some other items. But there are exemptions for groups such as pensioners, school children, and those dependent on social security. The bulk of the cost continues to be met from general taxation, and the services of hospitals and doctors are still entirely free.

The main branches of the National Health Service are shown in Fig. 13.8. Though the service is available to everyone, some people prefer to pay personally for medical consultation and treatment. Doctors are thus allowed to have private practices and hospital beds are made available for private fee-paying patients or those covered by private insurance schemes. This raises controversial questions for discussion. Should each person have the right to buy his own medical treatment? Does it lead to preferential treatment to the disadvantage of health service patients?

Housing

Britain contains about 20 million dwellings – flats, houses, maisonettes, and bungalows. About 60 per cent are owned by their occupiers. About 20 per cent belong to councils and the remainder are mostly rented from private landlords. The number of owner-occupiers has risen rapidly, partly due to the Conservative government policy of selling council houses to their tenants. At the same time, there has been a persistent housing shortage and many councils have long waiting lists of families in need of accommodation.

Encouragement of home ownership through council house sales is generally approved though Labour party policy stresses the need to maintain an adequate stock of rented accommodation for those who cannot afford to buy. Poor households are entitled to a housing subsidy in the form of rent and rate reliefs on a scale related to income. Rate reliefs are also available to owner-occupiers.

Education

Important developments in the 1970s included the raising of the school leaving age to 16 and the extension of the comprehensive system – eliminating selection at 11 plus – to most state secondary schools. The high cost of education has made it a prime target for public expenditure cuts in the 1980s. Also controversial is the government policy of encouraging the private sector by financing 'assisted places' in independent or private schools.

Attitudes to the welfare state

Some people still criticize the whole idea of the welfare state. It is accused of encouraging laziness as opposed to independence and self-reliance. However, few would deny the duty of a civilized community to look after its weakest members, and the social responsibility of governments is now widely recognized. All the main British political parties accept the idea of the welfare state though there is disagreement on important matters of finance and strategy.

There has been concern over the rising costs of social services and the resulting burden on taxpayers. This feeling is strong in the Conservative party and explains policies such as the extension of health charges and withdrawal of the general housing subsidy. The aim is to make people pay more directly for the services they use. At the same time, means-tested exemptions or reliefs are given to those who cannot afford to pay.

Underlying the controversy over charges is an important difference of attitude. Labour generally supports the principle of *universality* – that the main facilities and benefits of the welfare state should be available to everyone without conditions attached. Conservatives have argued for *selectivity*–concentrating taxpayers' money on helping those in greatest need. Thus, assistance to families is given through the means-tested family income supplement rather than a general increase in family benefits.

Arguments for selectivity are that it relieves the tax burden, concentrates on those in real need, and encourages others to help themselves. Its opponents emphasize the objections to means tests and the problem of 'take-up' or how to ensure that those in need actually claim and receive the benefit to which they are entitled.

A difference of approach is also apparent, since 1980, in Conservative government support for the *privatization* of activities such as hospital cleaning and laundry services–by contracting work out to private firms. In the field of retirement pensions, government proposals issued in 1985 aim at encouraging private pension arrangements while modifying the benefits of the state earnings-related pension scheme (SERPS) introduced by the preceding Labour government.

1 Make a list of the benefits that a person might obtain from the welfare state during his lifetime 'from the cradle to the grave'.

2 Do you agree or disagree with the view that the welfare state is too generous and that taxation is consequently too high? Explain your attitude.

Multiple choice

1 All the following statements are true except
- A Income tax is the largest source of government revenue.
- B Social services form the largest item of government expenditure.
- C Rates are the largest source of local government revenue.
- D Education is the largest item of local government expenditure.
- E Direct taxes provide more government revenue than indirect taxes.

2

Income	*Tax payable*
£1000	£100
£2000	£150
£10 000	£500

The above figures illustrate
- A a progressive tax
- B a regressive tax
- C a proportional tax
- D an indirect tax
- E none of the above

3 Which of the following measures is most likely to reduce general unemployment?
- A reducing government expenditure and increasing taxation
- B reducing the supply of money in the economy
- C discouraging bank lending and raising the rate of interest
- D reducing taxation and increasing government spending
- E a budget surplus

4 Indirect taxes tend to be regressive because
1. rich people spend more than poor people
2. poor people spend more than rich people
3. poor people save a smaller proportion of income than rich people

- A 1 only is correct
- B 1 and 2 only are correct
- C 1, 2 and 3 are correct
- D 2 and 3 only are correct
- E 3 only is correct

5 Which of the following would be identified as a transfer payment under the classification of public expenditure?
- A road maintenance
- B construction of a hospital
- C salaries of civil servants
- D unemployment benefits
- E the cost of a military aircraft

6 Money used to pay for local government services can come from
   1 national taxes
   2 local rates
   3 borrowing

   A 1 only is correct
   B 1 and 2 only are correct
   C 1, 2 and 3 are correct
   D 2 and 3 only are correct
   E 3 only is correct

7 Which of the following is NOT classified as a form of direct taxation?
   A corporation tax
   B inheritance tax
   C excise duties
   D national insurance contributions
   E income tax

8 A government might reduce the pressure of demand-pull inflation in the economy by reducing
   1 taxation
   2 the budget deficit
   3 public expenditure

   A 1 only is correct
   B 1 and 2 only are correct
   C 1, 2 and 3 are correct
   D 2 and 3 only are correct
   E 3 only is correct

Data response

Central government revenue

	£ billion	
	1975/6	*1984/5*
Income tax	17·4	33·8
Other direct taxes	3·4	10·1
VAT	3·9	18·0
Oil, tobacco and alcohol	5·5	14·2
Other indirect taxes	1·2	3·5
Miscellaneous revenues	2·4	9·8
Total revenue	33·8	89·4

1 Why does total tax revenue increase?

2 Calculate the percentage of total revenue obtained from income tax in each year and comment on the change.

3 What is a direct tax? Name three direct taxes not specifically included in the table.

4 What is an indirect tax? Which indirect tax has provided the most expanding source of revenue?

5 How do excise duties (on oil, tobacco, and alcohol) differ in character from VAT? Why are those products specifically selected as sources of revenue?

6 Estimate the approximate percentages of total revenue derived from direct and indirect taxes respectively in each year. Comment on the change in the balance between them and indicate (a) the government's motive in changing that balance, (b) whether the change is likely to have made the tax system more or less progressive.

Essays

1 With reference to particular categories of government expenditure and taxation, show how both sides of public finance can be used to either reduce or increase inequalities of income and wealth.

2 Compare the features of VAT and income tax and discuss whether it is desirable to reduce income tax by increasing VAT.

3 Why and how does central government contribute to the cost of local government? Should we abolish local rates and meet the whole cost of local government from national taxation?

Chapter 14

International trade

14.1 The theory of trade

In Chapter 3 (on the division of labour) we saw how people specialized in their work, and in Chapter 6 (on the location of industry) how areas of the country and consequently their inhabitants specialized in particular industries. International trade is an extension of the same principle of specialization to countries. However, national frontiers create special problems, such as the existence of different currencies and customs barriers, which make it necessary to treat trade between countries as a separate topic.

Advantages of trade

1 Variety of products
Trade enables countries to obtain products they cannot produce for themselves. For example, Britain obtains food products such as rice and tropical fruits which could not be grown in quantity at home. Similarly, some of the raw materials essential to British industry are not available in this country. Until North Sea oil became available, every motorist relied on trade.

In any case, foreign products widen our range of choice in all sorts of things. An enlightening exercise is to think of all the things we consume which either come from abroad or contain materials from abroad.

2 International co-operation
In the past, trade rivalry has sometimes been a cause of international conflict. But trade makes countries more dependent on each other, and recent experience suggests that it now leads to co-operation rather than conflict. Evidence of this is seen in the growth of trading alliances and the creation of international organizations to promote trade and break down the barriers to trade.

3 Economic efficiency and growth
The development of export markets stimulates production and enables a country's industries to obtain economies of large-scale production. Competition from foreign products may also act as a stimulus to home industries to become more efficient. Greater efficiency means lower costs of production, which can give home consumers the benefit of lower prices. Competition from abroad also helps to keep prices down by reducing the possibility of monopoly.

4 The advantage of specialization
The main advantage of trade is that it enables each country to specialize in the products for which its resources are most suited. It can export these products in exchange for the specialist products of other countries. Such specialization and exchange enable the trading countries to improve their living standards through greater output and lower costs of production. We must examine more closely how this comes about.

Specialization and trade

The gains from specialization and trade are illustrated in Table 14.1 by an example using two countries and two products. For simplicity, we assume that the two countries are neighbouring islands of equal population called Northland and Southland and they can both produce rice and coal.

Position 1 shows how much each island could produce if all its workers were employed in either the rice fields or the coal mines. Thus, Northland can produce either 20 tonnes of rice or 10 tonnes of coal. If it divided its workers equally between the two products it would get 10 tonnes of rice and 5 tonnes of coal. But it could also produce other combinations on the basis that it can always obtain an extra 2 tonnes of rice at a cost of 1 tonne of coal. (Economists call this the opportunity cost of a

Table 14.1 Gains from trade

			Weekly production (tonnes)		
			Rice		*Coal*
1	Production possibilities:	Northland	20	or	10
		Southland	4	or	8
2	Combinations under self-sufficiency:	Northland	12	+	4
		Southland	2	+	4
3	Production under specialization:	Northland	20		
		Southland			8
4	Effect of trade— 4 coal for 4 rice:	Northland	16	+	4
		Southland	4	+	4

product – that is, the cost in terms of other products that could be produced with the same resources.) For instance, it can produce 12 tonnes of rice and 4 tonnes of coal. Southland can similarly produce a range of combinations within its much lower production possibilities at a cost of 2 tonnes of coal for every 1 tonne of rice.

Position 2 shows the combination of the two products that each island would produce for itself on the assumption that each wants 4 tonnes of coal for fuel and would use its remaining manpower for rice.

Positions 3 and 4 show the consequences of specialization and trade. Although the figures show that Northland is superior in both products, its advantage over Southland is clearly greater in rice than in coal since it can produce five times as much rice but only one and a quarter times as much coal as Southland. Northland thus specializes in rice and Southland in coal. It can be seen that by trading 4 tonnes of rice for 4 tonnes of coal, each is better off (position 4) than under self-sufficiency (position 2). In fact, total production of both goods is greater than under self-sufficiency (position 2).

Our illustration shows that both countries gain from trade even though one (Northland) has an absolute advantage over the other in both products. It specializes in the product (rice) in which it has the greater comparative advantage while the other country (Southland) specializes in the product (coal) in which its comparative disadvantage is smaller. The case for specialization and trade presented in this way is called *the principle of comparative costs*.

The case for trade is even clearer if each country has an absolute advantage in different products – for example, if Southland's production possibilities were 20 tonnes of coal or 10 tonnes of rice. A further possibility is that of enforced specialization – for example, if Northland could produce only rice and Southland only coal. Trade is then the only means by which both countries can obtain both products.

Limits to specialization

In spite of the benefits, countries do not specialize completely. Britain, for example, produces some of its own food as well as the manufactured goods in which it specializes. This can be explained in a number of ways.

i) Foreign supplies may be insufficient to meet all our needs.

ii) Governments may consider it undesirable to rely entirely on imports of certain goods such as food and essential materials. A home supply of such products could be vital in a war or other emergency.

iii) Transport costs may outweigh the advantages of specialization and trade, particularly in the case of heavy or bulky goods.

iv) A country may produce a limited quantity of certain products very efficiently and cheaply, but additional supplies may be better obtained from abroad. For example, Britain could grow more wheat for itself but only by extending cultivation to less fertile land at a cost greater than that of imported wheat.

Terms of trade

The amount of benefit a country obtains from trade depends on the terms on which it buys from and sells to other countries – in other words, the relationship between import and export prices. Index numbers for both sets of prices are calculated monthly on similar lines to the retail price index described earlier. *The terms of trade show the export index as a percentage of the import index.*

$$\text{Terms of trade} = \frac{\text{Export index number}}{\text{Import index number}} \times 100$$

For example, the figure for August 1984 was

$$\frac{138.3}{142.7} \times 100 = 96.9$$

Table 14.2 UK terms of trade

Year	Export index	Import index	Terms of trade
1980	100·0	100·0	100·0
1981	108·8	108·1	100·7
1982	116·2	116·7	99·6
1983	125·7	127·5	98·6
1984	136·0	139·5	97·5

Table 14.2 shows recent movements of the index numbers concerned. The fall from 1981 was largely due to rising import prices associated with the downward float of sterling.

A rise in the terms of trade figure indicates that the general level of export prices has risen relatively to import prices. Such a movement is referred to as an improvement in the terms of trade. It means that a given quantity of exports will buy a larger quantity of imports. A reduction in the terms of trade figure is described as unfavourable because it means that the same amount of exports now exchanges for less imports.

However, it must not be assumed that a country always gains from an improvement in its terms of trade or loses from a worsening of the terms. Much depends on the causes of the movement. For instance, inflation raises export prices and so improves the terms of trade but is also likely to reduce the volume of exports and cause unemployment. Conversely, greater industrial efficiency, reducing the costs and prices of exports, would worsen the terms of trade but boost export volume and the economy in general. Both the terms of trade and the economy would benefit from increased world demand for our exports (raising their prices) or increased world supply of our imports (reducing their prices).

Restrictions on trade

In spite of the advantages of trade, most countries put some restrictions on imports with the effect of reducing the total amount of international trade. Restrictions of the following kinds have been used.

1 Tariffs

Customs duties or tariffs are the most common form of import restriction. As noted in the preceding chapter, such duties are of two kinds. Some are intended purely to raise revenue and consequently are balanced by equal excise duties on the goods produced at home. Others are deliberately designed to protect home industries from foreign competition. The purpose of a protective tariff is to raise the price of the imported article so that it does not undercut the home product.

2 Quotas

Whereas tariffs reduce imports by raising their prices, quotas put direct limits on the quantities imported. This is usually done by some form of licensing or rationing by which each importer is limited to a fixed amount of the product concerned.

3 Exchange controls

Imports normally have to be paid for in the currency of the country of origin. For example, an importing firm buying from the United States would probably require dollars. Governments can thus restrict imports by restricting the quantities of foreign currency they make available to importers for their purchases abroad. Such restrictions were widely used during and after the Second World War when a huge demand for American goods resulted in an acute shortage of dollars.

4 Subsidies

This was the typical method used by the government to assist farmers in Britain before entry into the EEC. Subsidies normally take the form of grants of money to home producers related to the quantities they produce. The object is to encourage production and at the same time keep down the market prices of the products concerned. By making home-produced goods cheaper they also tend to reduce the quantity of imports.

Arguments for protection

Most industries would like the security of a home market protected from foreign competition, and governments are often under pressure to provide such protection. A variety of arguments is used to justify the claims, some more convincing than others.

1 Social and political reasons

It has already been pointed out that countries sometimes protect their agriculture to ensure essential supplies of food and raw materials during wars or at other times of emergency. The same argument could be extended to other basic industries such as coal mining.

In an urban industrial country such as Britain, protection for the farming population is sometimes also justified on the grounds that it is important to preserve the rural way of life as an element in society. In other countries, such as France, the agricultural population remains a large and influential section of society able to exert political pressure on its government to act in its interests.

Tariff systems are used to strengthen political links between countries. An outstanding example was the principle of Commonwealth preference incorporated in Britain's tariff arrangements before entry into the EEC. The external tariff of the EEC itself is valued by some chiefly as a means of promoting the ultimate aim of political unity for Western Europe.

2 To avoid overspecialization

We saw that trade encourages specialization. But this could be a major drawback if a country became too dependent on the export of one or a few products. A decline in the foreign demand for those products could then be socially and economically disastrous, leading to widespread unemployment and poverty. Thus, a country whose economy relied largely on the export of a primary product such as cocoa or sugar might be justified in introducing protection to assist the development of a wider range of industries.

3 To develop infant industries

New industries take time to develop and may need to be protected from the competition of established industries in other countries during the period of infancy. As the new industries grow, the protection can be reduced by stages until they eventually stand on their own feet. This argument is particularly relevant to young developing economies. Unfortunately, experience suggests that industries which have grown up with the help of protection are sometimes reluctant to do without it even when fully grown.

4 To reduce unemployment

A distinction should be made between general unemployment affecting the whole economy and structural unemployment which affects certain industries only.

During the period of slump and *general unemployment* in the 1930s, most countries raised tariff barriers to keep out foreign goods that competed with their own industries. Britain thus abandoned a long tradition of free trade and began to protect its manufacturing industries.

Of course, if you buy foreign goods instead of your own, jobs are created for foreign workers at the expense of your own. But a policy of restricting imports has an obvious weakness. Foreigners also buy your goods. Protection may cause them to retaliate and, in any case, weakens their buying power. The most probable consequence is then declining trade and rising unemployment in each country. This appears to have happened in the 1930s.

Protection is commonly used to relieve *structural* unemployment when an important national industry is hit by foreign competition. This particularly applies to concentrated industries on which the prosperity of whole areas largely depends. A tariff then helps to resist the decline of the industry and the areas of concentration. But it also deprives consumers of cheap foreign products. Economists generally prefer such problems to be solved by regional policies to attract alternative industries into the areas concerned.

5 To correct a trade deficit

A deficit occurs when a country is paying out more for its imports than it is earning from its exports. This is similar to the position of an individual living beyond his income and cannot be allowed to go on indefinitely. An obvious solution is to reduce imports through some form of protection. However, protection would not help if it simply led to retaliation against the country's exports. Alternative measures are explained in the next chapter.

General Agreement on Tariffs and Trade

The desire of countries to move towards free trade is seen in the formation of trading alliances such as the Common Market and also wider international co-operation, particularly through the General Agreement on Tariffs and Trade (GATT).

GATT started after the Second World War as a treaty signed by nearly all trading countries outside the Communist bloc. Its members agreed to observe certain rules of conduct in trade and co-operate in removing restrictions on trade. Its rules generally ban a number of practices which obstruct free competition in international trade.

Among the condemned practices are quota restrictions on imports, subsidies to exports, and discrimination between the products of one country and another. However, the rules made allowances for existing arrangements, the creation of customs unions such as the Common Market, the needs of developing nations, and other special circumstances.

Tariffs are an accepted form of protection, but the aim is to reduce them through a process of consultation. Though hard bargaining between countries makes the process difficult and slow, substantial tariff reductions have been achieved through GATT negotiations. The best known of these was the Kennedy round resulting from negotiations initiated by the President of the United States in the 1960s.

1 How does international trade differ from domestic trade? What benefits do countries gain from international trade?

2 What does the principle of comparative costs show? If specialization is beneficial, why does a manufacturing country such as Britain also grow some of its own food?

3 Define the terms of trade and note the method of calculation. What is meant by (a) favourable and (b) unfavourable movements of the terms of trade?

4 Explain briefly each of the methods by which countries may protect their own industries from foreign competition.

5 Note the arguments for protection. Which ones could be used to justify the following cases?
(a) Britain's adoption of a general tariff in 1931.
(b) Tariff protection for the British textile industry.
(c) Zambia protecting its steel industry.
(d) The EEC system of protection for agriculture.

6 What is GATT?

14.2 Britain's trade

Since 1945 international trade has expanded rapidly between advanced industrial nations such as the United States, the countries of Western Europe, and Japan. The growth of world trade has naturally been accompanied by a rise in the volume and value of British exports and imports, though Britain's share of the total has declined disappointingly. Within the general expansion, there have been marked changes

Suggest likely cargoes for this container ship carrying exports from Britain.

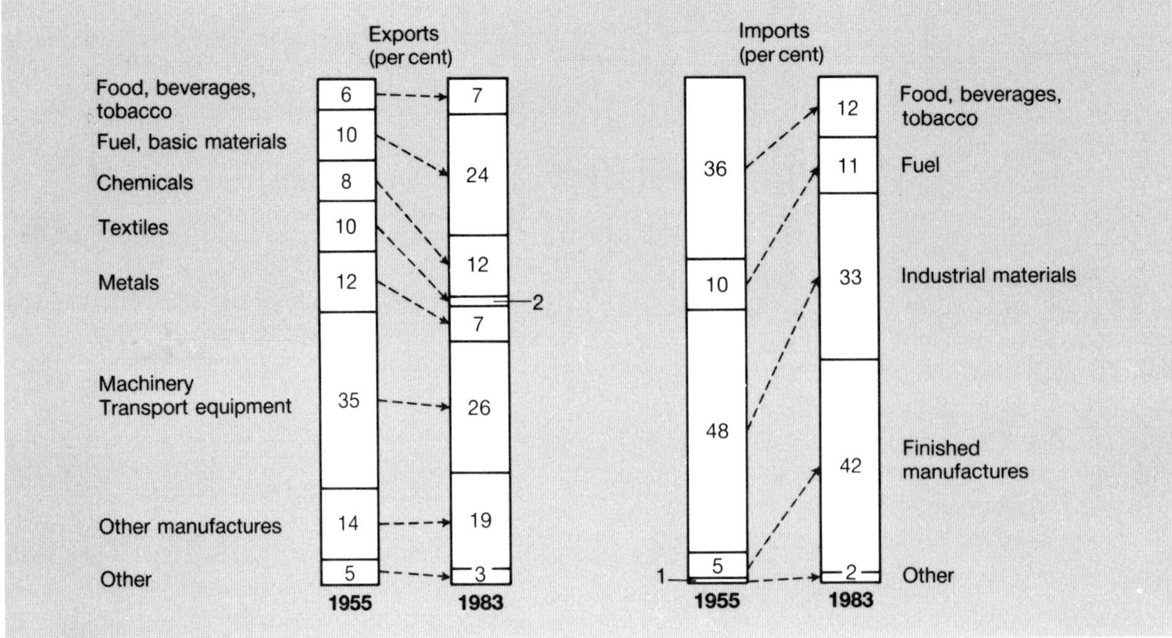

Fig. 14.1 UK exports and imports

affecting both the composition of products entering into Britain's trade and the geographical direction of that trade.

Composition of trade

The commodity composition of Britain's exports and imports is shown in Fig. 14.1. It is important to remember that we are looking at proportions and not absolute quantities exported and imported. The quantities have almost always risen with expanding world population and trade. But trade has not expanded at the same rate in all products and so their shares of the total have changed, in some cases significantly. A number of features can be observed. Look at the diagram and check them yourself.

1 Exports

The bulk of Britain's exports continues to be *manufactured* goods. However, the share of this group has been in decline for some years, though fortunately compensated by North Sea oil in the 1980s.

The composition of manufactured exports has changed radically since the Second World War. The growth of foreign competition has caused a large reduction in textiles, once the backbone of Britain's exports. Instead, trade has come to be dominated by *new industries*, such as chemicals, based on modern technology and science. The largest classes of exports are machinery, transport equipment, and motor vehicles. These are the products in which world demand has generally grown fastest.

2 Imports

The decline in the relative importance of the *food* category does not mean that we import less food – about half Britain's total food consumption continues to be imported – but the growth of imports has been larger in other commodity groups. In addition, home production of food has increased rapidly since the Second World War: technical progress has enabled a large rise in productivity; at the same time, production has been encouraged by government subsidies and, more recently, by EEC farm price policy.

Industrial materials have declined as a percentage of total imports largely because of the development of home-produced synthetic or manufactured materials such as plastics and man-made fibres.

The huge growth of *manufactured* imports is at first sight surprising since Britain is a specialist producer and exporter of such products. The explanation lies in the fact that rising living standards, above

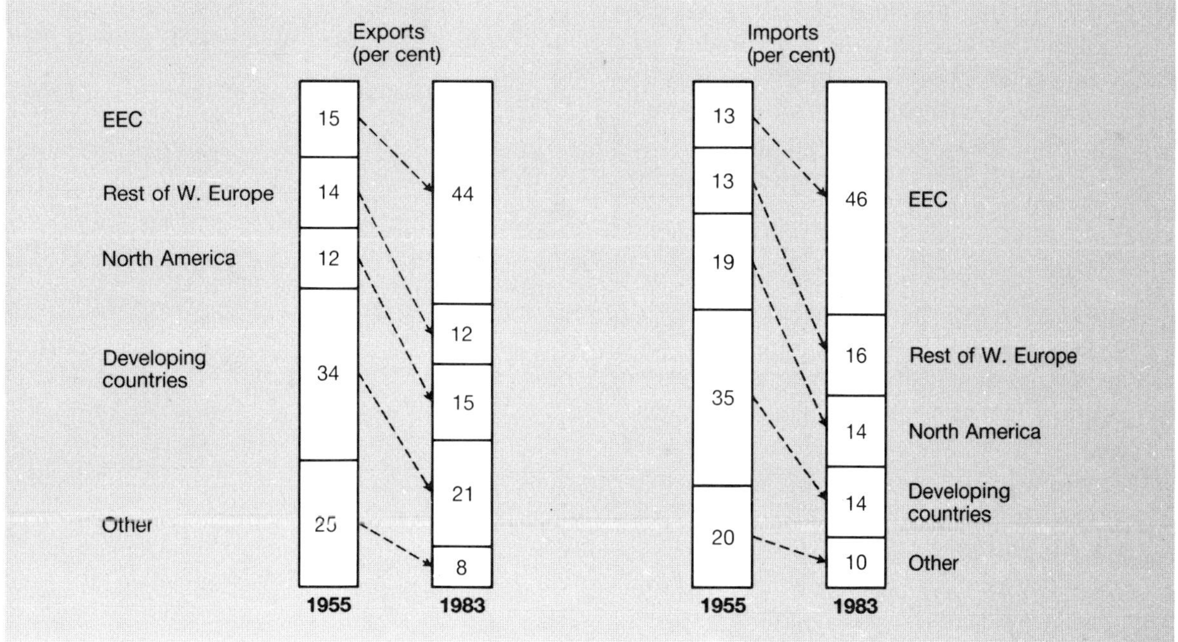

Fig. 14.2 Area distribution of UK trade

a certain level, create a demand for manufactured goods (cars, television sets, etc.) rather than food. At the same time, industrialization and technical progress create a demand for more machines and equipment. The growth of world trade has thus come about largely through the exchange of industrial products between advanced nations whose living standards have risen most rapidly.

With rising manufactured imports and flagging exports, UK trade in manufactured goods recorded its first ever peace-time deficit in 1983. However, North Sea oil ensures virtual self-sufficiency in fuel which now earns a substantial surplus of exports over imports.

Direction of trade

Fig. 14.2 shows the changing area distribution of Britain's exports and imports. It is noticeable that the main areas to which Britain sends its exports are also, in general, the areas from which it obtains most of its imports.

Britain's trade was traditionally based on the exchange of its manufactured goods for food and materials from the developing countries of the Commonwealth. This trading relationship was reinforced by the use of a common currency (forming the *sterling area*) and a system of *Commonwealth preference* involving tariff discrimination against the products of other countries. In 1950 about half of UK exports went to Commonwealth territories. Since then British trade has grown most rapidly with other European countries and the Commonwealth share has declined to a minor proportion.

There are a number of explanations for the changing pattern of Britain's trade. As already noted, the most rapid trade expansion in recent years has been in industrial products among advanced industrial nations. Furthermore, Britain's entry into the EEC has obviously influenced the direction of exports and imports. It has also had the effect of weakening Commonwealth links, and the removal of Commonwealth preferences encouraged Commonwealth countries to seek trading opportunities elsewhere. Australia and New Zealand, for example, have expanded their trade with countries such as the United States and Japan.

Trade with Western Europe has grown very rapidly since the early 1960s and now forms the largest part of Britain's total trade. This again fits the pattern of the growth of trade between the advanced industrial nations themselves. The reorientation of Britain's trade towards Europe began well before entry into the Common Market – a fact that was used to support the case for membership and also to argue that it was unnecessary. Integration into Europe has also reduced the share of trade with North America (the United States and Canada) on which Britain was particularly dependent following the Second World War.

There remain large areas of the world with which Britain still does little trade. Latin America and Eastern Europe (including the Soviet Union) still only account for small fractions of British trade, though attempts have been made to establish closer ties with the Communist countries. Japan has become a major trading nation and now plays a significant part in the trading pattern of the United Kingdom. There has also been a noticeable growth of trade with the rich Arab oil-producing countries.

1 Refer to Fig. 14.1 and (a) describe and account for the changes in the composition of Britain's exports, (b) note and explain the growth of manufactured goods as a percentage of Britain's imports.

2 Refer to Fig. 14.2 and explain the main changes in the direction of Britain's trade.

14.3 The Common Market

The Common Market had its origins in the European Coal and Steel Community created in 1951 by the six founder members – France, West Germany, Italy, Belgium, the Netherlands, and Luxembourg. Its scope was extended to form the *European Economic Community* under the Treaty of Rome in 1958. Britain, Denmark, and the Republic of Ireland joined in 1973, followed by Greece in 1981 and Spain and Portugal in 1986. It has thus expanded into a community of 12 member nations with a total population of about 320 million (Fig. 14.3).

Community aims and features

The development of the Community was planned to proceed by steps starting with the creation of a customs union and ending with political union – though not all its supporters want or expect it to reach that final stage.

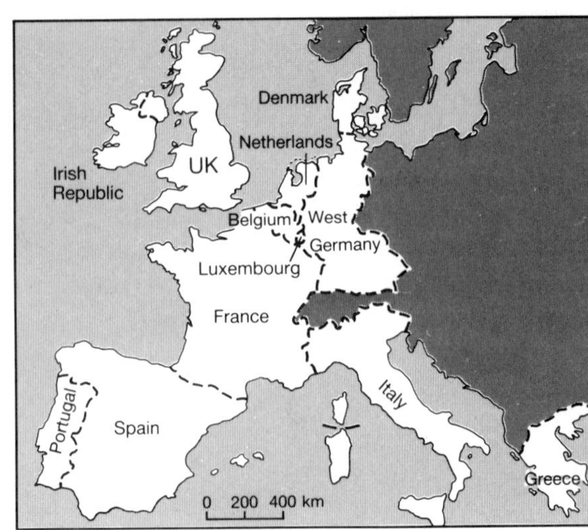

Fig. 14.3 EEC membership (1986)

1 Customs union

The customs union was completed in 1968 when the six countries established themselves as a free trade area with a common external tariff (CET). A *free trade area* allows goods to move between the member countries without any tariffs or other restrictions. The *common external tariff* means that any product entering the area from outside pays the same tax whatever the point of entry – that is, the whole area is surrounded by the same barrier of customs duties, forming a customs union.

The customs union was put into operation through a series of adjustments to national tariffs, bringing them into line over a period of time. Similarly, the new members including Britain were allowed a transitional period (generally about five years) to make the necessary adjustments.

2 Common agricultural policy

The common agricultural policy (CAP) is an important and controversial part of the Community's arrangements. In general, agricultural products can be moved freely between the member countries. But the main purpose of the policy is to ensure the Community's farmers good market prices for their products.

Farm prices are supported in two main ways. First, a variable customs tariff or levy on imports prevents their prices from falling below the required level. Secondly, if necessary, the Community's agricultural fund is used to hold up the market price

The European Parliament in Strasbourg. What could it be discussing?

of a product by buying it when the price falls too low. Stocks of goods acquired in this way are intended to be released on the market when prices rise again. The money for the agricultural fund is obtained from the import levies and also tax contributions from member countries.

3 *Economic union*

The Community still has a long way to go to reach the full economic union at which it aims. This requires completely free movement of labour and capital as well as goods, uniformity of certain taxes (including VAT and corporation tax), more uniformity of social policies, a common transport policy, and eventual monetary union with a uniform currency.

4 *Political unity*

An important driving force behind the creation of the EEC was the desire to end the divisions in Europe which produced two world wars in this century. It was thought that a more united Europe would also exercise greater influence on world affairs. Some of the founders thus envisaged an eventual association of states organized on similar lines to the United States of America. This would require the European Parliament to be made into a law-making assembly with effective control over the Community's budget and its various organs of government (Fig. 14.4).

Britain and the Common Market

The effects of membership cannot be measured and there is a deep division of opinion between supporters and critics. The arguments can be briefly stated as a basis for discussion.

The advantages claimed are generally those of free trade outlined at the beginning of the chapter. Supporters of membership thus emphasize the export opportunities in a large growing market, the scope for economies of scale, and the competitive incentive to British industry. To some, the chief attraction is the ideal of a politically united Europe. There

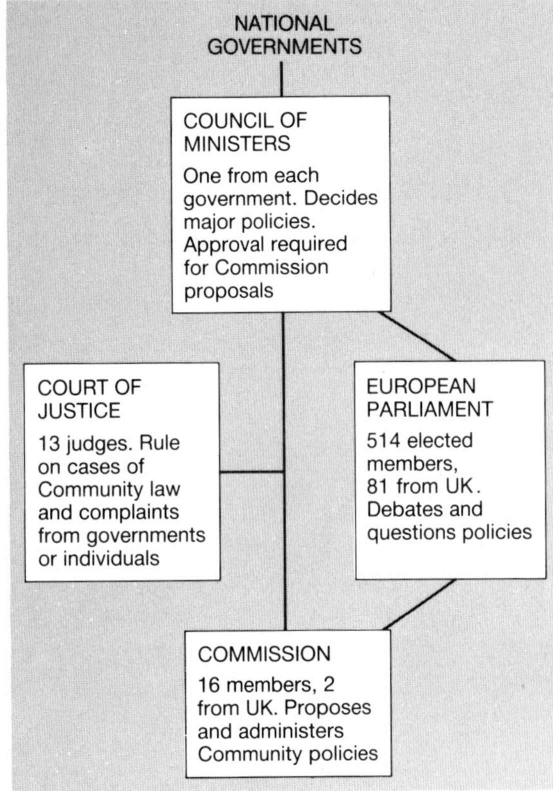

Fig. 14.4 European Community institutions

is also the fear that the alternative would have been both economic and political isolation.

The criticisms can also be summarized. It is argued that the conditions of entry imposed too high a cost on Britain. As a major food importer, Britain bears a large share of the payments into the agricultural fund and receives less than others out of it. Moreover, the method of agricultural support by buying surplus farm produce has resulted in costly accumulation of food stocks – the notorious butter mountains, milk lakes, and so on – providing visible evidence of the defects of the policy.

The effects on industry depend on the ability of British firms to compete with their European rivals. While efficient industries have gained, the less efficient have lost ground, and imports from other EEC countries have risen faster than our exports to them. Growing competition from Europe may also have added to unemployment in some areas. Another more fundamental objection is that membership means a loss of control over national economic policy.

1 When was the EEC formed? Which countries are now members? How can Britain influence its decisions?

2 The EEC is a *free trade area* with a *common external tariff* and a *common agricultural policy*. Explain the terms in italics. What further aims does it have?

Multiple choice

1

	Export index	*Import index*
Year I	100	100
Year II	126	105

The terms of trade index figure for year II is
A 21·0
B 95·0
C 120·0
D 126·5
E 131·0

2 Britain's largest export market is now
A the Commonwealth
B Western Europe
C North America
D Eastern Europe
E Latin America

3 The major category of UK exports comprises
A manufactured goods
B basic materials
C food, drink, and tobacco
D North Sea oil
E coal

4 Which of the following was an original member of the EEC?
A Greece
B Belgium
C Norway
D Denmark
E United Kingdom

5 Which of the following explains the benefits that countries can obtain through specialization and trade?
A the terms of trade
B the balance of trade
C the theory of comparative costs
D the law of diminishing returns
E the common external tariff

6 International specialization is hindered by
  1 tariffs
  2 quotas
  3 subsidies

A 1 only is correct
B 1 and 2 only are correct
C 1, 2 and 3 are correct
D 2 and 3 only are correct
E 3 only is correct

7 A favourable movement in the terms of trade occurs when
  1 export prices rise relatively to import prices
  2 import prices fall relatively to export prices
  3 import prices rise relatively to export prices

A 1 only is correct
B 1 and 2 only are correct
C 1, 2 and 3 are correct
D 1 and 2 only are correct
E 2 only is correct

8 The advantages of international trade do NOT normally include
A larger markets
B increased competition
C increased specialization
D more consumer choice
E reduced inflation

Essays

1 'Countries benefit from trade and yet impose restrictions on trade'. If so, why?

2 'International trade is simply an extension of the principle of specialization or division of labour'. Explain.

3 Explain precisely what is meant by an improvement in the terms of trade. What could cause it and is it necessarily desirable?

4 What particular adjustments did Britain have to make in becoming a member of the EEC? Outline the benefits and drawbacks of membership.

Data response

UK trade in manufactured goods

	1955	*1982*
Share of world manufactured exports (per cent)	20·0	9·0
Direction of manufactured exports (percentage of total):		
Western Europe	25·7	49·2
Other developed economies	39·4	21·5
Developing countries	34·9	29·3
Manufactured goods as a percentage of UK exports of which:	78·8	67·2
Machinery, vehicles and transport equipment	35·3	32·6
Metals	11·8	7·1
Textiles	10·1	2·1
Chemicals	7·8	11·0
Other	12·6	14·4

1 Note the change in the UK share of world manufactured exports and suggest reasons for it.

2 Note the main changes that have taken place in the direction of UK manufactured exports and give reasons.

3 Comment on the fall in manufactured goods as a percentage of UK exports, indicating which other exports you would expect to have increased their share of the total.

4 Describe and account for the changes shown in the composition of UK exports.

5 Briefly sum up the general trend of UK trade in manufactured goods as shown by the figures.

Chapter 15

International payments

15.1 The balance of payments

The balance of payments is a national account of all movements of money, to and from other countries, over a period of time. It therefore shows how a country is paying its way in relation to the rest of the world. If the total of payments to other countries exceeds the total received from other countries, the balance is said to be unfavourable, adverse, or in deficit. If the total received is greater than the total paid out, the balance is said to be favourable or in surplus.

The total balance of payments account is made up of a number of separate balances. Table 15.1 shows each of these balances as a single figure (plus or minus) arrived at by subtracting money outflow from inflow. To judge the state of a country's balance of payments it is necessary to look at each part of the total account and understand its importance.

The current account

The current account is generally regarded as the most important part of the balance of payments because it shows how much the nation is earning and spending abroad. It includes all payments for visible trade (goods) and so-called invisibles (chiefly services).

Table 15.1 Summary of UK balance of payments

	£ million 1984
Visible trade	- 4255
Invisibles	+ 4879
Current balance	+ 624
Investment and other capital transactions	- 3287
Balancing item	+ 1342
Balance for official financing	- 1321

1 Visible trade

The largest part of the total account consists of exports and imports of goods or merchandise. As we saw in the preceding chapter, Britain's exports are mainly manufactured products. Its imports include large quantities of food and raw materials as well as manufactured goods. The balance between the two is called the *balance of trade*. A plus figure means that earnings from exports exceeded spending on imports, resulting in a visible trade surplus. A minus figure means that export earnings fell short of import spending, resulting in a deficit.

In most years of this century Britain had a visible trade deficit – sometimes called the trade gap. Such a deficit is not necessarily undesirable. Since imports are greater than exports, it means a higher standard of living. But a deficit has to be paid for somehow. Britain is fortunate because it can normally offset a trade deficit by its invisible earnings.

2 Invisibles

Payments are regularly made between countries without any visible movement of goods across their borders. For example, foreign tourists come and spend money in Britain and foreign firms buy services such as insurance from British firms. Such inflows of money are essentially the same as our earnings from exports and are counted as invisible exports. Similar payments made by us to foreign countries are counted as invisible imports. These invisibles have the same effect on the balance of payments as the payments for visible exports and imports.

A substantial surplus on invisibles has been a feature of Britain's balance of payments for many years. As noted above, this surplus has helped to pay for a normal deficit in the visible trade balance. Fig. 15.1 shows the main items in Britain's invisible earnings and these are described below.

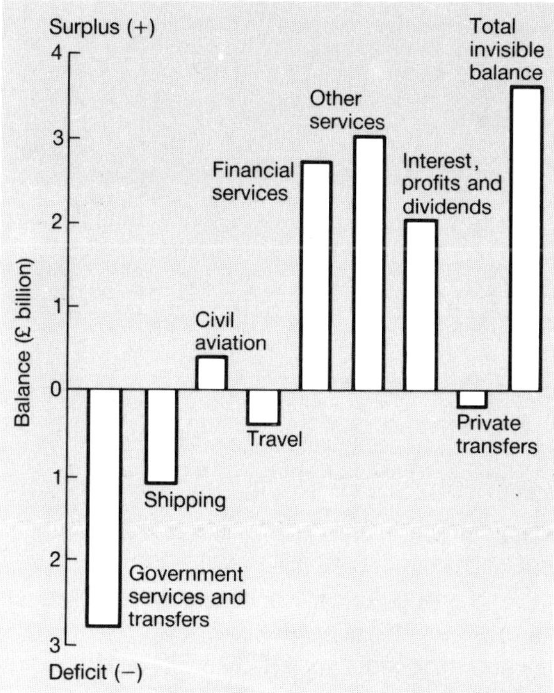

Fig. 15.1 UK invisibles (1983)

i) *Government*. Heavy overseas expenditure by the British government makes this a large minus item. It includes the cost of maintaining embassies and consulates in foreign countries, contributions to international organizations, assistance to developing countries, and other expenses connected with foreign relations. But the largest proportion comprises military spending on overseas bases and forces stationed abroad. A heavy burden of payments now also arises from Britain's financial contributions to the EEC.

Of course, foreign governments also spend money in Britain, but the British government's overseas spending is particularly high because of its traditional role as a world power and centre of the Commonwealth.

ii) *Transport*. *Shipping* charges for the transport of both goods and passengers have always been an important item of invisibles. At one time, British shipping companies were the world's leading sea carriers and the country made a large surplus on this item. In recent years, however, the earnings of British shipping have been exceeded by our payments for foreign shipping. *Civil aviation* now makes a useful contribution to Britain's invisibles.

iii) *Interest, profits, and dividends*. The surplus under this heading dates from Britain's former industrial supremacy. British people then lent or invested large sums of money abroad, and British firms built factories, railways, etc. in many parts of the world. These past loans and investments provide an annual income in the form of interest, profits, and dividends. Of course, there is now also an outflow of money to foreigners who have bought shares, set up firms, or made loans in Britain. Moreover, many of Britain's overseas investments were sold to raise foreign currency during the Second World War. Nevertheless, this item normally continues to provide a substantial surplus.

iv) *Financial services*. The large invisible earnings under this heading can also be traced to Britain's historical position established in the nineteenth century. As the world's leading financial and commercial centre, the City of London built up a large overseas business in activities such as banking and insurance. In spite of the rise of other financial centres, London's financial institutions continue to contribute strongly to the surplus on invisibles.

v) *Other services* include royalties or profits from books and records, and income from films shown abroad. Internationally successful pop groups thus make their contribution to the balance of payments.

vi) *Travel*. This covers the expenditure of tourists and businessmen on trips abroad. It includes their hotel bills, fares, entertainments, and other expenses. Although many foreigners come to Britain, their expenditure is offset by the growing number of British people taking their holidays abroad. Countries such as Spain and Italy thus earn large surpluses in this connection.

vii) *Private transfers*. Money is transferred across national borders in the form of gifts, inheritances, and other such personal payments. Migration also results in a flow of funds to homes and families in the countries of origin.

Investment and other capital transactions

Large international movements of money take place not to pay for goods and services but in the form of investments and other capital flows. These transactions are sometimes referred to as the *capital account* in the balance of payments. They include government loans or overseas aid, direct foreign investment by firms setting up new factories abroad, and purchases of foreign shares or securities.

Because of Britain's world position, it usually lends and invests abroad more than it receives in this way. The figure is therefore usually a minus – that is, the annual outflow of capital exceeds the inflow in most years. However, the annual interest and profits from such overseas investments contribute to Britain's invisible earnings on the current account.

International capital transactions also include monetary movements of a more temporary nature such as the transfer of bank deposits from one country to another. Such transfers are sometimes undertaken for speculative reasons connected with foreign exchange rates (to be explained later) or to take advantage of higher interest rates in other countries. These temporary movements can have disturbing effects on the balance of payments and the rates at which currencies are exchanged.

Balance for official financing

The current account and capital transactions together determine the balance for official financing. The official statistics also include a *balancing item* allowing for unrecorded transactions the size of which only becomes known when the accounts are finally made up.

The nation must somehow cover the difference between monetary movements into and out of the country. Like an individual, a country cannot pay out more than it receives over a period without obtaining the extra funds from somewhere.

An individual who overspends might draw on savings or obtain a bank loan. A country with a deficit on its total payments must similarly draw on its reserves (of gold and foreign currencies) or borrow temporarily – for example from the International Monetary Fund (see page 179). Conversely, a country with a surplus may add to its reserves or pay off past debts. As the guardian of the reserves, the Bank of England is responsible for these transactions which make the final adjustments to the balance of payments and are described as *official financing*. Through official financing, the account as a whole is brought into exact balance (Fig. 15.2).

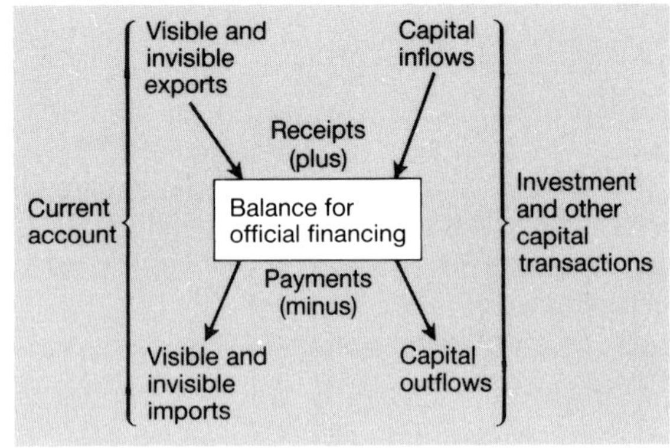

Fig. 15.2 Transactions in the balance of payments

Correcting a deficit

Countries normally aim at a surplus, and a deficit is usually considered a matter for concern. However, the effect of a deficit depends partly on its cause. If it is due to loans or investment overseas, it may mean that the country is increasing its wealth abroad and so strengthening its future current account through the resulting inflow of interest and profits.

On the other hand, a deficit on current account means that the nation is spending more than it is earning abroad. This is similar to an individual living beyond his income. It may be sound policy for a young couple setting up home or for a young (developing) nation borrowing from abroad to develop its natural resources. But a country in Britain's position is generally expected to lend rather than borrow abroad, and should aim at a current surplus. Special attention is consequently given to the current account, and when we refer to the balance of payments we often mean the current account (Fig. 15.3).

Since one nation's surplus must have its counterpart in other nation's deficits, it is not possible for every nation to achieve a surplus every year. But a country cannot go on having deficits without using up reserves or accumulating foreign debts. Sooner or later, action must then be taken to correct the deficit.

1 Controlling the flow of capital

If a deficit in the balance of payments is placing a strain on the nation's reserves, this may be relieved by government restrictions on investment and other capital flows abroad. Alternatively, foreign capital

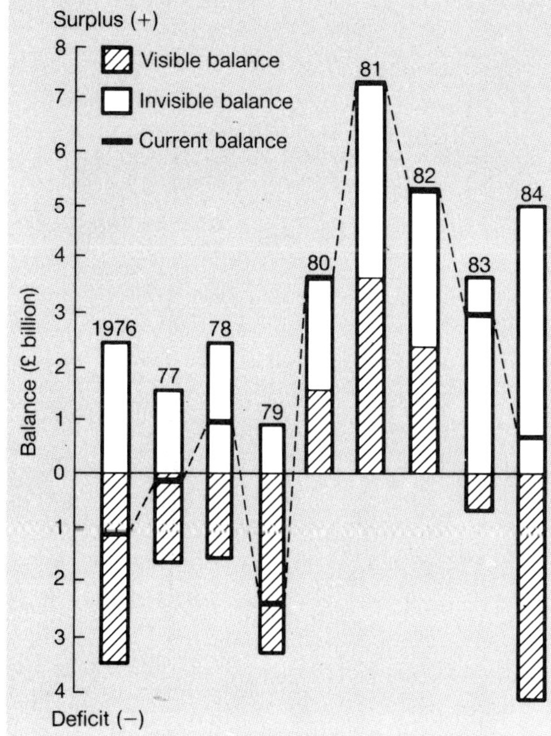

Fig. 15.3 UK current balance (1976-84)

might be attracted by raising interest rates at home. However, we have seen that overseas investment adds to a country's wealth and provides invisible earnings in the form of interest, profits, and dividends. In any case, restricting the flow of capital does nothing to relieve a deficit on current account which is the crucial part of Britain's balance of payments.

2 Expanding exports

Export growth is the ideal solution to a current deficit since it avoids the need to cut back on imports. Direct government subsidies to exporters are against GATT rules but it is possible to encourage firms to export by giving tax incentives. For instance, an argument in support of VAT is that exported goods are exempt from the tax.

Governments also try to assist exporters by helping to promote advertising facilities in trade fairs or exhibitions, providing information about overseas markets, arranging loans at favourable rates of interest, and so on. In Britain, the Department of Trade and Industry is active in these ways. However, such methods take time to produce results and governments are usually forced to seek other means of dealing with immediate balance of payments problems.

3 Reducing imports

The most obvious solution is to restrict imports through the use of tariffs or quotas. General tariff increases were thus imposed by Britain in 1964 and the United States in 1971 when faced with large payments deficits.

The objection to import controls is that they are contrary to GATT regulations and are likely to lead to retaliation which damages exports. However, other countries may tolerate them as a means of temporary relief. Thus, Britain's tariff surcharge on imports in 1964 was accepted as a temporary measure and abandoned within two years.

4 Deflation

The effect of a deflationary policy is to reduce the level of spending. Governments usually do this by reducing their own spending, increasing taxes, and curbing bank lending. Since a part of our spending is always on imported goods, it can be assumed that such measures will lead to a reduction in imports. At the same time, manufacturers find it harder to sell their products in the home market and are likely to make greater efforts to sell abroad. The effect of deflation on prices should also help exports.

Since the Second World War, deflationary policies have been adopted by successive British governments to deal with balance of payments crises. The objection to such policies is that they slow down the growth of production and sometimes create unnecessary unemployment. If a payments deficit appears when there is already too much unemployment, the deflationary remedy becomes unacceptable. Devaluation or exchange rate depreciation is then the most likely solution.

Devaluation

Devaluation simply means a reduction in thc foreign exchange value of a nation's currency – that is, the rate at which it can be changed into other currencies. Its effect is to worsen the terms of trade, making exports cheaper and imports dearer.

Suppose that the rate of exchange between the pound and the dollar is originally £1 for $2. A British product priced at £100 would then sell in the United

States for $200 (assuming that there are no transport costs). Now suppose that the £ is devalued to $1·5. The same product would now cost only $150 in the United States.

By devaluing its currency, a country makes its products cheaper to foreigners and so encourages its exports. It must be remembered, however, that each unit sold now earns less in foreign currency and so a comparatively small increase in the quantity sold would not be enough to expand total export earnings. The success of devaluation thus depends on how well foreign demand responds to cheaper export prices. In the language of economics, it is necessary for the demand to be relatively elastic.

At the same time, devaluation makes imports more expensive. Using our previous example, an American product priced at $200 would sell in Britain for £100 before devaluation and £133 afterwards. We should therefore buy fewer foreign products at higher prices. But the full effect again depends on elasticity of demand.

Devaluation has usually helped to correct a balance of payments deficit but its other effects are clearly unpleasant. For example, by making imports more expensive it raises the cost of living, particularly in a country such as Britain which imports a large part of its essential food supplies. It also makes us worse off by diverting goods from the home market into exports.

Britain devalued in 1949, 1967, and again in 1972 when the pound was left to float (and floated downwards) (Fig. 15.4). The process of devaluation should become clearer in the next section.

1 Note the definition of the balance of payments. Copy Table 15.1 and add more recent figures if available.

2 What is meant by the current balance and why is it considered most important?

3 Distinguish between visible and invisible trade. Why is a deficit on visible trade not necessarily considered a matter of concern for Britain?

4 What are invisible exports and imports? Refer to Fig. 15.1:
(a) Why is government a large deficit item in Britain's invisibles?
(b) Which items are mainly responsible for Britain's invisible surplus, and why?
(c) Note the other invisible items.

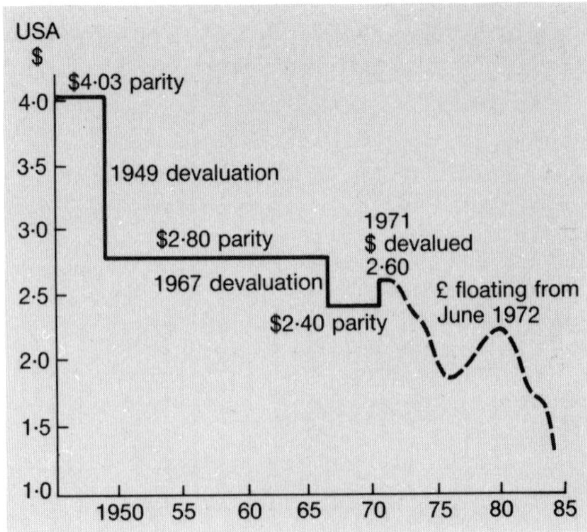

Fig. 15.4 Sterling exchange rate movements against the US dollar

5 What kinds of movement of money are included under the heading of investment and other capital transactions? Why are they separated from the current account in the balance of payments?

6 What is meant by the balance for official financing? How can the Bank of England finance a deficit on this balance, and what can it do with a surplus?

7 Note the different methods of correcting an adverse balance of payments and indicate the problems or drawbacks of each method.

15.2 Exchange rates

Foreign exchanges

Payments between countries normally involve an exchange of currencies. For example, goods purchased from the United States would normally have to be paid for in dollars because Americans naturally want dollars. Consequently, if we are making payments to people or firms in the United States, pounds will have to be changed into dollars. Conversely, in the case of American payments to Britain, dollars must normally be changed into pounds.

The exchange of currencies is carried out mainly through banks which operate in the foreign exchange market. Thus, by telephone or telegraph, sterling deposits in a London bank can be exchanged for dollars in a New York bank or vice versa. But what

Name three major currencies that could concern these dealers in the foreign exchange department of a bank.

determines the price or rate at which currencies are exchanged in the market? This depends, in the first place, on whether the rate is floating or fixed.

Floating rates

During the 1930s, and again in 1972, the pound, in common with many other currencies, was left to float. *A free, flexible, or floating rate of exchange is one that is allowed to find its own level according to demand and supply forces in the foreign exchange market.*

1 Determining the rate

In the foreign exchange market there is always a demand for pounds from foreigners requiring to make payments in Britain and a converse demand for foreign currencies by British residents requiring to make payments abroad. Foreigners are prepared to supply their own currencies in exchange for pounds and the British will supply pounds in exchange for other currencies.

If the foreign demand for pounds exceeds the British demand for other currencies, the pound will become relatively scarce and its value will rise in relation to other currencies. But as pounds become more expensive, the excess demand will be choked off. Thus, in a free market, the rate of exchange will settle at a level at which demand and supply are equal. In this respect, it behaves like any other market price (Fig. 15.5).

What determines demand and supply in the foreign exchange market? The answer lies basically in the balance of payments. As we saw earlier, a surplus means that the inflow of money is greater than the outflow. The demand for your currency is then relatively strong and its value is likely to rise against

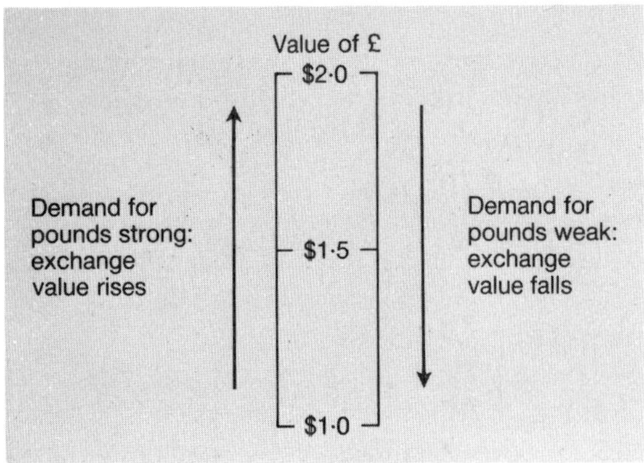

Fig. 15.5 Exchange rate fluctuations

other currencies. Conversely, a deficit generally means a weakening or *depreciation* of the currency amounting to devaluation.

2 *Effects of floating*

The advantage claimed for floating is that it keeps international payments in balance or equilibrium through normal movements of exchange rates. These movements have the effect of eliminating deficits and surpluses in the balance of payments. For example, a deficit can be expected to produce the following chain of events.

i) Unfavourable balance (deficit)
ii) Fall in the currency exchange rate (devaluation)
iii) Exports become cheaper and imports dearer
iv) Exports expand and imports contract
v) Elimination of deficit.

Note the consequences of a favourable balance (surplus) by reversing each of the above steps. An international balance can thus be secured through automatic adjustments of exchange rates in both deficit and surplus countries. Of course, such adjustments take time to work and payments may go out of balance in the meantime, but floating rates may be expected to restore the balance, at least in the long run.

The disadvantage of floating is that fluctuations in exchange rates increase the risks of trade and may consequently discourage international trade. We saw earlier how devaluation raises import prices. For example, devaluation of the pound from $2 to $1·5 causes the price (in pounds) of a $200 American product to rise from £100 to £133. Under a floating system, price changes of this nature could occur whenever a country's balance of payments weakened and its currency floated downwards. Businessmen might then become afraid to place orders for goods from foreign countries and trade would slow down.

3 *Stabilizing exchange rates*

The instability of floating rates can be further magnified by speculation or panic selling. For example, if people rush to sell a weak currency – perhaps intending to buy back at a lower price – its price is forced down even more sharply.

However, the drawbacks of instability may be exaggerated. Traders can guard against the risk of exchange fluctuations to some extent – for instance, by buying currency in advance of their needs through what is called the *forward market*. Moreover, governments themselves take steps to offset the most violent fluctuations such as those due to speculation.

Governments can stabilize exchange rates by using national reserves to offset market fluctuations. This method was adopted by Britain and other countries during the period of floating in the 1930s. For example, if heavy sales were causing the pound to fall in value, the Bank of England would use gold or foreign currency from the reserves to buy pounds and so hold up the price. Conversely, a strong demand for pounds, forcing up their value, could be countered by selling pounds in exchange for foreign currencies.

The gold and foreign currency reserves used for stabilization are held by the Bank of England in a special fund called the *Exchange Equalization Account*. This account now holds the whole of the nation's reserves and is still available for its original purpose of stabilizing the exchange value of the pound.

Fixed exchange rates

Instead of being left to market forces, exchange rates can be fixed or rigidly held between limits. The advantage is that it removes the risk of fluctuations and so encourages international trade. But it also rules out the normal adjustments that help to keep international payments in balance under a floating system. A country with a deficit may thus be forced to undergo deflation as an alternative to devaluation.

Exchange rates used to be fixed through the operation of the gold standard. In more recent times, the same purpose was achieved through the arrangements of the International Monetary Fund.

1 The gold standard

The gold standard operated in Britain through most of the nineteenth century and was not finally abandoned until 1931. Its essential condition was that the Bank of England was prepared to change notes into gold at a fixed price. Since other countries such as the United States similarly tied their currencies to gold, the relative gold prices (or parities) automatically determined the rates of exchange. For example, if an ounce of gold exchanged for £7 in Britain and $35 in the United States, the rate of exchange between the two currencies could hardly vary from £1 = $5.

Under a gold standard, the supply of money in a country depended on the central bank's reserves of gold – a commodity that became scarce in many countries. This restriction became a serious drawback in times of high unemployment such as the 1930s. When countries agreed to maintain stable exchange rates after the Second World War, it was not by returning to the gold standard.

2 The International Monetary Fund

Towards the end of the Second World War, plans were being prepared to help post-war recovery. A monetary conference held at Bretton Woods in the United States produced two new international bodies – the International Monetary Fund (IMF) and the International Bank for Reconstruction and Development. The latter, better known as the *World Bank*, is not concerned with exchange rates as such. Its main purpose is to provide aid to developing countries for schemes such as road construction and hydroelectric power. Funds are obtained from government contributions and from private sources through the issue of bonds.

The principal aims of the IMF were to promote international monetary co-operation, establish a system of stable exchange rates, and provide a fund from which members could borrow when faced with balance of payments difficulties.

As a basis for stable rates, each member initially adopted an agreed rate (or parity) between its own currency and the dollar. This automatically determined their rates against each other on similar lines to the gold standard. The central bank of each country undertook to use its reserves – in Britain, the Exchange Equalization Account – to keep its rate within narrow margins (orginally 1 per cent) on either side of the agreed parity.

A country with severe payments difficulties could devalue, by altering its exchange parity, with the approval of the Fund. But this came to be regarded as a last resort. The consequent rigidity of exchange rates began to create strains leading to the widespread abandonment of parities and the period of floating which began in 1972 (Fig. 15.4). However, the Fund itself continues to operate as a base for international monetary co-operation and a source of financial assistance to its members.

To supplement their reserves, members have the right to borrow temporarily from the Fund. To provide the necessary resources, each member was required to make a contribution (called its quota) partly in gold and the rest in its own currency. The Fund thus possesses gold and currencies of many kinds.

An important extension of the Fund's facilities was made in 1971 when it began to introduce *special drawing rights* – a kind of international currency of its own creation. These are allocated to members in limited quantities and are recognized as additions to the reserves of their central banks. They have been described as 'paper gold' and are considered capable of development to become the main international currency of the future.

1 Note the definition of a floating exchange rate. Explain the influences that determine the level of a floating rate.

2 How do floating exchange rates help to promote international equilibrium in the balance of payments? Refer to the effects in both deficit and surplus countries.

3 Why have countries sometimes tried to maintain fixed exchange rates? How was this done under the arrangements of the International Monetary Fund? What would a country have to do if its currency was weak and it could not hold its exchange rate?

Multiple choice

1 Which of the following would be included in Britain's invisible imports?
- A the cost of a factory built in Britain by an American firm
- B payment for American goods bought by a British firm
- C payment to an insurance company in the United States by a customer in Britain
- D money received by someone resident in Britain as an inheritance from a rich American uncle
- E expenditure by an American tourist in Britain

Questions 2 and 3 relate to the following table of items in a country's balance of payments

Exports	700
Imports	600
Government services	+50
Other invisibles	−200
Investment and other capital transactions	+200

2 Which of the following is the only correct description of the country's balance of payments?
- A visible trade deficit
- B surplus of invisibles
- C surplus on current account
- D surplus in the balance for official financing
- E a net outflow of capital

3 The country's balance of payments on current account is
- A −150
- B −50
- C 0
- D +50
- E +100

Questions 4 and 5 relate to the following organizations
- A International Monetary Fund
- B World Bank
- C GATT
- D Foreign exchange market
- E Bank of England

4 Which organization lends to countries facing temporary balance of payments difficulties?

5 Which organization would have its rules broken if a government gave export subsidies to firms?

6 A recognized remedy for a UK current account deficit is to reduce
- A tariffs
- B taxes
- C interest rates
- D the sterling exchange rate
- E subsidies to exporters

Data response

Items in the UK balance of payments, 1983

	£ million
Exports	60 625
Imports	61 341
Government services and transfers	−2 839
Private services and transfers	+4 523
Interest, profits, and dividends	+1 948
Investment and other capital transactions	−3 648
Balancing item	−84

1 Using the above data, calculate:
(a) the visible trade balance
(b) the balance of invisible items
(c) the balance of payments on current account
(d) the balance for official financing

2 What action was likely to have been taken in that year under the heading of official financing?

3 Comment on the state of the balance of payments in that year.

4 Discuss the significance of the figure for investment and other capital transactions. What action could be taken to stem an outflow of capital?

Essays

1 We talk of deficits and surpluses in the balance of payments but, in fact, the balance of payments always balances. Explain this statement.

2 Distinguish between the balance of trade and the terms of trade and show how they are related.

3 Why do countries need foreign currency reserves? What could cause the reserves of a country to fall and what steps could be taken to check such a fall?

4 In 1972 Britain and other countries allowed their currencies to float. What did this mean? Outline the advantages and disadvantages of a floating exchange rate.

Chapter 16
Britain's economy

Rate of inflation on target

Reserves used to support the pound

House prices 'rise by 10% with boom in the South'

Oil price slump likely to continue

Job prospects fail to improve

Record exports lift current account surplus to £2bn

Which three aims of economic policy are illustrated by these newspaper headlines?

The economic policies of successive British governments have had four main aims: a high level of employment; stable prices; rapid growth of production in order to improve living standards; and a healthy balance of payments. Sometimes added to these is the social aim of relieving poverty and reducing the gap between the very rich and very poor.

Economic theory indicates means of achieving each aim. The difficulty is that the aims often conflict with each other. For example, measures to boost spending in order to stimulate production and employment have frequently aggravated inflation and affected the balance of payments. However, economic success or failure is judged to a large extent by the performance of the economy in each of the four areas concerned.

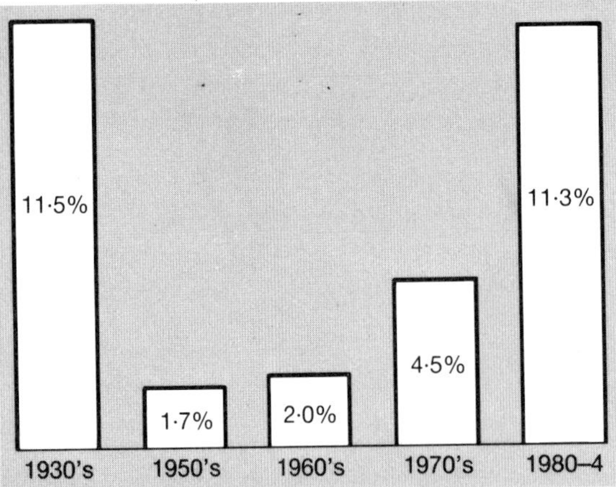

Fig. 16.1 The trend of unemployment: average percentage unemployed in the working population

16.1 Employment

General level of employment

The national level of unemployment largely depends on the level of spending in the economy. Spending leads to production and so creates jobs. War-time military spending virtually eliminated unemployment in the 1940s and unemployment remained generally low, with both government and private spending on a rising trend, throughout the next two decades.

A significant change in world economic conditions was brought about by steep increases in the price of oil, imposed by the producing countries in the 1970s. The dependence of modern economies on oil was immediately apparent. The burden of high oil prices not only gave a fresh boost to inflation but also reduced spending power and so depressed the economies of oil-importing industrial countries. World slumps in the mid-1970s and early 1980s consequently pushed unemployment up to levels that had not been experienced since the depression of the 1930s (Fig. 16.1).

Despite the development of North Sea oil, Britain felt the full force of industrial depression with unemployment rising to over 3 million (about 13 per cent of the working population) in the 1980s. Government policies designed to bring down inflation by reducing the level of spending in the economy may have added to the total of unemployment. New technology, encouraging the substitution of capital for labour, could also be a cause of job losses.

Regional unemployment

1 Assisted areas

In spite of the government's policies designed to assist depressed areas, there are still wide geographical variations in general prosperity and opportunities for employment (see Chapter 6).

For the purpose of regional assistance, areas are classified into the main categories shown in Fig. 16.2. For a long time, regional policy has been related to particular *development areas* qualifying for various forms of government aid. *Intermediate areas* also receive assistance but on a lesser scale. Intermediate areas do not have such high levels of unemployment but suffer from a degree of economic slackness that qualifies for financial assistance. Such assistance may also come from EEC funds.

2 Regional policies

The methods used to get a better balance between the regions were outlined in general terms in Chapter 6. We now refer more specifically to some of the measures in operation.

i) Firms investing in development areas qualify for *regional development grants* of 15 per cent towards the cost of new plant, machinery, and buildings.

ii) *Selective financial assistance* is further available for capital developments that create or safeguard employment in assisted areas. This includes loans on favourable terms and grants towards certain costs of moving an undertaking to an assisted area.

iii) The government builds *advance factories* for sale or rent in the areas concerned.

iv) *Special employment measures* such as the Youth Training Scheme and Community Programme provide work experience for young people and take them off the unemployment register. Although these measures are nationwide, they are particularly helpful in assisted areas.

v) Areas are made more attractive to industry by improving their general facilities or *infrastructure*. Government grants may be given for such purposes as land clearance and development.

vi) A number of *enterprise zones* have been established by the government in order to attract new industry into depressed areas, particularly declining city centres. Firms setting up in these areas are granted generous tax concessions such as exemption from local rates for a period of ten years. Other

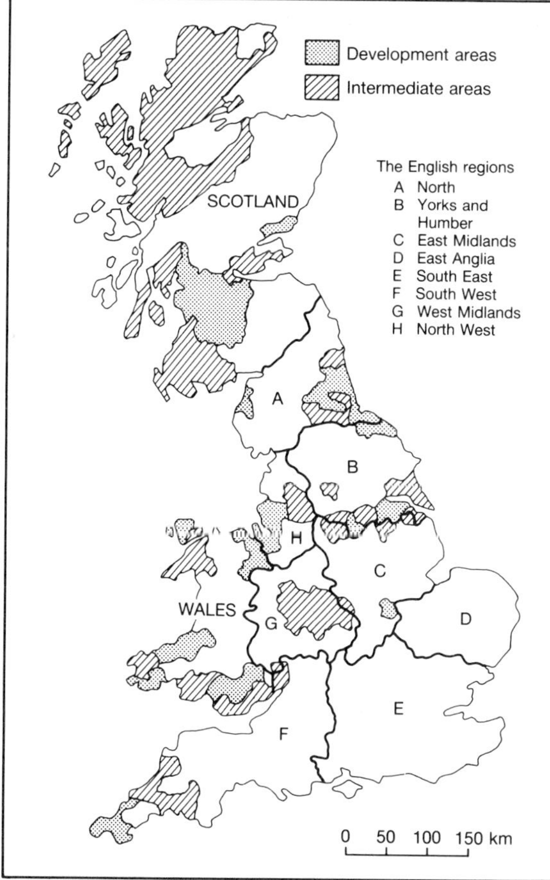

Fig. 16.2 Assisted areas (1985)

attractions include relaxation of administrative restrictions such as planning controls over new factory building. The aim is to encourage business enterprise and help to create new jobs by allowing greater freedom and opportunity for making profit.

The change of government in 1979 was followed by a reduction in the scale of regional assistance as part of a general policy of cutting government spending. The number of assisted areas was consequently reduced with the intention of concentrating aid where it was most needed. The uneven impact of economic slump has also affected the map of assisted areas. For example it now includes the once prosperous West Midlands region.

1 Describe and account for the trend of unemployment since the early 1970s.

2 Note the classification of assisted areas and give examples (Fig. 16.2).

16.2 Inflation

The problem of inflation

Inflation has created recurring problems for the British economy since the Second World War but did not rise into double figures until the 1970s (Fig. 16.3). A feature of the rapid inflation of the 1970s was that soaring prices were accompanied by a high and rising level of unemployment. This contradicted the assumption that inflation is most likely to occur when there is a strong pressure of demand in the economy and unemployment is consequently low. A possible explanation is that the inflation stemmed from cost-push forces unaccompanied by demand-pull.

Many factors contributed to rising costs and prices during this period, but the exceptional severity of Britain's inflation may be traced to two particular origins – devaluation of the pound and the cost of oil.

The weakness of Britain's balance of payments had led to devaluation in 1967, and the floating of the pound in 1972 was followed by further downward slides. Devaluation means that more pounds have to be paid for any given value of imports and so the sterling cost of imports automatically rises. Since Britain relies on imports for a large proportion of its food and raw materials, this can be a significant factor in inflation.

Before the North Sea development, Britain's oil had to be entirely imported. Towards the end of 1973, the oil-producing countries began to raise their prices sharply, pushing up not only the price of petrol but also fuel costs in many important sectors of the

Fig. 16.3 Inflation since 1970

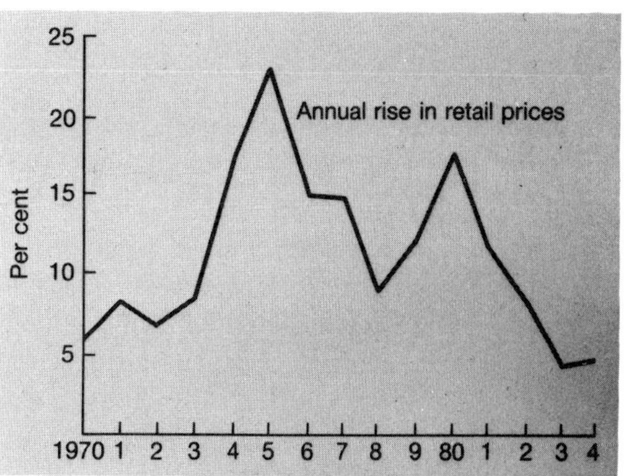

economy. With the cost of living rising steeply, trade unions increased their wage claims, so giving a further boost to production costs and the rate of inflation. The inflationary surge at the end of the decade was similarly preceded by a sharp rise in the world price of oil.

Control of inflation

The slackening rate of inflation in the early 1980s is attributable to government policy combined with a stronger pound and more stable oil prices.

Monetary and fiscal policies to control inflation have been outlined in earlier chapters. Conservative counter-inflationary strategy is derived from the economic doctrine known as *monetarism* and relies essentially on monetary policy. The central proposition of monetarism is that the root cause of inflation, whether demand-pull or cost-push, is an excessive quantity of money in circulation. The solution is then to restrict the growth of the money supply by methods indicated in Chapter 11. The role of fiscal policy is merely to assist monetary control by reducing government spending and borrowing.

Fiscal and monetary restraints on spending add to unemployment, and governments have consequently been unwilling to use them too harshly. If inflation is primarily cost-push, the obvious remedy is to curb cost increases. The cost of imported materials is largely beyond our control, but wages are a large element in industrial costs which governments have tried to influence either as employers of labour themselves or by interfering in other wage settlements.

The Labour government in the 1960s and the Conservatives from 1972 to 1974 operated statutory *incomes policies* empowering the government to prevent or limit wage and price increases by law. These policies had some success, but it was generally agreed that they could only work for a time and could not hold back the flood of wage demands indefinitely.

The Conservatives' statutory policy was abruptly ended by a clash with the miners which brought about the general election and defeat of the government in 1974. Labour had meanwhile renounced statutory methods and adopted a voluntary policy based on a 'social contract' with the trade unions. Withdrawal of union co-operation caused the collapse of that policy and also led to electoral defeat in 1979. The succeeding Conservative government has since rejected any formal incomes policy but intervened to curb pay increases in the public sector.

1 Why did inflation accelerate sharply in the mid-1970s and again at the end of the decade?

2 Why did the rate of inflation fall in the early 1980s?

16.3 Economic growth

Britain's slow growth compared with that of other advanced industrial countries is illustrated in Fig. 16.4. As we saw in Chapter 1, a rapidly growing economy does not necessarily mean that people are correspondingly better off, but the slow growth rate does suggest that the standard of living in this country has not risen as fast as it might have done. In the deep slump of 1980-1 output actually fell.

Obstacles to growth

It is difficult to explain Britain's poor growth performance because there are so many influences that cannot be calculated. For example, how can one measure the effect of the education system on the efficiency and productivity of labour? One possible explanation of Britain's comparative failure is that this country was the first to industrialize and others have since been catching up. But a number of countries have clearly caught up and forged ahead, and so other reasons must be sought.

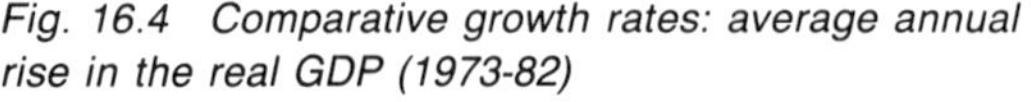
Fig. 16.4 Comparative growth rates: average annual rise in the real GDP (1973-82)

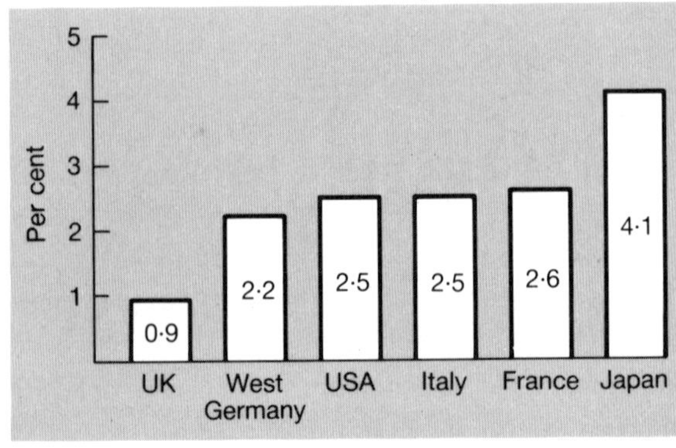

1 Investment

Since a country's productive capacity can be increased by adding to and modernizing its capital (factories, machines, etc.), the proportion of national resources devoted to capital accumulation or investment is obviously important to growth. In this respect, Britain has noticeably lagged behind many of its rivals. British industry has also been slow to invest in new technology compared with competitors in countries such as the United States and Japan.

2 Deflation

The most important influence on businessmen when deciding whether to invest is their expectation about future sales. In this connection, the confidence of British business may have been undermined by frequent doses of deflation on the part of governments faced with balance of payments problems brought on by inflation. The resulting instability of the British economy, which came to be known as 'stop-go', has almost certainly contributed to the sluggishness of investment and economic growth.

3 Management and labour

Britain's slow growth rate is often blamed on human factors including the attitudes of trade unions and workers or, alternatively, inefficiency and lack of initiative on the part of managements. Unfavourable comparisons are again made with other countries such as West Germany and the United States.

1 Define economic growth and classify the main influences affecting it.

16.4 The balance of payments

The Second World War left Britain with reduced reserves of foreign currency and a seriously weakened balance of payments. Exports had fallen by about two-thirds, and some of the overseas markets that Britain could not supply during the war were permanently lost. Although the country's balance on invisibles remained substantially in surplus, it could no longer be relied upon to cover the deficit on visible trade. Export expansion thus became a national priority, and 'export or die' was a post-war slogan.

With international trade becoming increasingly competitive, a major obstacle to exports was the effect of inflation on prices. Successive balance of payments crises were consequently met by deflationary measures associated with 'stop-go' policy. Such measures helped the balance of payments by contracting Britain's demand for goods, holding back inflationary pressures, and reducing our demand for imports. However, as we have seen, they also held back employment and production.

A possible alternative to deflation, as a remedy for an adverse balance, is to reduce imports by means of tariff protection. But this is contrary to international agreements, provokes retaliation against exports, and could only be used as a temporary device in exceptional circumstances.

The other main alternative is devaluation. British governments have generally resisted this measure, partly because maintaining the exchange value of sterling came to be regarded as a matter of national prestige. Nevertheless, Britain's trade competitiveness was assisted by devaluations in 1949 and 1967 and a downward floating pound after 1972 (Fig. 15.4).

Relatively high inflation and low productivity soon cancelled out any competitive advantage to British industry from a depreciating pound. The current account was thus heavily in deficit during most of the 1970s. By 1980, however, the trade balance was clearly showing the benefits of North Sea oil and moving strongly into surplus (Fig. 15.3). But large deficits in non-oil trade must give cause for concern as the flow of oil begins to decline.

1 Account for the problems of Britain's balance of payments in the decades following the Second World War. Why did it cease to be a problem in the early 1980s?

Multiple choice

1 The recognized aims of economic policy do NOT include
- **A** a reduction in taxation
- **B** full employment
- **C** higher living standards
- **D** a healthy balance of payments
- **E** stable prices

2 Which of the following statements is generally true of the UK economy in the early 1980s?
1 Unemployment was falling.
2 Inflation was falling.
3 The current account of the balance of payments was in surplus.
- **A** 1 only is correct
- **B** 1 and 2 only are correct
- **C** 1, 2 and 3 are correct
- **D** 2 and 3 only are correct
- **E** 3 only is correct

3 Regional policy is concerned with all the following EXCEPT
- **A** reducing unemployment
- **B** relieving urban congestion
- **C** improving the balance of payments
- **D** reducing regional inequalities
- **E** reviving depressed areas

4 A new firm could claim assistance under regional policy if it located in the vicinity of
- **A** London
- **B** Glasgow
- **C** Bristol
- **D** Norwich
- **E** Southampton

5 The rate of inflation may be reduced by
- **A** increasing money supply
- **B** increasing public expenditure
- **C** increasing direct taxation
- **D** relaxing pay restraint
- **E** devaluing the pound

6 Improvement in the UK balance of payments could have been due to
1 the development of North Sea oil
2 a reduced rate of inflation
3 reduced taxation
- **A** 1 only is correct
- **B** 1 and 2 only are correct
- **C** 1, 2 and 3 are correct
- **D** 2 and 3 only are correct
- **E** 3 only is correct

Data response

The period since 1945 has been one of rising production and, until the 1970s, a low level of unemployment (generally around 2 per cent). But economic growth, averaging 2 to 3 per cent, was slower and more erratic than in most other western European countries. There were also periodic difficulties with the balance of payments, especially during periods of relatively high pressure of demand. A steep rise in the price of imported oil, imposed by the producing countries in 1973, put new strains on the balance of payments, initiating a surge of inflation, and also added to a rising level of unemployment. Another surge in the world price of oil, in 1979, was this time beneficial to Britain's balance of payments but again was followed by both soaring inflation and unemployment. Government policy, pursued in the early 1980s, helped to reduce the rate of inflation but not unemployment.

1 Name four important government aims indicated in the passage.

2 Why should balance of payments difficulties occur especially during periods of high pressure of demand?

3 Why should the oil price rises have accentuated both unemployment and inflation?

4 Why did oil price rises weaken the balance of payments in 1973 but strengthen it in 1979?

5 Explain how government policy helped to reduce inflation but not unemployment in the 1980s.

Essays

1 Monetary and fiscal policies that help to reduce inflation may also cause unemployment. Explain the nature of the policies concerned and the dilemma implied in the statement.

2 'Regional policy merely obstructs the market forces that should determine the location of industry'. Discuss the aims and forms of regional policy in the light of the quotation.

3 What is meant by the rate of economic growth? Account for Britain's slow growth and suggest how it could be increased.

4 Write an account of the state of Britain's economy indicating its problems and prospects.

Appendix on coursework

The coursework component of GCSE examinations requires students to work independently on selected tasks, assignments, or projects related to the syllabus objectives. The form of work, method of presentation, and choice of subjects are prescribed by the appropriate examining group whose regulations must be consulted. There are considerable differences in syllabus requirements, and this appendix can do no more than indicate general points for consideration by students in their approach to coursework.

Forms of coursework

Economics coursework options may be divided into the broad areas of local studies, aspects of the national economy, and the world of business.

Studies related to the local economy provide scope for practical fieldwork through observation, surveys, questionnaires, visits, and interviews. In some cases temporary work experience can be utilized.

Wider national and business subjects offer fewer possibilities of fieldwork but provide ample opportunity for research involving use of newspapers, periodicals, government reports, and other published sources. A diary of relevant information recorded over a period of time can provide a foundation for some coursework topics.

Specimen topics

Some syllabuses require several units of coursework on fairly specialized topics. In any case, it is advisable to avoid topics of such a general nature that they cannot be treated in sufficient depth. The following classified examples indicate the kind of options available.

Study of a local industry or firm

1 A manufacturing establishment. One or more of the following aspects could be covered: locational influences; organization, size, and capital structure; production methods and division of labour; wage structure and labour relations; range of products and markets, including exports; impact on the national and local economy, with possible reference to social costs.
2 A service industry, such as tourism, with reference to structure, employment effects, local significance, etc.
3 A primary industry, possibly concentrating on a particular local development, e.g. a change in the structure of agriculture from dairy to arable farming.

Economics of local government

1 The local authority budget: its sources of revenue, allocation of expenditure, and the impact of central government policies.
2 The effects of local government activity on industry and commerce, including impact of rates, council spending and assistance to local industry.
3 Actual or potential consequences to the community of privatization of services such as refuse collection and school meals.

The local economy

1 Local employment opportunities: the diversity of employment, trends and prospects, and the effect of government policy.
2 The housing market and house prices, with reference to demand and supply influences and the effect of council house sales.
3 Impact of regional policy on the local economy.
4 Transport use by households: for commuting and social purposes, and the effects of changes in family income, fares, petrol prices, etc.

Aspects of the national economy

1 Analysis of current movements of exchange rates, interest rates, terms of trade or trade balance.
2 A current industrial dispute or wage claim with reference to reasons, background, and bargaining influences.

3 Import penetration into the UK car market: growth, causes, remedies, etc.
4 Impact of the United States's economy on Britain's economy in relation to trade, unemployment, etc.

The world of business

1 A merger or takeover, actual or proposed, with reference to motives and consequences to workers, consumers, and shareholders.
2 Price fluctuations in a specialized market, e.g. oil or commodity markets.
3 Non-price competition (including advertising) in the markets for products such as petrol and breakfast cereals: methods, motives, and effects.
4 Public ownership versus private enterprise, e.g. in relation to privatization of gas or water supply.

Sources of information

Local information may be obtained from the library service, local newspapers, council offices, job centres, and other local agencies or organizations.

The statistical background to the national economy is covered by a range of government publications some of which should be available in a well-stocked reference library. The most comprehensive statistical sources are the *Annual Abstract of Statistics* and the *Monthly Digest of Statistics*. Another government publication, *Economic Trends*, contains commentary on specific aspects of the economy together with a selection of tables and charts. The Treasury also produces a brief monthly *Economic Progress Report*.

An official handbook on *Britain*, published by HMSO, is brought up to date annually and contains descriptive chapters on the economy. Topical articles on aspects of the economy are also to be found in quarterly reviews produced by the main banks.

Index

Answers to multiple choice questions

Chapter	Question 1	2	3	4	5	6	7	8	9	10
1	E	C	D	C	E	B	B	C	B	D
2	D	C	C	D	E	A	D	D		
3	D	E	A	D	C	D	C	C		
4	A	E	B	D	C	B	C	C		
5	B	E	C	D	D	D	E	C		
6	B	D	C	A	D	C	D	A		
7	E	A	B	D	B	C				
8	C	C	B	B	D	C	C	E	D	E
9	D	B	A	B	A					
10	D	B	A	C	E	C	D			
11	E	C	D	C	B	D	D	D	B	B
12	D	B	E	A	C	D	D			
13	C	B	D	E	D	C	C	D		
14	C	B	A	B	C	C	B	E		
15	C	D	B	A	C	D				
16	A	D	C	B	C	B				

Numerical answers

Chapter 8

Page 98, Exercise 1: $\frac{1}{2}$
Exercise 2: $1\frac{3}{5}$
Page 99, Data response, Exercise 2: £12
Exercise 4: £13

Chapter 10

Page 122, Exercise 2: a) 122, b) 106
Page 123, Data response, Exercise 2: 1980-1, 12 per cent

Chapter 11

Page 136, Data response, Exercise 2: a) 50, b) 20 per cent
Exercise 3: a) 50, b) 100

Chapter 13

Page 156, Exercise 3: a) 80p, b) £240

Chapter 15

Page 180, Data response, Exercise 1:
a) −716, b) +3632, c) +2916, d) −816

Acknowledgements

The publishers wish to thank the following for permission to reproduce photographs:
Age Concern/Thanet Times p. 147 (bottom right); Airviews (M/C) Ltd p. 70; Ashmolean Museum, Oxford p. 115; Austin Rover Group Ltd p. 55; Bank of England p. 131; Ben Line Steamers Ltd p.165; British Coal p. 49; British Petroleum Company plc p. 16; Central Press Photos Ltd p. 140; Co-operative Retail Services Ltd p. 47; Ercol Furniture Ltd p. 31 (middle); FAO/F. Botts p. 26 (bottom left); Forestry Commission p.31 (top); Sally and Richard Greenhill p. 147 (top left and right); Golden Wonder Ltd p. 37; Imperial Chemical Industries plc p. 59; International Planned Parenthood p. 26 (top left); London Transport Executive p. 21; Massey Ferguson p. 6; Manpower Services Commission p. 33; Midland Bank plc pp. 127 and 177; Milton Keynes Development Corporation p. 68; Network Photographers: Laurie Sparham pp. 103 and 106, John Sturrock pp. 109 and 147 (bottom left); Oxfam p. 26 (bottom right); Paul Popper Ltd p. 154; J. Sainsbury plc p. 121 (top); SavaCentre Ltd p. 75; Universal Pictorial Press p. 169.

Cartoon on p. 5 by Kate Charlesworth.
Additional photography by Chris Honeywell.

The publishers also thank the following for their co-operation: Pine and Cane, Oxford; Marks & Spencer plc; Warlands Cycles, Oxford.

Cover photograph by Susan Griggs/Julian Nieman.